ONE SIGNAL
PUBLISHERS

ATRIA

THE MAGA DIARIES

MY SURREAL ADVENTURES
INSIDE THE RIGHT-WING
(AND HOW I GOT OUT)

TINA NGUYEN

ONE SIGNAL
PUBLISHERS

ATRIA

NEW YORK • LONDON • TORONTO • SYDNEY • NEW DELHI

To my mother, who taught me to be brave,
and to John Homans, who taught me to be bold.

(And to Batman, from whom I swiped the phrase
"The Brave and The Bold.")

ATRIA

An Imprint of Simon & Schuster, Inc.
1230 Avenue of the Americas
New York, NY 10020

First One Signal Publishers/Atria Books hardcover edition January 2024

ONE SIGNAL PUBLISHERS / ATRIA BOOKS and colophon
are trademarks of Simon & Schuster, Inc.

Simon & Schuster: Celebrating 100 Years of Publishing in 2024

For information about special discounts for bulk purchases,
please contact Simon & Schuster Special Sales at 1-866-506-1949 or
business@simonandschuster.com.

The Simon & Schuster Speakers Bureau can bring authors to your
live event. For more information or to book an event, contact the
Simon & Schuster Speakers Bureau at 1-866-248-3049 or visit
our website at www.simonspeakers.com.

Interior design by Dana Sloan

Manufactured in the United States of America

1 3 5 7 9 10 8 6 4 2

Library of Congress Cataloging-in-Publication Data has been applied for.

ISBN 978-1-9821-8969-3
ISBN 978-1-9821-8971-6 (ebook)

CONTENTS

AUTHOR'S NOTE

There are hundreds, if not thousands, of books about the history of the Republican party, the history of the American conservative movement *inside* that party, and the history of Donald Trump and his administration and January 6th and militant white nationalists and whatever other right-wing insanities have emerged in American politics over the last eight years.

This is not one of those books.

The MAGA Diaries is a coming-of-age memoir, one of those tales wherein the main character goes on a transformational journey from childhood to adulthood—a political book with a curveball, really. And yes, as the title might indicate, it's about the MAGA movement. *But Tina,* you might point out, *you were born in 1989. MAGA didn't even exist when you were a child!* Your mind might also be shattering into apoplectic fragments at this point. *Also: you're a woman! From Boston! You went to prep school! Your parents had PhDs! You're not even Christian! You're not even white!!!*

Obviously, I don't fit the stereotype of someone who'd be fluent in right-wing American politics, much less a former adherent. But this is also the story about the conservative activist movement at the dawn of the twenty-first century, and the people who've been inside it ever since they were teenagers in the 1960s: a secret world and hidden power structure inside the Republican party with a unique culture of fellowship, drive, and purpose, like being in a political version of summer camp with your best friends forever. (And yes, there were summer camps. Lots of them.) That sense of unshakeable loyalty to your community, even as the diehards of your movement do increasingly horrifying things and make everyone wear MAKE AMERICA GREAT AGAIN hats, and that addiction to victory, even if you must poke holes in the social fabric to keep your power, is something that the history books and the nonfiction bestsellers from *New York Times* reporters could never capture. They write *about* it, as do I, but at one point, I *lived* it—and it coincided with the very beginning of the MAGA movement in 2008, the year I turned nineteen and went off to college.

I guess this is a book about life in a very, very weird political gray zone.

Admittedly, saying something is in a "gray zone" might come off as a headache-inducing cop-out in these hyperpartisan times, and perhaps it makes me, a member of the spooky mainstream media, look somewhat evasive and noncommittal. But it's made me a better chronicler of the conservative movement, and hopefully, a more trustworthy one. Unlike conservative activists, especially the ones who were trained to become journalists to promote a set of values, I never became a true believer and cannot profess to be one. But sometimes, I wonder if my career in the mainstream resulted from a massive cosmic oversight: it's a rapidly shrinking industry of newsrooms, clinging to survival in blue states and blue cities, staffed by people who generally come from networked, privileged backgrounds with very expensive name-brand schooling. It's so exclusive, in fact, that the conservative critique of the media sometimes makes sense—and I wouldn't have fully comprehended this critique, much less its ability to resonate with the American public, if I *hadn't* been a part of the professional right.

A few housekeeping notes: the quotations in this book prior to 2015, when I started formally reporting on the activist and MAGA right as cultural and civic institutions, are either reconstructions of conversations to the best of my memory or, when possible, drawn from contemporary documentation (emails, etc.). Conversations and quotes post-2015 are drawn from interviews and transcripts. Names of nonpublic individuals have been changed for their privacy. And I've endeavored to keep things as even-keeled as possible, because let's face it, these days, writing about politics can easily tilt into hyperventilating and hyperbolic pronouncements that some side or another is trying to destroy the country. But I've spent fourteen years dancing and hopping across the cracks dividing America, even as they've become ravines and canyons, and I'm prepared to be subject to cancellation from all quadrants of the political divide.

So if you're a liberal wondering why all this nativist populism seemed to come out of nowhere, to the point that it's on the precipice for subsuming American civic life, this book is for you. If you're a Republican who thought the GOP looked like a Mitt Romney paradise in 2012, believed that Trump was an aberration in 2016 and 2020, and have no idea why he's still a presence in 2024, this book is for you. If you're a MAGA conservative, this book might be a good hate-read, but please trust that I tried to capture the nuances of your beliefs and motivations without bias, to the best of my ability.

And if you're a right-wing career activist who would have preferred this all remain under the radar: sorry for pulling the curtain back. I just thought people should know.

PRELUDE:
START THE SHOW

July 23, 2022
Entrance to the Tampa Convention Center
Turning Point USA Student Action Summit

I t was 2 p.m. when the Nazis showed up, with their swastika flags and signs praising Ron DeSantis, their skull masks and their SS armbands, their shirts emblazoned proudly with the word ANTI-SEMITE, stubbornly camped between two concrete pillars, two stories tall, draped in Turning Point USA banners. They were swarmed by angry college students, still in their summer business-casual wear, who'd come there that weekend to network and see Donald Trump speak, but instead were confronted with these unexpected interlopers. Across the street, staffers were quietly panicking—this was, apparently, not the first time people in Nazi outfits had shown up to one of their events, and they were now imagining the vicious headlines that would be published in mainstream press—but they were relieved that the students were screaming back at the Nazis.

"Nobody fucking wants you here, get out of here!" yelled a man in a striped shirt.

"We've got free speech too," drawled a man with a megaphone and a skull mask, standing among less than a dozen of his Nazi peers. "*Sieg heil,* brother, *sieg heil.*"

I'd chugged my Starbucks, left my room at the Embassy Suites, taken the disconcertingly open-glass elevator down a vertigo-inducing eighteen stories into the lobby, and darted across the street with my phone out. When I'd made the decision to fly down, I'd expected to spend my weekend with five thousand bright young MAGA activists who were so eager to see speakers like DeSantis, Don Jr., Ted Cruz, and Josh Hawley that they'd willingly flown to Tampa in the middle of July. I'd suspected that I'd hear a lot of talk about *the libs* and how socialism was the worst, and I expected at least one Truth Social booth and several parties. But I hadn't expected to walk straight into a metaphor.

It was evident that the students didn't want the Nazis to be there either: most were recording them on their phones, several were in heated arguments with the masked men. But something fascinating was happening: the majority of the kids didn't seem to believe the Nazis were Nazis at *all.* They accused them of being leftists, of being antifa infiltrators sent to make them look bad; they demanded that they pull down their masks and identify themselves. It seemed to amuse the Nazis that the students thought they were anything *but* what they said they were. "We're not mad," the megaphone guy said casually through his megaphone at one of the screaming students. "It sounds like you're the ones who're mad."

Hours later, I heard from another reporter that the group *were* really Nazis: they were known as the Goyim Defense League, an honest-to-goodness antisemitic online troll organization. They'd leave flyers on people's doorsteps, blaming the media for being controlled by Jews; they'd drop banners from highways claiming that whites were being replaced; they'd dress up like Orthodox Jews, sideburns and all, and claim that the Holocaust was faked. Later, I'd read a report from a conservative outlet suggesting that they'd shown up in an attempt to "cancel" DeSantis by associating him with Nazis. The point, buried underneath the next several days of vicious headlines and a feud between TPUSA and *The View*, was that real Nazis had shown up at the conference: they really hated Jews, they really believed in the supremacy of the white race, and they were more than happy to needle Turning Point, which, for all its pro-Trump nationalism, was *still* loathed by the extremist wing of the right for being pro-Israel.

But that distinction was lost. Chalk it up to the fact that just months prior, an anti-Trump group known as the Lincoln Project had installed fake Nazi protesters at an event for Glenn Youngkin, attempting to portray the Republican gubernatorial candidate as being pro–white supremacist. Maybe tie it to the fact that the Nazis never *did* pull down their masks, arousing more suspicion in the minds of the TPUSA students that the fake Nazis had an ulterior motive. Maybe even acknowledge the bizarre stuntlike nature of the GDL's appearance: Why would they have a poster with nothing but the pro-Israel DeSantis's *face* on it, or a flag declaring that Florida was "DeSantis Country," if not to tie DeSantis to their twisted brotherhood? Were they sure that DeSantis would not condemn them? Or were they just chaotic, postmodernist trolls, gleefully muddying the public debate between what was true and false? But even in the face of evidence that the Nazi group *was* real—one unmasked man was eventually identified as David Howard

Wydner, who had attended several GDL protests in the past—the narrative could not be changed. "We are on a mission to find and unmask the 'Nazis'—aka paid leftists—who tried to ruin the lives of 5K patriotic young American students," Benny Johnson, Turning Point USA's chief creative officer, tweeted five days later.

———

I grew bored and reentered the convention hall, trading the smell of sweaty Nazis on the breeze for the scrubbed-clean air of a convention hall. Apart from the white supremacist stunt, it had been a normal student conference so far, except for the bright colors and corn dogs.

I'd covered about nine or so right-wing activist conferences in the past—big yearly confabs that could consume entire conference halls, with thousands of people flying in from all over the world to meet fellow activists, watch speeches and panels, pick up swag, and plot the takeover of the American government in their spare time as their badges dangled from their necks on lanyards. But this was my first Turning Point USA event. The group was specifically geared toward wooing young people into the conservative movement. They loved khakis and lightweight dress shirts and sundresses. And right now, about five thousand of them were watching twenty-nine-year-old founder Charlie Kirk pontificate about how they, the most dedicated members who'd decided to spend their summer vacations in sweltering Tampa, were going to save America.

TPUSA branding was everywhere on the building, from the pillars outside to the grand staircases leading to every floor, to the massive LED screens behind Kirk: the color palette leaning more "Margaritaville happy hour" than the red, white, and blue star-spangled display I'd come to expect. There were branded step-and-repeats with ring lights at each booth leading up to the main exhibition hall: Patriot Mobile, Truth Social, Turning Point Action; some with massive cardboard cutouts of Donald Trump and Marjorie Taylor Greene, ready to be photographed and tagged for Instagram. (Conservative activists would rarely use TikTok, save for deliberate marketing campaigns to "normies," since, in their belief, it was a Chinese-government-backed spyware app and not to be trusted.)

The crowd had clearly been to enough conferences to know that when a VIP with Secret Service protection came in, all the doors to the venue would be locked for security purposes. No one could go in, no one could go out, and that was the perfect time to sell corn dogs and caffeinated beverages to the sweaty, exhausted students lined up at the concession stand inside the venue. (If they weren't hungry, the smell of fresh popcorn would surely lure them over.)

I settled onto a box on the media risers in the back, crammed with correspondents and cameramen from decidedly right-wing outlets—names like Rebel News, Audacious Liberty, Real America's Voice, and the Right Side Broadcasting Network. Fox Nation, Fox News' attempt to ape Disney+ for right-wing youngsters, hadn't been left out—in fact, they had a booth on Media Row in the hall outside, streaming the entire conference live and scoring interviews with Lauren Boebert and Matt Gaetz. There was one woman from the Associated Press, but apart from her and some local Florida reporters awaiting a speech from state governor Ron DeSantis in a few hours, as well as some cameras from CNN, no other mainstream outlets were reporting from the ground.

Thank goodness for that concession stand, I thought, and beelined toward the fresh corn dogs, waving at Andrew, the comms director, as I thought about all the times I'd survived on granola bars and soggy gift shop sandwiches at other conferences.

Who's speaking next? I pulled up the agenda. It was DeSantis, the Republican governor from Florida, and a man as MAGA as they came. Sure, he'd graduated from Yale and dabbled in Tea Party–era conservative measures as a member of the House Freedom Caucus, but he'd only gone full MAGA during the initial weeks of the COVID outbreak in March 2020. Sniffing out a strategic opening to the rightmost flanks of his party, he'd reopened the beaches and schools and restaurants, he'd railed against mask mandates and compulsory vaccinations, and he'd later switched his focus to "wokeism"—the idea that liberals were trying to institute some great social leveler on behalf of minorities and underrepresented groups, to the ultimate detriment of white Americans. That August, he was fresh off yanking Walt Disney World's tax-exempt status after the company publicly opposed his bill preventing elementary school students from learning about same-sex relationships, known then as "Don't Say Gay." I leaned back, watched a video introducing DeSantis, reconsidered my corn dog choices, and—

BOOM!

Plumes of sparks and smoke shot fifteen feet into the air, exploding and crackling and fizzing across the fifty-foot stage. The crowd erupted into a fever pitch as DeSantis emerged from the center of the stage, amid a glittering storm of lights as furious as the tropical hurricane about to hit Tampa that night. Between the jet-engine roar of the sparklers and the screams of thousands of college kids, cheering as if the tightly wound governor had been replaced by Taylor Swift, my eardrums nearly blew out.

"YOU HAVE PYROTECHNICS?!" I shouted to Andrew. He nodded mischievously.

"JESUS," I responded, bewildered and agape. "THEY SURE AS SHIT DIDN'T HAVE PYROTECHNICS AT *MY* STUDENT CONFERENCES."

———————

I'd come to the Student Action Summit to get a sense of what the next generation of conservative activists were shaping up to become. And this group, generationally speaking, was new to me. Founded in 2012, right after I'd graduated from college, Turning Point USA had become the most prominent student group in campus conservative activism, thanks to Kirk—startlingly young but politically savvy—and his bond with the Trump family. Young college conservatives I met swooned over their lineup of MAGA celebrity affiliates (Jack Posobiec, Benny Johnson, Kirk himself) and champed at the bit to become official Turning Point Ambassadors.

Everyone knew about the Ambassadors program: it was their digital street team of right-wing social media influencers: a group of savvy, well-groomed, well-compensated Zoomers who posted conservative memes and took pro-America selfies and hosted live streams for millions of their followers. But the majority of the kids who were at *this* specific summit were the kids working behind the scenes. These were the student officials running the TPUSA college chapters—the heads, the secretaries, and so forth—and the point was to network, network, network.

I floated these observations to Savannah Harrison and Hannah Poltorak, TPUSA campus leaders at Louisiana State University, who nodded solemnly along. "Coming to school, I thought that I would be surrounded by more conservatives," Poltorak, the chapter secretary, told me. "And it's very much the opposite, where we are the silent minority. But this year, I think we're really amped up to really bring ourselves into the light, because on campus, we are shoved with mask mandates and vaccine mandates. And it's honestly been enough." Her mother was a left-leaning labor lawyer, her father was with the Los Angeles Police Department; the past two years of start-and-stop COVID regulations had tipped her over to her father's side. All told, she said, there were about 240 students at the LSU Baton Rouge chapter—one of the largest student chapters in the country. And according to Hannah, there were no other conservative groups on campus, a fact that befuddled me, considering what she'd told me afterward. "There are so many people I've met in my economics class that have whispered to me, 'I like your button that says "guns are groovy."' And I wear my pins with pride. I don't post necessarily, because I'm not so big on social media. But I'm confident somewhat in what I say. And so I want students on campus to be as confident as the blue-haired chicks that stand up and yell."

Hannah, the group's president, was about to be a junior, and wasn't sure what she would do with her life. But Savannah was driven and had a clear path to the top: she'd already interned for Louisiana's state attorney general Jeff Landry. She was applying for scholarship after scholarship to pay for graduate school and had just interviewed at Pepperdine for their public policy program, with plans to perhaps pursue a law degree at the same time. And then there would be a run for office one day. "That's something that Turning Point does exceptionally well," she told me. "Like, anything you need, they have it for you. Any resources you need, they have for you. They will network you with anyone that you need to succeed, as long as you have that drive and you have that passion for the movement."

Suddenly, I had a flashback, to a time when I was their age.

It was 2009, the first week of June, and a group of kids my age were sitting around a sunken living room in a college dorm, drinking beers and huddled around a famous columnist who had spoken earlier that day. Several boys had come in from outside from smoking cigars and cigarettes, smelling of tobacco, eagerly chattering about the ways they'd clashed with the liberals at their respective colleges. I kept brushing my bangs out of my face, watching in awe as the columnist took a swig of amber liquor out of a crystalline bottle.

"So how does one get to be where you are?" a student asked.

"Well, you have to keep writing," he said. "Keep writing, take any job you can, but keep in touch with the network. We're always here to hook you up with any opportunities to get your byline out there. Churn out enough, you'll be like me one day."

"Good luck," I said to Savannah and Hannah, sincerely, instinctively, as they beamed.

————

Whenever someone asks me why I cover the far right instead of the far left—particularly my conservative sources, irked that a mainstream reporter is chasing after them—I have two answers. "First of all, the left is *incompetent*," I told a source once who'd asked me that question as we tore through slices of Sicilian-style pizza. "They have no idea what they're doing but they just want to get there *immediately*. It's like, the left has an airplane, and they want to get from Point A to Point B, but there's a mountain in the way. One would think you'd fly *around* the mountain. Or take a longer route. It might take some time and burn fuel, but it'll get you there safely. But the far left? Nope. They're like, *the shortest way from here to Point B is a straight line, and no one can tell us otherwise,* and then, BOOM." (The source delicately mopped a tomato sauce drop that had splashed onto his plate.)

But the second answer is that sometimes, I don't think the left—or even people who consider themselves centrists, center-right, or even a regular card-carrying Republican who's wondering why everyone went batshit over the past five years—understands, even now, the scale or geography of the mountain that's in their way. I'd even go so far as to mix metaphors and say it's a mountain that's *also* a perfectly calibrated Rube Goldberg machine: a bit too elaborately constructed, with hundreds, if not thousands, of different pieces that need to be placed just so in order to achieve a specific outcome. It was constructed over decades, placed in the right places at the right times, with the proper protections from being set off too early, but when it was ready—and at the right moment—it would begin cascading under everyone's noses into a political avalanche. (The first time I read *The Handmaid's Tale,* I knew that its author, Margaret Atwood, got the premise wrong. Conservative activists in America, as I knew them, wouldn't have seized their power through a violent coup—they were going to do it gradually and slowly, using the Constitution as a clever road map.)

I'll give everyone else a pass on not knowing about the sheer scale of the right inside American civic life, because when I was a young conservative activist, *I* didn't know what they were trying to do either. Between 2008 and 2012—from college until my early twenties—I was simply a politics nerd with an unnerving obsession with the US Constitution and American history, who dated an odd but highly ambitious conservative boy in high school and followed him to Claremont McKenna College, a renowned college with a notoriously conservative government department, and a deep affiliation with a right-wing think tank whose scholars and papers formed the backbone of the Trump doctrine. From there I found some interesting internship opportunities through a local think tank, got involved in some weird ghoulish groups in Washington, DC, met Tucker Carlson, wanted to *be* Tucker Carlson, went to work for Tucker Carlson, had some bad early career experiences while working for Tucker Carlson, experienced an identity crisis (as one does in their early twenties), and then left the movement to pursue a career in *normal* journalism (assisted by a nice favor from Tucker Carlson). In a bizarre twist, it brought me back to covering the movement: when Donald Trump was elected, my *Vanity Fair* editor started gasping at my offhanded observations about the people I recognized in his orbit, and I suddenly realized exactly how unusual my background was. To the rest of the world, the things I'd taken for granted were actually obscure, esoteric, and hidden knowledge.

It would be easy to dismiss it as a fabricated "Astroturf" movement, funded by the rich and powerful, but it's more complicated than that. Conservative activism is like a kudzu plant: a movement, meant to grow as quickly as it can across every American civic and cultural institution, from school boards to Congress, from the judicial system to the newsrooms, choking out everything in its path. If you'd been able to look around the corners of America's right you'd have seen Donald Trump coming from a mile away. Or understood that the coordinated hashtag #StopTheSteal was playing with forces the mainstream media wouldn't understand until it was far too late. Or January 6th, the events of which an extremist researcher and I had hypothesized about on January 4th. Or the slow-then-fast repeal of *Roe v. Wade,* which, for nearly fifty years, had been strategized over whiskey glasses at cocktail parties and political seminars. By the time this book is published, who knows what new visions will have turned into reality?

Plenty of ink's been spilled over what happens as a *result* of conservative activism: districts suddenly get gerrymandered, strange new laws appear on the books, a cascading domino effect of judicial rulings suddenly leads to civil rights getting repealed. And there are so many articles and books about the ideological warfare inside the right, which seems far more intense and personal than any quibbles the left has with itself. But missing in their work is something that a journalist looking in from the outside would never quite understand: the way the conservative movement makes itself immortal, turning idealism, friendship, and ambition into the same thing. It draws in young people with promises of stability, purpose, and career summer seminars full of new, like-minded friends; it invites them into a world of power, full of eager mentors and cocktail hours, who want to help them mature and grow; it gives the most promising kids internships and research projects to fill out their resumes. Their loyalty becomes organic, their ideas become similar, and eventually, those young people occupy the positions of power: Like my ex-boyfriend, who became a hatchet man for Peter Thiel, introducing the billionaire to white supremacists. Or my old boss who became, for a time, the most hated (and popular) man on Fox News. Or that one woman who was at that seminar my friend attended, who became a federal judge repealing mask mandates at the tender age of thirty-three. Or that one guy I met at a thing who became a Trump speechwriter, or that other guy I met at that other thing who's now running that GOP candidate's campaign, or that guy whom I made memes with who now gets paid to churn them out. Or the time you met Ginni Thomas in the bathroom at work and watched her, ten years later, try to dismantle Joe Biden's election from the inside.

Acknowledging that I see these figures as real, living humans—not monsters, but people—has taken a toll in my life. I've lost left-leaning friends who hate the way that I report, infuriated that I haven't used my platform to take a side (meaning, their side) in this particular era. For instance, I've probably lost professional opportunities because of this too: I will never be able to work at the *New York Times* without every single one of my sources dropping me, thinking I work for "enemy press." There were times I felt like a zoo animal inside the mainstream media social scene, or among general friend groups in liberal enclaves (*Look at the ex-conservative, can you* BELIEVE *she's not a Nazi?*) and there were too many people who asked me the one question I'm not qualified to answer, nor could I ethically give, as a journalist: *How do we stop all of this?* On the flip side, I've grappled with this lingering sense—probably one ingrained in me by countless mentors and past friends—that by writing about the right as a movement, even as I strive for objectivity, I am betraying the community I grew up in, because I wanted to be a journalist without binding myself to an ideological obligation. (They would have preferred it be their side.)

I guess those programs did what they were supposed to do: familiarize me with the structure of the American right and how to make a successful living inside it, while helping the cause come to fruition. All those mentors and acquaintances who let me in on its secrets probably didn't expect me to end up chronicling it from the outside, and frankly, they might be sort of mad that I'm doing so in a book literally titled *The MAGA Diaries.* But I believe that knowledge has kept me sane throughout the past decade of writing about politics: I know the layout of the conservative movement and the characters who live in it, as if it were the hometown I'd left and could still navigate blindfolded if you asked, and it's not totally surprising if you know which research institution is lurking behind the corner to spring something—say, the legal justification for a riot on Capitol Hill—on an unsuspecting public.

14   *THE MAGA DIARIES*

So here's everything I know about how this movement works—not the GOP, or Republican voters per se, but the *movement*—wrapped in a hell of a coming-of-age tale. Some of the things I'll reveal about the activist right may seem convoluted, harebrained, and ridiculous. And sure, they may (will) claim that they're doing so in order to protect the principles of life, liberty, and the pursuit of happiness, and dismiss me as a shrill harpy with an axe to grind. But at its core, the conservative movement wants to master and restructure America's civil institutions: the free press, the judicial system, the education system, democratically elected legislatures, and elections from the presidency down to the local school boards. And they are very good at it.

————

As I finally got my second corn dog the next day to watch Donald Trump Jr. speak, I made my way to the front of the stage, observing the audience he was about to address: thousands of children in thousands of MAGA hats, sitting on the floors and in chairs they'd claimed hours before, eyes glued to the president's son, just as they had been glued to Matt Gaetz, Greg Gutfeld, even Kimberly Guilfoyle, when they'd spoken earlier. Kat Timpf, a Fox News blonde with Tina Fey glasses who'd attended the same journalism program as I had, was now a cohost on the late-night show *Gutfeld!* and a keynote speaker at Turning Point, idolized for her acid lib-burning wit. Earlier that day, she'd delivered an address telling the young ones how to persevere past failures in life.

Maybe I'd forgotten what it was like being that young. I was still unsure why this specific generation of activist needed Timpf's encouragement to keep going in their careers. I had no doubt that they loved the free food and neon-lit mixers, tote bags and cute Don't Tread On

Me T-shirts and packets about freedom and liberty and political organizing, the new friends they were making at the photo booths and the lobby Starbucks. But there *had* to be an underlying imperative. For my generation, the Koch-era Tea Party generation, it was fighting the rise of federal involvement in everyday life, with the Affordable Care Act front and center, but within the boundaries of traditional politics. For the activists of the Reagan era, it was to bring an end to the Cold War. What did the kids want *now*?

It was at that moment of puzzlement that Don Jr., the raven-haired eldest son, took the stage. His mother, Ivana Trump, had passed away earlier that week, and he apologized if he seemed tired. "But she would have wanted me to be here," he reassured the audience. "Because the reason I got political [so] young was because she escaped from communism . . . she literally shipped me to communist Czechoslovakia in the eighties for like, six weeks, every summer, so that I could see with my own eyes what that shit was like." The crowd imperceptibly leaned in as Don Jr. spoke about his time being questioned by Soviet guards as a six-year-old for wearing a denim jacket, and how it had calcified something for him: "I understood very quickly what oppression was all about. And when you look at what's going on in America, right now, you have to ask yourself the same questions. Like: if you were trying to destroy America, and everything that it stands for, would you do anything differently than what this administration is doing?"

He listed off several current events: the soaring cost of energy that summer, the border crisis that had leaked thousands of pounds of fentanyl from Mexico into the US, the corrupt Ukrainian government siphoning billions from American aid, the collapse of the Afghan government last month, and the return of the Taliban's reign of terror under Joe Biden's incompetence. "I'm shocked that we allow them to get away with it[, but] we're pretending to live in a world that does not exist," he continued. "You see it day in and day out. You see it with the lies that they're pushing on you. You see it with the attacks on conservatives. You see it in the censorship, each and every day. But that's why it's awesome to be in crowds like this, groups like this, right? You would have never said this about conservatives in history—*you guys are actually the rebels.* You're not buying the narrative, you're not believing the nonsense, you're fighting against the man, each and every day."

The battle lines he drew were very specific to the summer of 2022: social media algorithmic censorship, COVID restrictions, and the eighty-year-old Biden's deteriorating attention span, with one mention about the military's obsession with pronouns. Transgender issues were not on the horizon yet, nor were woke corporations. But I realized at that moment that Don Jr. could have been discussing *anything* the liberals were doing that year or the next—or the Deep State, or Hollywood, or the federal government—and he would have exhorted them to be zero-sum rebels all the same, hell-bent on razing every element of liberalism and progressivism from American culture, from the biggest acts moving through Congress to the smallest conversations in their college classrooms—the battlefield where these students now fought, every single day. And that was a very, very, *very* broad mandate.

President Trump finally took the stage, and according to the schedule, there was no set time for his speech to end. By now, this wasn't a surprise to me, and I'd bought a second Diet Pepsi to steel myself. I'd heard him speak at countless rallies and events before, and watched him ramble on television, and I'd always been impressed with his stamina: the man can go onstage without a single talking point or written script, and rattle out, for two exhausting hours straight, whatever culture war marbles are rattling his brain. There's no internal structure inside it—no signposting, no classifications, nothing that I'd learned in oratory class in school—but it takes whoever listens to it on an adrenaline-juiced journey through the raging id of MAGA populism. Its incoherence is, oddly, compelling in its own way, and I noticed that it was perfect for the attention span of Gen Z. For one hour and forty minutes, he packaged up tiny, snackable bits of self-aggrandizing anecdotes and culture war outrages into miniature rants, from trans swimmers, to China, to a story about a general named Raisin Caine, to corporate wokeness, to Dutch farmers worrying about the government stealing their farmland, to Ukraine, to China again. A tired teenager with a short attention span could zone out briefly, snap back to attention, and feel like they hadn't missed a beat. But stringing them all together was his repeated insistence that they were the future, and that they were needed to fight the system:

"Each of the young Americans here today is coming of age at a pivotal time in our nation's history. Like so many generations before you, you are the front lines of a momentous struggle that will determine the future of America."

"No matter how big or powerful these radicals may be, you must never forget this nation does not belong to them, this nation belongs to you."

"Their extreme ideology has nothing to offer for the next generation. The radical left is the past. our movement Make America Great Again, America First, it is the future."

"Our movement needs young people to help push back on woke corporations, and their cowardly surrender to the radical left."

"And our American liberty is your God-given right," he rasped, and the crowd broke into wild screams. "As great as the challenges are, as great as the threats appear, all you have to do to rekindle your hope in our future is to look around this room, the incredible people in this room, at the thousands of proud young American patriots with spines of steel and hearts full of faith and love. You have love, you're tough and you're strong and you have love . . . I have no doubt that it will be young, courageous freedom-loving patriots of America like you who once again lead the way to greatness."

That benediction was more meaningful than the one Don Jr. could give them. It was the rebel leader—the elderly man who had nevertheless snatched the reins of the conservative movement from the corrupt Washington elites and handed it to the ignored populace—bestowing his life mission to the next generation. And as the students leapt to their feet, cheering and whistling and clapping until their hands were sore, I knew that they had fully accepted it.

———

It was 9:45 when the Secret Service finally let us leave the convention hall. I'd been wrung out from days of travel and convention-hall traipsing, but surrounding me was a sea of amped-up college students flowing toward the exits, most of whom had heard Trump address them directly for the first time. They chattered about how amazing he'd been as a speaker, how much better he was as a speaker than Ron DeSantis, how they were going back to their chapters and bringing the MAGA gospel to their colleges.

Suddenly, unprompted, a few students broke into a call-and-response:

"LET'S GO BRANDON!"

"WE WANT TRUMP!"

More students joined in.

"LET'S GO BRANDON!"

"WE WANT TRUMP!"

The chants grew louder.

"LET'S GO BRANDON!"

"WE! WANT! TRUMP!"

Five thousand students bellowed their loyalty as they spilled out of the building, onto the streets, into the night, streaming toward their hotels across the street. The farther out they got, the more the chants faded into chatter about the afterparties they were going to attend. Most of the crowd headed back into the Embassy Suites with me, and I crammed myself into the elevator with about fifteen other students wearing Trump hats and lanyards. As the doors closed on us, I looked around at their glowing faces, still awash in the awe of seeing Trump speak live. It was the first time for many of them.

"I thought he was going to announce he was running tonight," one student said earnestly.

The elevator shuddered, and we all soared high into the air, trying not to look at the plummeting abyss below.

1

THE YOUNG CLAREMONSTER

Milton, Massachusetts

1994

I grew up with the sounds of Vietnamese in the background, but my parents never spoke it to me. Nor did they say much about what their life was like back in Saigon, before they fled during the war. My only interactions with my family's culture were through VHS children's tapes of Viet nursery songs, taped performances of the variety show *Paris by Night,* incomprehensible visits to a cobbled-together Buddhist temple in Dorchester, and the occasional song my mother would play on her guitar, the lyrics of which I never knew, with a sad look in her eyes. But her eyes would light up whenever she had the chance to bring me to Harvard University, where she was finishing her doctoral dissertation.

We would always go to Gutman, the main library at the Graduate School of Education, and as long as I didn't disturb other students— they were working hard, she told me, just like her—I could have the children's to myself. I got to read all the books my tiny baby hands could pull off the shelves, going through at least five or six while sitting on the floor in the stacks; if I behaved Mom would reward me with a big, flaky croissant and an Orangina on the side. But my absolute favorite part was when she would take me out to the bronze statue of John Harvard in the middle of the Yard. There she would retell me the story of how the university was founded, 350 years before. These places, Mom tried to impress upon me, were not mysterious lands in the sky meant for the privileged few. She fully expected me to follow in her path to Cambridge, Massachusetts. I was more fascinated with the idea that Harvard University was so old, that it was here before my parents were even born.

My mother was one of twelve; my father, one of seven. They'd met in Utah, relocated by the US government after fleeing Vietnam, and though I never quite understood why they'd been in love in the first place, they had one thing in common, likely drilled into their heads when they grew up in a Confucian society: entering the best schools in the country (and only the best) guaranteed financial and societal success. My charismatic father had somehow clawed his way into the University of Utah's computer science doctoral program, putting to- gether a thesis so brilliant that Harvard soon came knocking, offering a position teaching pediatrics at the medical school. They immedi- ately moved to Boston, my mom soon enrolled at a graduate program at Harvard, and in their minds, they were set for life. My mom wore Harvard sweaters; my father framed his letter offering him a position teaching in the medical school. They toted me through the campus as a four-year old, to the point that I knew the interiors of the lecture halls and the stacks of the libraries by memory; my father got a membership to the Harvard Faculty Club, where we would brunch on fancy china on Sundays. And they introduced me to one of my father's colleagues, who mentioned that I would be perfect for a kindergarten at Milton Academy.

It all flew over my head at the time. My classmates shared the same last names as all the buildings I saw at Harvard—Taylors, Warrens, Kennedys, Forbeses, no Nguyens. But nothing seemed weird about it to me—not the names, not my parents, not the fact that I lived in a cramped apartment while my friends lived in mansions. I went to horseback-riding camp and cotillion right alongside them, and tore through all the American Girl books in the elementary school's library. I begged my mother for Felicity, the one that lived through the American Revolution (and shipped with a colonial tea set), or Josefina, the one who lived on a hacienda in the Wild West, or Addy, the one who escaped a slave plantation. But Mom insisted that I get a custom Asian doll, to my despair. It did not come with a storybook.

The older I got, and the more Milton let us enter the older buildings now that we were less accident-prone, the more I realized that I, too, lived in history: in the old paintings on the wall at school and the weather-thinned gravestones in the nearby cemetery, where generations and generations of Boston families, some whose ancestors fought in the American Revolution, were laid to rest; in the spines of delicate dusty books and the well-worn grooves in the wooden floors; in the photos of squash teams lining the gymnasium walls dating back to the 1910s; in the battered leather briefcases my teachers had used ever since the 1970s. We were trundled into school buses every other week for field trips through Boston, to the re-creation of the Pilgrims' first settlement at Plimoth Plantation, to the sites of the first battles of the Revolutionary War, to the coastal museums about the beginning of the whaling industry, to the trip to Fenway Park to learn about the great American sport of baseball (and become naturalized citizens of Red Sox Nation). But everything changed when I was cast as Martha Jefferson in our fifth-grade production of the musical *1776*. There were songs about John Adams and Abigail Adams writing letters back and forth, his frustration mounting; songs about the Virginian Richard Henry Lee helping John Adams get a *Resolution! For in-de-pen-den-cy!*; Benjamin Franklin and Robert Livingston cornering Thomas Jefferson into drafting the Declaration of Independence. The debate between the northern and southern colonies over whether to denounce slavery was cut in our school production—the song about the slave trade in the original musical, apparently, had inappropriate lyrics—but we did have a line with Jefferson reluctantly striking a passage concerning slavery from the final draft of the Declaration.

And then we burst into joyous song, which I sung with pride and a sense that I was home:

> And as just as Tom here has written
> Though the shell may belong to Great Britain,
> The eagle inside belongs to us!

————

My earliest *shittiest* memories, on the other hand, were about money, and the increasing lack of it that became apparent around the fifth grade. My father, for reasons unknown to me often told me that he was a genius. "There are four vats of knowledge in the universe," he'd say, "and I have three of them. Maybe you can have one." In his brilliance, he quit his lucrative job to enter the world of dot-com start-ups. I didn't catch on at first—I was distracted with summer camps, trips to the water park, my first computer and AOL account, and two little baby sisters who were wholly unexpected additions to the family. Every other month, it seemed, my father had some new job afloat, or had started some new company. There was one time he took a job that flew him off to Toronto every week until he stopped; another short stretch at some consulting firm; a period when he convinced my friends' parents to join a technology consulting company he started in his basement. Later, to my puzzlement, those parents stopped letting their kids hang out with us.

Suddenly, the self-helpy business books started to show up: Dale Carnegie seminar materials, Robert Kiyosaki's *Rich Dad, Poor Dad* (that one had a board game too), and Donald Trump's *The Art of the Deal.* Mirrors and crystals appeared over all the windows and doors, and my father bought a dragonfish and dug a koi pond in the backyard, determined to use feng-shui principles to direct wealth into the house. Then there was the Milton parent who introduced him to a company called Melaleuca ("She drives a Lexus," he bragged), and he promptly jumped in, procuring dozens of boxes filled with all-natural beauty, skin-care, and cleansing products derived from the power of tea tree oil. The idea was that you would sell these products to other potential partners—friends in your social circle, ideally—who would then sell it to *other* potential business partners. He would demonstrate this opportunity in a presentation to my friends' parents, and one slide had a chart showing the business structure. It looked awfully similar to a pyramid. Eventually, they stopped talking to my father.

By ninth grade, things were *really* bad. My mother was now muttering about $200,000 worth of low-interest student loans that she'd taken out to support my father; my father was now rambling about investing in a Laundromat and tearing holes in the wall for better feng shui. My naïve mother found a tenure-track position at a local state college, blanching when she discovered her salary was only $40,000 a year— but didn't she get a PhD from *Harvard*?!—and my father declared he'd never work for anybody again, dead set on being his own boss.

"Just work at Home Depot," my mom would beg, repeatedly, her voice rising to a fever pitch. My father would run off to the Vietnamese Buddhist temple instead, meditating there for hours and chatting up the local monks and flirting with the impressionable young immigrant women. (Having a PhD, it seemed, was a huge deal to them.)

The inevitable divorce arrived in tenth grade, and my mother, juggling liens, a second mortgage, her student loan repayments, and whatever financial disaster my father had left for her, took her first meeting with the Milton Academy financial aid office, begging them to reconsider our scholarship packages. There was no way she could afford to pay $30,000 a year for one of us, let alone three. Plus, Milton was a rich-person school: it came with free lunch and dinner, and afterschool activities, counselors who could handle her children's academic trajectories and emotional well-being while she struggled to keep the bank from taking our house. It became an annual event for our family for the next decade: every January was Financial Aid Armageddon, when Mom was scrambling for her tax returns, more stressed-out than usual, trying to figure out whether she should teach an extra course to send us to SAT prep camp, or whether that would disrupt the equation that arbitrarily determined how much aid we'd receive. It was also a good way to keep us in line if we misbehaved or deviated from her rules: "I should withdraw you from Milton," she'd threaten us. "You'll go to public school."

As for Dad, he disappeared from our everyday lives, chasing dreams of fast money, easy women, and spiritual fulfillment at various cheap meditation retreats in Vietnam. He would only show up for parent-teacher conferences and graduations, wearing old suits during the cocktail mixers with the rich parents, snapping photos of us from afar (we refused to talk to him), telling anyone who'd listen that his children had inherited *his* smarts, and then leaving immediately whenever Mom would approach to ask about child support.

———

As my home life crumbled, my school life suddenly became more daunting. My class of thirty-two doubled in seventh grade, bringing in dozens of new, wealthy students from the greater Boston area, all of whom my mother furiously looked up online: *Tina, did you know that Elizabeth's father is a billionaire? You should befriend her.* The class of 2007 doubled again in ninth grade, when Milton started accepting boarding students from around the country and the world. There were plenty of scholarship students in the mix—locals, underrepresented minorities, bright kids from rural areas, and a kid from Ukraine—but their tuition was subsidized by a hefty number of extremely rich and extremely powerful people, the kind that even I hadn't seen growing up. The wealthy New Englanders I'd grown up with were modest and thrifty: their L.L.Bean totes were battered and worn, their houses were old and charming but unassuming, the cars were (largely) sensible Subarus. And then, suddenly, I learned that Elizabeth's family owned a *personal helicopter.*

More signifiers of wealth popped up around me as I flailed: Coach bags, North Face fleeces, hockey-playing boys wearing layers upon layers of Ralph Lauren polos. My old friends were suddenly visiting family vacation houses and name-dropping summer programs that I'd never heard of—debate camp at the University of Texas, summer ski training at Mount Hood in Oregon, unofficial internships at the Woods Hole Oceanographic Institution on Cape Cod.

Around this point, my mother had become obsessed with the idea of the *career track record*. Every decision from that period on, she'd read somewhere, would dictate how successful one would be straight out of college, and how quickly they'd be able to achieve it. Naturally, she thought, this meant we had to start building our track records early, and that was the moment she began calibrating my resume for maximal outcome, A/B testing my skills, cramming me into Milton's arts program in hopes in would compensate for my unremarkable math skills. "I can't believe they didn't cast you in the lead," she'd fume after every one of my failed auditions for school plays. "You have such good stage presence. You did TV commercials as a baby! What happened to you?"

I didn't go to summer acting camp at Interlochen like my friends did, I thought. *That's what happened.* Borderline poverty and "oblivious immigrant tiger mom" parenting, I learned, are a bad combination.

———

I didn't know that my first boyfriend would eventually become known as "Chuck Johnson," and that his name would be said by congressmen, journalists, and Trump White House officials with a shuddering revulsion. His phone number would be in the address books of famed white supremacists, his redheaded visage would be seen darting between right-wing billionaire donors at secret parties, his antisemitic blog posts would go viral among disinformation researchers and progressive activists monitoring extremism. His name would appear in the *New York Times* in stories about billionaire Peter Thiel's creepy political donations, and in therapy sessions among victims of his. Roger Stone and Steve Bannon would rant about him but accept his help; Russian intelligence officials would feed him intel meant to destabilize trust in American institutions.

I only knew him as Charlie Johnson, the only boy at Milton just as poor as me.

He'd come to Milton amid the ninth-grade bumper crop and quickly established himself as our token angry Republican. He was prone to picking fights with everyone over some perceived anti-American slight, and was so incandescent in his remarks that the school once had to cancel classes when he nearly sparked a race riot: he said on a web forum that high abortion rates in Black communities meant that there should be a decrease in crime. (I don't remember much of it. I was most likely watching online comedy videos in the AV Club basement, or in the middle of a depressive crying spell, during said race riot.)

I deeply admired Charlie's drive, and so did my mother. "He works for *Alan Dershowitz*," she gasped. Even *she'd* heard of the famous super-lawyer, and she knew that he was a Harvard law professor. Charlie had interviewed him for the school paper in our junior year, and Dershowitz was so impressed by his smarts that he immediately offered him a research position in his office. That summer, during our respective internships in Boston, we would meet at the Harvard Law School's library to do research on potential college scholarships. We went to Charlie's office at Dershowitz's office to print out sheafs of our own personal research—top floor, perfectly air-conditioned, stuffed with books and photos of the professor with various Israeli politicians and an entire wall where the Dersh had taped up his hate mail. Another was full of shelves containing records of Dersh's life—volumes of books with *The People of the State of California v. Orenthal James Simpson* inscribed on their spines, framed photos with Bill Clinton. Charlie would tell me eagerly about the phone calls he fielded from famous people, like Eliot Spitzer and Jeffrey Epstein, to patch through to the Dersh. And then we'd head back to Milton and our threadbare, mildly hovering-above-the-poverty-level homes, both of which we found tense and miserable. Both our mothers were teachers in the public school system, and both our fathers were failing entrepereneurs with connections to Harvard University. (Charlie's dad, specifically, had graduated in the 1970s and now ran various businesses involving music festival paraphernalia.) We were both the eldest of three, too smart for our own good. Too bristly to make many friends, and too poor to feel secure of our place in the world. It was inevitable that one day, we decided to start dating, something my exhausted mother approved of begrudgingly. "Maybe he can help you get focused and into Harvard," she'd say.

But all the verbal whipping and passive-aggressive remarks about my career track did little to correct my path into Harvard. By December of senior year, when my final grades for the semester were already submitted, and when all of my applications had alrcady been filed, my college counselor was grim. Harvard was a pipe dream, he told me, with my *one* bad grade in calculus impossible to overlook despite my A's in everything else that year. So was everything else on my list. In their recommendations to the college admissions boards, my teachers had done their best to explain my divorce-era academic record prior to my junior year. They could lean on every relationship they had, but had warned me my scores needed to be absolutely perfect for the next two semesters. And I'd failed. "Do you have any other options?"

I did. Tulane University in New Orleans was struggling to attract students after Hurricane Katrina, and earlier that year, had sent me an expedited online application that I'd completed in five minutes between classes. Within a week, they'd accepted me, and threw in a hefty scholarship. Frankly, I'd forgotten about Tulane entirely until the moment I realized it was my only option. "I've never *heard* of Tulane, though," I admitted.

"Well, that's probably where you're going," he said kindly.

"The *South*!?" my mother shrieked when she heard.

I sobbed in Charlie's room for days, staying as far away from my shattered mother as I could. I had been competing against the sons and daughters of billionaires and Nobel Prize winners, kids whose parents paid for acting summer camps in Interlochen, Michigan, and knew that a summer at the Martha Graham School of Contemporary Dance would launch their careers in the arts. *They* didn't have to fill out their own financial aid forms, or chase down school officials who could give proof of "Sustained Lack of Financial Support from the Non-Custodial Parent." And in the hypercompetitive halls of Milton, where smarts and talent were valued a hair above wealth and status, bitter students whispered about undeserving classmates with the right last names whose well-connected parents could make the right donation to the right Ivy—whispers that I picked up on, and my mother never quite did.

But Charlie, I thought, was special, and I prayed that he could make it.

He was bringing me out into a real world of intellectuals, outside the confines of our Milton homes. He had taken me to talks hosted by conservative speakers like Daniel Pipes during our relationship, brought me to movie night at the Dersh's house while Alan was away, introduced me to John Derbyshire's podcast, listening to his dulcet, soft British voice as he urgently discussed the ballooning size of government.[1] The Drudge Report was always open in a tab on his web browser, cluttered behind about thirty other windows, *National Review* and John Derbyshire's podcast and a new right-wing website aggregator called Hot Air. He believed in me, in meritocracy, and that he was set to attend Harvard, because he *deserved* it. He had Alan Dershowitz's recommendation, after all, and he was a legacy student, with a father who'd gone to Harvard.

If *he* could perform just as well as them, then maybe there was hope for me.

————

Thirteen college rejections later, as I was glumly clicking through Wikipedia's page on the history of New Orleans and processing the profundity of my failure, I heard shrieks of joy suddenly bursting out of the computer lab. Harvard admissions decisions, it seemed, had landed in everyone's inboxes at the same time. The brilliant Kenzie had gotten in. So did Sam, the student body president. Annie, the scientist; CeCe, the squash player. I got rejected, *again,* but that was to be expected, and my mother, watching my rejections roll in, had already upbraided me for that D+. She could stomach my failure by now.

Wait. What about Charlie?

I scooped up my backpack, ran across campus, up the stairs of Warren Hall, bursting into the student paper office . . . "What happened?!"

He was staring blankly at the screen in disbelief. "I didn't get in," he said.

Within days, he'd rationalized several excuses that I suspected were bullshit, but didn't challenge because I felt bad: he'd actually been wait-listed, not rejected. Dershowitz had worked out a way for him to transfer into Harvard next year. And of *course* our wealthy classmates had bought their way in, they *must* have. He had, however, been a finalist with the Questbridge Scholarship, eligible for increased financial aid at several colleges that had accepted him. One immediately caught his eye. "I think I want to go to Claremont McKenna," he told me as we sat in front of his home computer one day in May, plotting out our prom outfits.

I was confused. "The one in California?" It seemed so far away from the prestigious East Coast schools drilled into our heads, the kind of college our friends' parents would deride as a *safety school*.

CMC, as it's known, apparently had a famous government department. The program took students to Washington for a semester of classes and internships for credit, and the school operated student-run research institutions covering everything from state politics to leadership and political economy. Then he pulled up the website and pointed to the faculty bios: professors who worked in the Reagan administration, former GOP staffers who were now teachers. There was even a research center—and my jaw dropped—called the Salvatori Center for the Study of Individual Freedom in the Modern World, devoted to studying the works of the Founding Fathers.

"Wait," I said. "Can you pull up the section about transfer student applications?"

———

The more that Charlie told me about CMC during our year apart, over cell phone calls and Gchats and Facebook pages, the more I fell in love with it. I could recite its description to a small group of friends who, realizing that they weren't happy at Tulane, were also trying to transfer out: located right on the border of Los Angeles and San Bernardino County, Claremont Men's College was founded in 1946 with an initial class comprised of returning soldiers taking advantage of the GI Bill, went coed in 1976, and eventually became renowned for churning out Reagan-era Republican officials, Wall Street tycoons, Silicon Valley entrepreneurs, and several generations of policy dorks and investment bankers. Charlie and his new Claremont friends filled in the blanks about its student life. It wasn't uncommon for students to brainstorm their internship applications to the White House or the *New York Times* while waiting for their turns at beer pong or stay up until 3 a.m. to practice for their case study interviews with Deloitte or Bain, or put their foot in the door of the exciting new world of tech start-ups like Facebook (which I'd just discovered) and Google (which I'd heard provided beanbag chairs and free food for its employees).

And it was prestigious, which would make Mom happy; it was a *U.S. News & World Report*–ranked top ten liberal arts college. In any given year there were roughly 1,200 type A students on campus, who went on to lead wholesome, high-achieving lives (after, of course, learning how to party harder than most Big Ten frats). Charlie, himself, had gotten a work-study job at the Salvatori Center, and his description was exactly what I wanted to hear: a place to help our professors research the Founding Fathers *and get paid for it*, while rubbing elbows with the biggest names in politics. "People joke that Professor Rossum keeps name-dropping his friendship with Antonin Scalia in every lecture," he told me. I couldn't believe that real humans got to *be* friends with Antonin Scalia. Collectively, he told me, they were known as the Claremonsters: the political philosophy students and teachers of Claremont McKenna who studied the works of Plato, Socrates, Marcus Aurelius, and the Founding Fathers. And they seemed to like him too. Inspired by the *National Review*'s online blog, *The Corner*, he'd started his own blog called *The Claremont Conservative* to jot down his thoughts about various topics, ranging from the current state of the war in Iraq to musings on Barack Obama's ability to run for president, to campus goings-on. The professors had given him their hearty encouragement. "People are *reading it!*" he told me excitedly, showing me the page views and the IP addresses: people as far away as New York were visiting his site.

At Tulane I applied myself harder academically than I ever had before, shaping myself to be the perfect CMCer: I nailed all my English and Spanish and history classes, picked up a job writing op-eds for the *Tulane Hullabaloo*, organized a policy conference for the Roosevelt Institute (which was left-leaning, but I wanted to prove that I could organize a conference), and applied for internships with the new governor of Louisiana, Bobby Jindal, to bolster my CMC-worthy credentials. Charlie relentlessly curated my resume, from the work-study jobs I'd take to the people I hung out with, citing them as bad influences, and I obeyed, because he was successful. I clawed my GPA up to par to secure a transfer—quite an accomplishment in a year when over 300 people applied for 29 spaces.[2]

Though I kept telling Mom about how awesome CMC was, and all the networking opportunities that I could get, she had become suspicious of Charlie and kept hinting that I should break up with him. She watched warily when he told me not to go home for Thanksgiving or Christmas, saying he did not want to see his parents and that I needed to stay with him in California if I loved him, and blanched when he demanded I get a Verizon cell phone, getting off our family's T-Mobile plan, so his calls would be cheaper. And the moment I got the email accepting me into Claremont McKenna in May—"MOM I GOT IN OH MY GOD MOM," I shrieked, dashing down the stairs at home—she looked at me with shock and concern.

"Well, that's lovely, miss," she said finally. "What does the financial aid package look like?"

"It's loan-free."

She sighed, with some sort of disappointment. "Well, as long as you don't have debt, like me."

2

PRESERVING THE IDEALS OF THE AMERICAN FOUNDING

October 2008

Marian Miner Cook Athenaeum

Second-Floor Balcony

Being a research fellow at the Salvatori Center for Individual Freedom in the Modern World[1] had amazing privileges. Charlie had helped me with the application, since he worked there too, and apparently, the professors were charmed by my fondness for drawing cartoons about George Washington. For ten dollars an hour, with shifts twice a week, I was on standby for small errands certain gov professors needed that day: photocopying handouts for a class on natural law,[2] helping them research citations for academic papers, and so forth. Simple work, really. The main purpose was for us to simply *be* there and soak in all their knowledge. I'd do so on the second-floor balcony of the Athenaeum, aka the Ath, the mansion where CMC held its famed nightly dinner talks; I'd be reading my copy of Harold Bloom's *Plato's Republic* for class and trying anxiously to understand why everyone at the Salvatori Center was talking about Straussianism,[3] eating chocolate-covered strawberries and homemade Rice Krispies Treats from the Ath kitchen downstairs. The center was housed in the giant apartment suite on top of the Ath, boasting vaulted ceilings and outdoor patios overlooking the fountain, shaded by a giant old oak tree. I soon realized it was the best office out of all the other research centers. (The Rose Institute of State and Local Government was, essentially, a cinder-block closet next to the snack bar, where the research fellows compiled spreadsheets and data sets in a windowless room.)

One of my first assignments was to coordinate the travel plans for the upcoming Salvatori Conference. About fifteen or so academics and public thinkers were supposed to attend for three days of intense discussion over Leo Strauss's *Thoughts on Machiavelli* (I was auditing the event and reminded myself to read the first chapter) and they were flying in from all over the country. Elvia, the office assistant, had handed me a list of people who were attending and asked me to put together a spreadsheet of their travel arrangements and contact information. I emailed them, reached out to their assistants, and, a week later, handed in my spreadsheet. Out of the sixteen I'd confirmed, a few names had piqued my curiosity:

Harvey Mansfield—will need ride to LAX. The political philosophy legend at Harvard.

William Kristol—not staying Saturday. The editor of the *Weekly Standard.*

Peter Thiel—private plane—private transportation. I did a double take. The Facebook billionaire?

"So what's Thiel doing here?" I asked Charlie later. CMC students, keenly attuned to the school motto of "Civilization prospers with commerce," were obsessed with the goings-on of Silicon Valley and the world of start-ups and venture capital. Someone had been talking about how that Facebook thing I used to poke my high school friends was now worth $15 billion, and Thiel was apparently an angel investor, which I'd understood to be wealthy dudes who gave money to small start-ups in exchange for part ownership of the company. Passive income, my mom had told me during one of her entrepreneurial moments, was the rich person's way to make money.

"Yeah," he said, reading his own copy. "He's also really interested in philosophy. He loves coming to these things." *Oh, that's cool,* I thought.

———

"You wanna come to the Salvatori Awards with me?" Charlie asked me one day.

"Is it here on campus?" I asked, looking up from the book I was annotating.

"Nah, it's at the Claremont Institute. They're holding a dinner. We get to dress up."

I had no idea what the Claremont Institute was, but Charlie and the other fellows filled me in over the next several days: they were the home of the West Coast Straussians[4] and had some loose connection to *our* Salvatori Institute, largely because they shared the same professors and philosophical interests. They, too, studied the texts of the classical philosophers (every Western philosopher from Socrates to Machiavelli) and the documents of American Founding, in hopes to preserve the Founders' vision of America's values and liberties in the face of modernity's social relativism, whatever that meant. (It was here that I first heard the words *socialism* and *progressivism* outside the context of a history book, as if it were an imminent and looming threat.) They published a distinguished conservative magazine—the *Claremont Review of Books*, edited by our very own Charles Kesler—and they were about to give John Bolton, who had served as President George W. Bush's US ambassador to the United Nations, a prestigious award.

I'd learned how to behave at proper dinner parties, the kind with five types of forks and bread plates, thanks to a cotillion program my parents made me take in fifth grade. But when we walked into the five-star Island Hotel in Newport Beach and entered a massive ballroom, I realized that this was beyond cotillion class: this was the world of *important black-tie galas.* Crystal chandeliers hung from this ceiling, casting a golden light on the velvet drapes. The banquet tables here had frickin' *candles* on them. And *centerpieces.* And hundreds of people, old and young, several in tuxedos, eagerly talking about the election with tumblers of whiskey and glasses of champagne. I sipped the glass of red wine that had been placed at my table seat, and my eyes widened in shock at its complexity and nuance. This wasn't a Two-Buck Chuck party. This was a level of decadence and prestige I'd never experienced in my *life.*

As we sat down at our table way in the way, way back, someone caught my eye on the edges of the crowd: a man in a scrubby brown jacket with wild hair, madly going from tuxedoed person to tuxedoed person, deliberately out of place in the group. *Oh my god*, a friend pointed out, *that's Andrew Breitbart.*

What on earth is the internet guy doing here? I wondered.

At that point, Breitbart was the conservative movement's devil trickster god. Compared to the *National Review* or the *Weekly Standard,* or the *Claremont Review of Books,* which our puny libertarian publication tried to emulate, Breitbart.com had a screaming everyman sensibility. It didn't even exist in *print.* When Charlie introduced me to it, I knew he had become so obsessed with reading its articles, which seemed odd for someone who used to read *National Review* blogs regularly, and I never thought that Breitbart would be someone in the Claremont orbit. He was too plebeian, too unsophisticated for what I thought I knew about this world. But if Breitbart was in the room—indeed, he was holding *court*—there was clearly something important about him.

We absorbed Bolton's speech over wine, even though we were still too young to drink. Far away and mustachioed, Bolton thundered the American ideal across the room: a world of American might against the forces of darkness amassing weapons of mass destruction. "Defend America and its allies," he declared. "Defend the interests of America and its allies. And the rest will take care of itself."

We all stood to applaud, then soon stood again for Kesler's traditional toast in honor of Winston Churchill himself (*That's what the brandy was for,* I thought), and then it was all over. But as I readied to head home in the van and throw my shoes off, one of the other fellows soon came over with a giddy excitement. "We got invited to the after-party!"

We hopped in an elevator, zoomed up to the top floor, and gawked as we stepped into the Presidential Suite. The throng of people downstairs, who had paid hundreds, if not thousands of dollars to come to this event—*they* were not allowed in here. There were probably fewer than a hundred VIPs in the suite, helping themselves to the bottles in silver buckets dotting the room and delighting over the quality of cigars in the humidors. This wasn't a normal after-party: this was high-stakes networking, with real adults and real opportunities.

My savvier friends immediately got to chatting with several legal scholars with whom I was unfamiliar. Others peeled straight to Bolton. But Charlie snatched a cigar and beelined to Breitbart, who was smoking on the balcony with several others. Not knowing anyone else in the room, I clung to his side, grabbing a cigar from one of the humidors around the room as well, and hovering behind him as the two of them greeted each other familiarly.

I probably was the least likely person to be on that balcony, and I did not look cool with my cigar, but I waited for some opportunity to enter the conversation. *Look at me*, I prayed silently. Someone said something about race, and I took my opportunity: "I mean, Vietnamese Americans are the most likely constituency to vote Republican," I chirped.

Breitbart smiled, nodded, and then went back to talking intensely to Charlie. We'd all suspected it, but it was made clear that night: Charlie Johnson had been anointed as *the* promising young person.

Something overtook Charlie once he met Breitbart—a hastening of a subtle change I'd noticed ever since I started at CMC. It had manifested as soon as we learned who my new roommate was, whereupon he dug into her Facebook photos, saw that she had been drinking at a college party, and immediately demanded I put in for a room transfer. "She'll be a bad influence on you," he insisted. He suddenly saw the clothes I'd bought while I was at Tulane—spaghetti-strap tanks and sundresses—and told me they were inappropriate and low-class. Then he warned me to stop talking to the Democrats on campus—*But I thought the point of coming to CMC was that we coexisted?*—and soon he started talking about me interacting with the wrong kind of men.

The quirks were bearable when we were in a long-distance relationship, and I'd chalked them up to a romantic notion of us missing each other, but now that we lived less than a hundred yards from each other, it had grown to be too much.

As Election Day rolled closer, it had tilted out of a normal sort of possessiveness into outright paranoia. Obama was going to ruin the country, and the country was about to slide downward, and if I went outside his tightly controlled social orbit, I would have sided with *them*, whoever *they* were, and hasten its decline. "If you loved me and believed in me, you would understand," he said that week, as we headed back from the dining hall with a group of his friends. "People here hate my politics. I'm trying to protect you."

"I thought you believed in freedom of choice," I shot back.

He was quiet for a second. "They're going to hate *you* if you leave me," he finally responded. His friends said nothing.

The night of the election, hundreds of students watched the returns on a projector beneath a giant balloon arch. The Campus Democrats and Republicans were the joint hosts. Some sort of glass ceiling was about to be broken, and either way, there was plenty of fun to be had. One of our friends at our table wondered aloud about the future of universal health care under an Obama administration, and someone else made a racy joke about Kenyans. Charlie seethed silently, and I kept my thoughts to myself: *I* didn't think the world would end if Obama were elected. He seemed friendly, youthful, new; he was a pitch-perfect orator, which made the debate nerd in me sing; he had a similar background to me. I wasn't particularly a fan of his health care plan, but I was positive that Congress would find some way to hem back government excess. The allegations of terrorism? I found them baseless and sort of funny, in a *Daily Show* sort of way. And if he ate dog, so what? *I'd* eaten dog meat in Vietnam before.

There wasn't a singular explosive moment when it became clear that Obama would win, but a murmur of excitement built as the election map filled in. State after state turned blue, falling like a wall between the dark past and the hopeful, clear sky. The one student with the iPhone kept rapidly refreshing RealClearPolitics on his screen, shouting out election results before they even popped up on the screen. And CMC students were smart enough to add up the math: the screaming and cheering began five minutes before the network called it.

There was a glazed, distant look in Charlie's eyes as we walked out from the party, back to Stark Tower. *How does it make you feel, Chuck?* one student yelled on the way out. Charlie didn't respond. I desperately wanted to congratulate them, say that I was happy, at the very least, to see that a Black man had become president, but an unknown terror gripped me as I stood next to Charlie. *I voted Libertarian*, I demurred.

Over the next few days, Charlie got moodier, clinging on to me as if I were a security blanket he owned. "You don't understand how scared I am for this country," he kept repeating as his behavior became worse. "You have to do this for me. You're a bad girlfriend if you don't."

Finally, late on Thursday night in his room, he stopped. "I don't want to make you cry," he said, smiling as if he were doing me a kindness, and went to sleep.

I woke up in a daze the next morning, left his bedroom without speaking. I sat through a literature class, trembling as teenagers debated *Madame Bovary* around me. I wanted to cry everywhere I went, wondering what he'd told everyone at Claremont about me, wondering whether I still wanted to be his girlfriend, wondering if throwing myself off Stark Tower was a better option.

Instead, I broke up with him over Gchat.

I deleted the text thread over eleven years ago—long before Donald Trump tweeted his first tweet, before the Breitbart News site was launched, before Charlie became famous, and before we even graduated—as part of a therapeutic exercise. The hope was that by deleting the message, I would be able to let go of what happened that night—that I'd stop sending myself into a PTSD spiral whenever I read it, that I'd be able to move on one day. But I will always remember the last message he sent:

"I don't want to be your enemy. Can we say it was mutual?"

———————

"Just ignore him, miss," my mother told me over the Thanksgiving break. "You can't let him scare you out of Claremont." It was both her attempt at comforting me and a pragmatic observation. I was going to CMC without student loans, and my mother's life had been destroyed by the ones that she'd taken out for my father—a fate she wanted me to avoid at all costs, even before anyone had known the extent of the student loan crisis. At that point, she'd only started making a dent in what she owed to her debtors, and if I went back to Tulane, I would be taking out at *least* $10,000 a year to attend—possibly more, considering that my father had essentially vanished.

"I can't," I wailed, struggling to explain. No matter how hard I tried to get away from him, it was impossible to avoid him on the tiny campus, and he'd made sure that I knew it. I don't know his motives, but I know that I felt threatened. He would show up to my door with orange juice when he heard I'd been coughing; he would call me and rage when he found out I was drawing cartoons for a publication that was *not* his blog. He even tried to curate my dating pool: *Charlie told me that he would be fine with me dating you*, one of the Salvatori fellows told me, puzzled. But Charlie was *important*. He knew Alan Dershowitz. He knew the people who knew John Bolton. He had the number of Peter Thiel, and Andrew Breitbart, and the editors of the *National Review*, and whoever else read his blog. And he could not be touched: he had started telling people that he was downloading their Facebook photos for future collateral. The unsaid threat: he would ruin me if I didn't obey.

This meant nothing to my mother. She had survived a war and a refugee camp, stuck in Indonesia for two years while waiting for asylum, and though she never spoke about her experience while she lived, her tolerance for bad men doing monstrous things was quite high. Even if there was a part of her that felt bad, my trauma at a nice, safe American college, I learned after she died, barely compared to her worst days in Vietnam.

Perhaps I'd started to mirror her disdain for looking back at the past. All I knew was the example she set for me, and I clung to it like flotsam in the ocean: I would *not* let Charlie, Chuck, *whomever* he'd become, take away my choice to study what I wanted, where I wanted, or go down the path that I wanted. And despite my failures, Mom would never let me completely collapse.

That weekend, I pulled up the newest iteration of the Claremont Jobs Email, searching for journalism internships. At Milton, I'd consistently gotten A's in my English classes and won the school prize for nonfiction writing, and if I was good at something, I thought, I should make a career in it. Immediately, several opportunities leapt out: communications internships in Republican congressional offices, fellowships at the National Journalism Center;[5] several research jobs run by the Koch Foundation.[6] But the Institute for Humane Studies (IHS) at George Mason University stood out: it could place me at a high-quality publication for the summer—the *Wall Street Journal*, MSNBC, and Bloomberg were listed as options—and it was *paid*. I quickly hammered out an application, writing a long, Claremont-infused essay about the topic of liberty in the modern society, and uploaded it to the portal.

Please look at me, I thought, as I hit the "submit" button. *I'm a promising young person.*

3

RIGHT-WING
SUMMER CAMP

June 2009
Bryn Mawr College
The Suburbs of Philadelphia

I'd taken the Amtrak from DC to Philadelphia, the SEPTA train to the suburbs, and arrived at the secluded, misty Bryn Mawr campus aglow. I'd packed properly—six days' worth of clothes, notebooks, pens, toiletries, and a camera. ("Whether taking pictures of the campus and nearby sights, or capturing memories with your new friends, you'll be glad you brought one," the internship coordinator had written us in our orientation email.) I checked into my dorm—cozy, puritanical, reminiscent of the dorms at my prep school—received a packet full of documents, dropped off my bags, and headed over to the lecture hall.

I then spotted John Elliott, the official head of the Institute of Humane Studies' Journalism Program and the unoffical group mentor, for the first time: tall, thin, a head full of white hair, a pleasant face that looked straight out of a Dutch Old Masters painting, a blue oxford shirt that made him instantly professorial. I immediately darted over to say hello, bubbling with type A excitement. "It's great to meet you!" I said, shaking his hand. "I'm so excited to be here."

"We're happy to have you," John said with a warm smile.

It was time to kick off the start of my journalism career: I now had a paid journalism internship for the summer—a huge deal in the post-recession year of 2009—at Broadband Census, a tech policy publication in DC that covered the growth of high-speed internet. It wasn't as sexy as an internship at the *New York Times* (impossible to get) or as well-known as *The Hill* (which was unpaid), but it was an *internship* in *journalism* that *paid me*, and paid me well: $400 a week for eight weeks, a $350 reimbursement for travel.[1] As a condition of the scholarship, however, I had to attend a mandatory "Journalism and the Free Society" seminar.

This wasn't a big deal, and in fact, I was anticipating it. Back when my family could afford them, I *loved* nerdy summer camps whether it was theater camp or PSAT prep. And judging from the email invite, this just seemed like an even *better* version of it, especially since they paid for my travel and gave us free room and board.

"You know, the influences you listed on your application were one of the best we received this year," said John as we entered the lecture hall, rows of seats at an incline facing a pit and the desk where the teacher normally would stand.

"Yeah," I replied, mildly embarrassed.

"It was very sharp . . . I turned down students from Harvard who answered that question incorrectly." He scoffed. "They said things about being influenced by Oprah and Bill Gates."

I had listed *Notes on the Constitutional Convention,* James Madison's detailed accounting of every debate the Founders hit as they invented an unheard-of form of republican government. I'd read it as part of my American Constitution class that spring, and I'd devoured it as if it were a thriller novel: the wrestling over the Virginia Plan, the heated debates over the role of the presidency, the uncomfortable tragedy of the Founders weighing the inalienable rights of Black Americans over the economic benefits of keeping them as slaves for this young nation. "I mean, the idea of all those guys in a room trying to balance everyone's interests out to create something that outlasted the monarchy? It's so cool."

I took my seat, still slightly puzzled at John's enigmatic nod. *There was a* correct *answer?* But I quickly brushed it off: I'd beaten Harvard students for this internship. Mom would like that.

———

My resume had been perfectly calibrated for an aspiring college journalist-slash-essayist: I'd reported stories for the *Claremont Independent,* our conservative paper, wrote restaurant reviews for the *Student Life* at nearby Pomona, and occasionally drew cartoons for the *CMC Forum.*) I wasn't quite sure why the IHS Journalism internships had been buried in an email list of conservative internships (I immediately passed on PJ Media's[2] "Generational Theft" essay contest, even with its $10,000 prize[3]), but it seemed safe. Its interns went to places like ABC News, MSNBC, Fox News, or a scattering of muscular regional papers like the *Dallas Morning News* or the *Orange County Register.* The internship money traveled with me, too, if I found an unpaid gig elsewhere. And I shot applications everywhere else too. (For some reason, my email to the New Orleans *Times-Picayune*'s editor kept getting eaten—probably kept landing in a spam filter, and I was too young to realize that I could send things like follow-up emails.)

After several phone interviews earlier that spring, John Elliott set me up with an internship with the Philadelphia *Bulletin*. I quickly looked it up: established in 1847, the *Bulletin* had been a civic institution of Philly, and had once boasted the largest circulation of evening newspapers in the country. It eventually collapsed in the 1980s, when people stopped reading evening newspapers. In 2004, Thomas G. Rice, a Pennsylvania-based investment banker with pro-life views and a penchant for attempting to acquire newspapers, bought the rights to the *Bulletin*'s name and relaunched it as the *Evening Bulletin,* a paper promising "biting, conservative commentary" and run by editor in chief Kevin Williamson, a *National Review* editor and columnist. The launch had been ambitious—twenty-five-cent broadsheets, street hawkers screaming "Extra, extra!" on busy corners, an eventual staff of twenty-five reporters, as Williamson told the Associated Press—and I imagined myself as a scrappy young journalist, in an ink-stained newsroom straight out of *All the President's Men.* It would be a summer of beat reporting, interviewing Philly pols and reviewing new restaurants and covering local crime. "It's a done deal," Elliott promised me in April, the day of my birthday. I breathed a sigh of relief, happy to have that responsibility squared away, and gladly surrendered as my Salvatori Center friends, as per CMC birthday tradition, kidnapped me that evening and threw me in the fountain.

But as May rolled around, and finals week crept up, I started wondering about a sublet, and shot an email to John Elliott asking for logistical details. The email he wrote back punched me in the gut. "I sent you this email on April 24th. Did you not get it?"

I am afraid that I have bad news. The Bulletin has chosen only three interns for this summer and you were not among the candidates they chose. I sent them 6 resumes for 4 slots. But they decided to only fund three internships. That was a bit of a surprise.

The other two candidates they rejected were exceptionally gifted and experienced. So if it is any consolation, you were rated ahead of them.

I am afraid that I have even more bad news. **I don't think that I will be able to place you in an IHS funded internship.** *I am bound by financial considerations now and the loss of one slot at the Bulletin—which pays half the stipend—seriously upsets my planning. If one of the three chosen at the Bulletin drops out, then I can propose you as a replacement. But unless I can find an internship in which the media outlet pays half the stipend, then my hands are tied.*

You are technically a sophomore and very few sophomores get internships. You will be a stronger candidate for next year.

I nearly blacked out in the Poppa Computer Lab, head spinning. *No internship*, I thought, as my heart raced. *It's May 4. It's finals week. Internship applications are closed everywhere else. I'll have* nothing. The blood was draining from my face. *I'm going to have to go home to Mom.* I quickly emailed him back, telling him that I'd never received his email and that I was, in no uncertain terms, fucked for the summer. "I had been given every reason to believe that our four slots at the Bulletin were a done deal," he wrote back. "That is why I was so surprised to hear that. That is why I wrote you right after getting off the phone. I should have followed up with a telephone call. I feel terrible that that email did not arrive. I will have to see what I can do for you."

But what if he couldn't follow through? Studying for finals could wait—

had to wait—in a matter of life or death. Over the next several hours, I wrote desperate emails to everyone I knew. I ran to the Salvatori Center to beg Professor Blitz for any leads, cornered Professor Kesler in the hallway for asks, and kept sending email after email to Elliott to see if there was anything I could do to help him help me. I weighed the possibility of asking Chuck for a favor but remembering what a former friend of his had told me: *He heard you were dating someone else and called me a bad friend for not telling him.* At one point, I even called Elliott, nearly sobbing on the phone, pleading for *something to do* that summer. The *Times-Picayune* had already locked in their interns, and certainly did not have funding to match IHS; the local papers back in Boston didn't even *have* internship programs I could take on short notice. And where else could I go that would have a reporting-related skill—an ad firm, a political campaign—that would pay me, much less hire me? If I did nothing this summer, I thought, I would be doing nothing the *next* summer. And with nothing to do next summer, I would have nothing to do once I graduated. I imagined coming home to my mother in three weeks, and the look of rage and disappointment that would cross her face: *You're just like your father.*

I hardly slept that night, and jumped out of bed the next morning, manic, to start internship-hunting anew. But I'd barely sat down at my research station at the Salvatori Center when—*ding!*—John Elliott's name appeared in my inbox. "Drew Clark at BroadbandCensus.com is an ally of IHS. He has a news service aimed at following the high speed internet services industry," it read. "He needs an intern and we would like to place one with him."

For the past twenty hours, I'd felt like I had been shoved off a skyscraper and my life was in free fall. I now felt like I'd landed in a dump truck full of sponges that had appeared out of nowhere. "This would be a great opportunity!" I wrote back immediately. "But will I still get IHS funding? That's a major concern of mine."

"We would fund you. Yes."

Other strokes of luck soon followed. Professor Blitz carved out $2,000 from the Salvatori Center budget, beefed up that summer by a grant from the Koch brothers, to assist Professor Thomas on a project about American presidents and their views on civic education (with my focus primarily on Woodrow Wilson and Thomas Jefferson). I quickly secured a two-month sublet on a Wisconsin Avenue studio, overlooking the Washington National Cathedral, within walking distance of two friends who were also doing internships. My mom got off my back, happy that I was now *building a career track record*—and, I'd learned with glee, certain Washington bars were loose about checking IDs. And in 2009, $5,200 over the course of two months was more than what my mother made in the same period. My future was back on track. I was going to learn reporting skills. I was going to be out of suburban Boston. And most importantly, I had something to add to my resume—who *cares* if it wasn't the *New York Times*, I was a sophomore with a reporting internship!

I was so thrilled with my good fortune that I nearly missed the news that, two days before the June seminar, the *Bulletin* announced that it would stop publishing its print edition. Rice had laid off the entire staff, telling them that the paper couldn't afford to operate any longer; its managing editor, John Rossomando, told *Editor & Publisher* magazine that a crash in ad sales—an increasingly frequent phenomenon in post-recession newsrooms—had made funding the publication impossible. In a message on its home page, Rice promised that the *Bulletin* would return that August with a Sunday print edition and a daily online blog, and asked current readers to purchase $100-per-year gift subscriptions for schools and friends.

Whew. Guess I dodged a bullet, I thought, and kept packing for Washington.

The *Bulletin* never came back online.

————

With all the heart-stopping drama surrounding whether I'd have an internship or not, the seminar seemed like a fun if academic requirement compared to the near-death experience I'd just gone through. It was only a week of being on a college campus, learning the history of classical liberalism, the benefits of liberty, and the ways that the mainstream media sometimes got things wrong. But I was surprised when I met several other kids who didn't have internship placements.

"Oh, they just invited me to come," said Maxwell, a gangly boy who sat down next to me, wearing a suit in the sweltering heat. "They thought I was interested enough in the cause." *Allies? Causes? Right answers?*

It turned out that there were more than just aspiring journalists in the crowd. There were philosophy students who'd wanted to discuss free-market economics, economists who wanted to delve into the philosophy of the eighteenth-century British thinker Edmund Burke[4] and eagerly grabbed the free copies of Adam Smith's 1759 economics treatise, *The Theory of Moral Sentiments.*[5] There were budding activists who wanted to understand the inner workings of journalism and perhaps become speechwriters or comms officials. There were a few who had gone to other IHS seminars and were all too happy to attend another. But all of us, I could tell instantly, were mega-nerds who had been reading the latest blogs about the growing Tea Party movement, attenuated to the greater political world around us and eager to enter it, so eager that we gave up the first week of vacation to attend libertarian summer camp—though some, I thought as I watched Maxwell talk about cigars and the left, seemed more eager than others.

The professors at Claremont had approved of the Institute for Humane Studies since it was affiliated with George Mason University, whose economics and philosophy departments were on the bleeding edge of current libertarianism in those times. Founded in 1961, the institute hoped to promote the ideas of classical liberalism: free-market economics, freedom of expression and thought, a tolerant and pluralistic society that recognized and rewarded merit, civilized rebellion against the imperious academic and political elite that believed their degrees and privilege made them wise and prudent rulers. The institute had largely focused on fostering right-leaning scholars who studied topics like political philosophy, legal theory, economics, and the like, even offering yearlong fellowships and stipends for graduate students to pursue their careers in academia, courtesy of the Koch Foundation. As far as I could tell, the journalism program was relatively new—perhaps a few years old or so—and, if I did my math correctly, had a budget of well over a million dollars if they were accommodating interested nonjournalists, which made up roughly half the attendees at this seminar.

It was a good time to be a libertarian, too, especially a millennial one, in the years before the iPhone's ubiquity and when Facebook's functionality was limited to pokes and tagged photos. We'd all shared a keen suspicion of George W. Bush's administration, tired of the war in Iraq as it grew blatantly pointless, unnerved by the expansion of the post-9/11 security state and the paranoia of our elders. We were still too young to understand what the hell a subprime mortgage was, but we could see that our friends and family were suddenly losing their jobs and homes. But it had only been mere months since Barack Obama had taken office and immediately announced bailout packages for homeowners who'd taken out bad mortgages—using *our damn taxpayer money* to save the idiots who couldn't afford houses in the first place—and the thought that he'd do the same with universal health care was unnerving. This libertarian moment gave us a morally clear path down the middle, between two parties we could not stomach: rejecting the authoritarian surveillance state of the Bush era, and dragging the country away from the potential authoritarian communist state of a well-meaning Obama era. *Where were you when Rick Santelli declared the beginning of the Tea Party?* could have been a getting-to-know-you game among us. (I was personally in the Salvatori Center office, watching a grainy CNBC clip with my friends in which the anchor ranted about the people's anger.)

The next few days were sheer heaven for me. By day, we'd sit and listen to lectures from famous libertarian and right-leaning writers—Williamson from *National Review* (and formerly the *Bulletin*), Megan McArdle from *The Atlantic*—alongside actual, living, breathing journalists, such as Gretchen Morgenson from the *New York Times*, and philosophy professors, discussing the works of David Hume. We'd break out for discussions, debating and hashing over what we'd learned and putting together mini-presentations. I met young journalists who were striving as hard as I was—Lachlan Markay, interning at the *Washington Examiner*; Rachael Bade, interning at *The Hill*; me, interning at some random weedsy policy blog—as we flocked around the professors and teachers at lunch, seeking more of their insight, before going back to lecture for the afternoon. At night there was a lot of free booze (beer and wine only) and no one particularly cared how underage we all were. Sometimes Williamson, fresh off his recent layoff from the Philadelphia *Bulletin*, would come out to join us, dressed in black and swinging around a bottle of something amber in a crystal cut bottle, which we thought was totally badass. It vaguely reminded me of being on the balcony with Andrew Breitbart the previous year, with a twist: this time, IHS had *wanted* me to be there, so much so that the very director of the program had *fought* for me to have a job that summer. I looked around at the beaming faces of my fellow nerds on the couches, as Williamson gave us an informal seminar on what we *needed* to know about whiskey. For a twenty-year-old always kicked into the cold, I thought belonging somewhere felt *great.*

When I went back to CMC that fall, with a summer's worth of dull reporting on broadband internet policy on my resume, another email from Elliott soon landed in my inbox. "I'm writing to invite you to participate in one of IHS's most selective, invitation-only opportunities—the IHS Mentoring Program," it read. "You have been selected for participation based on your interest in classical liberal ideas and your interest in a career with the potential to advance those ideas. . . . Navigating the world of journalism and staying aware of opportunities to advance your career can be daunting. Through the Mentoring Program, I would work closely with you to craft a game plan and do everything I can to help you achieve your intellectual and career-development goals."

I broke into a grin. I couldn't believe my luck. "I think my future looks a little bit brighter," I wrote to my mother, forwarding her the invite. She'd always wanted me to have a mentor.

Every time I sent my resume out, or found a new job listing, or prepared for an interview, I would send it to Elliott first, and he gave me

quiet encouragement and gentle feedback. Professional presentation, he told me, was just as important as the entries on my resume,
and he'd forward as many journalistic career development seminars as
he could: the "Journalism Career Workshop," where a young woman
named Mollie Hemingway[6] would teach attendees how to hone pitches
to editors, or "TV for Print Journalists," hosted at the Leadership Institute,[7] where we were trained on how to be camera-ready at their
journalism center. (I quickly signed up, remembering the various di-
sheveled journalists I met during my internship who had lacked social
graces and hit their professional ceiling ten years earlier.)

But internships still mattered, too, and Elliott was more than happy
to edit my cover letters and give me leads. "The Collegiate Network[8]
[CN] wants to support students who desire to be full-time journalists,"
he told me, sending me a link to a website. "I think it is good to stress
that you have been politically active but really want a career in journalism. That is what they are looking for." He gently warned me to stay
away from a job with Andrew Sullivan, the famous libertarian blogger,
who was in the market for a researcher: "He is all over the place politically. He was for the Iraqi war. Yet IDs as a kind of liberal. It would
be an interesting job. If you could get it, it would be a great start in
DC." My eye was on the golden internship: the Eric Breindel Collegiate
Journalism Award, funded by News Corp,[9] came with a summer job at
the *Wall Street Journal* or Fox News, a $10,000 stipend, and free lodg-
ing in a Fifth Avenue apartment. Several other *Claremont Independent*
writers had won the award, and I couldn't imagine that a mainstream
publication would turn away someone who'd interned at the freaking
Wall Street Journal. Elliott delicately told me it was a long shot, with college editors in chief and opinion editors having the most likely chance,
and sent me more achievable opportunities in libertarian-world with

right-leaning publications with a decent amount of respect—*National Review, Reason*, the *Washington Examiner.* (But never the *Weekly Standard*, which, as everyone in his circles kept telling me, was neoconservative garbage hell-bent on waging a Forever War in the Middle East.) I kept getting spammed with tempting offers in my inbox, which may have not aligned with my interests but seemed good enough for the ol' resume: The Heritage Foundation[10] sent me an invite to a free seminar called "What Every Job Seeker Should Know About the History of the Conservative Movement." The Leadership Institute sent me numerous opportunities to apply for the Youth Leadership School, a two-day "comprehensive campaign and activist training" course.

But I was eager to cultivate a relationship with John Elliott, my best shot at a career in journalism—so much so that when he told me he was coming to Los Angeles for an IHS cocktail event, I begged my friend Elise to borrow her car and drove the two hours from Claremont to a ballroom at the Marriott Marina del Rey. I got there, had a glass of hotel wine, spent face time with Elliott, who seemed pleased to see me, had another glass of hotel wine, met several other activists, exchanged contact information, and drove back to Claremont slightly tipsy after the happy hour wound down. *That was networking,* I told myself, focusing intently on the dark road ahead. *Networking is important.*

Remembering the brutal lesson I'd learned with the *Bulletin* in 2009—the news industry had become even more battered in the months since—I started applying for internships in quasi-related industries as backup plans: law firms, tech companies, public relations shops, anything that looked good to recruiters and future editors. At one point, I met Heidi Cruz, a CMC alumna and the wife of the new Texas Solicitor General, Ted Cruz, and she immediately offered to help me out if I wanted to interview with Goldman Sachs: "You have lots of promise, I can tell!" (I then remembered I had no aptitude for math and didn't follow up.) I landed an internship at Wexler & Walker Public Policy Associates, making enough money for my mom to be satisfied, and returned to DC that summer. In the mid-1980s, founder Anne Wexler, a former Jimmy Carter aide who'd given Bill Clinton his first job in politics, stumbled across the game-changing revelation that corporate clients could accomplish more if a lobbying firm hired both Democrats *and* Republicans. As a result, she'd stacked her firm with a vast array of lobbyists from across the ideological spectrum. "As much as I'd love to work in journalism, nothing has really panned out this summer and by this point, I'm taking whatever I can get," I wrote John Elliott. "I'm hoping lobbying will give me a lot of contacts and teach me new research skills, as well as allow me an opportunity to see DC from the other side."

Elliott wrote that he understood the urgency. "The lobbying internship sounds interesting. You will get very useful experience and information. It will help you be a better journalist. I would apply to CN next year regardless. And why don't you look our way too."

Oh thank goodness he approves, I thought, and immediately set up a coffee date for when we both were in Washington.

Maxwell had come to DC that summer too, taking the same internship at the same blog writing about broadband internet, but journalism was the furthest thing from his mind. His goal, as he told me as we hung out over beers and cigars that summer, was to become a Republican speechwriter and eventually write op-eds for conservative publications. And he was drilling deep into the heart of Republican activism in a way that even I hadn't known about. "Wait," I sputtered when he told me about the people he interviewed for his thesis. "How the hell do you know *Grover Norquist?!*"

"Oh, I emailed him for a school paper," he told me lightly. "He helped me out and we kept in touch."

Grover Norquist, the head of the advocacy group Americans for Tax Reform,[11] was one of the most powerful activists in the current movement, famous for wanting to reduce the power of the federal government—in his own words, "to get it down to the size where we can drown it in the bathtub." He also ran an event called the Wednesday Meeting, a gathering so influential that it got its own profile in the *New Yorker* a few years before. Every week, Norquist would invite representatives from all the conservative and Republican organizations in Washington for coffee and bagels, where they'd update each other on what they were doing and where they were going at any given time. It was all off the record—*ooh, spooky,* I thought—and its goal was to make sure every conservative knew what the other conservatives were doing at any given time, so there wouldn't be any accidental overlap or crossfire. There would be representatives from the Senate, the House, and the White House (if there was a Republican president), the official GOP committee and its attendant arms (even the College Republicans sent an emissary), activist groups like the National Rifle Association and the Heritage Foundation, interested lobbyists with a Republican background, foreign guests from conservative movements around the world. And Maxwell, apparently.

I must have asked some of the Republicans at Wexler about the importance of the Wednesday Meeting, because they suddenly became interested in lending advice. Bob Walker, the former House minority whip and now a SpaceX lobbyist, told me war stories about him and Newt Gingrich learning how to use C-SPAN, and Monty Tripp, a sharp redheaded woman who served as general counsel, invited me to a Republican Women's Federal Forum luncheon at the Capitol Hill Club.

Maxwell freaked out when I told him about the lunch: that building, he told me, was *the* GOP's private club, a town house steps away from the Capitol complex, where aides and members of Congress mingled with other Republican power brokers.

Now *I* was nervous.

I put on my nicest outfit, dressed to impress, and teetered on high heels off the DC Metro escalator, up two blocks to the entrance of the Capitol Hill Club, where a woman asked for my name and who I was visiting. Oh my, I thought, walking up a grand staircase flanked by two carved wooden elephants and entering a large dining room. Monty waved me over to the table in the middle of the room, where several stately women with perfect bobs and crisp suits sat around a table. "Tina is a very promising young woman who works with me," she said.

"Pleasure to meet you," I said to the woman to my right as I sat down.

"Barbara Grassley. Pleasure to meet you as well."

Wait. Mrs. Grassley? As in, the wife of Iowa senator Chuck Grassley?! I sat up straighter. These were the wives of Republican senators, who chattered about the important things their husbands were doing. There were other powerful women, too, in federal positions, chatting about the news of the day and the policy they'd been working on. I listened eagerly, and with Monty vouching for me, they seemed happy to entertain my questions. *The things one could achieve by being a promising young person in the Republican Party,* I marveled, as Mrs. Grassley passed me the butter.

In my spare time, I was obsessively listening to YouTube song parodies. Maxwell and I had bonded over our love of musicals and song parodies, tooling around with a rewritten version of "My Fair Lady" titled "My Fair Palin." At one point, we got bored and created a music video parody wherein I pranced around in a bad Lady Gaga outfit and sang our own lyrics to "Alejandro" about the summer intern season (*"You know you're an intern, boy / still in college, unemployed"*). It had gone viral that summer, with a whopping forty thousand views in DC—Wexler & Walker seemed okay with it, as long as I hadn't mentioned the firm's name—and Maxwell had forwarded it to Grover Norquist. "He wants us to show it at the Wednesday Meeting!" he said the next day.

I was more nervous for this breakfast conference than I was for the Republican women's luncheon, putting on my best Going to the Athenaeum face as I entered a bland, gray conference room on the top floor of Americans for Tax Reform. Roughly eighty or so people were milling about, gnawing on bagels and pounding box coffee. Maxwell and I had printed out roughly forty sheets of paper describing our project—*UnBeltway, a political song parody duo more risqué than the Capitol Steps*—and deposited one at each seat, atop a pile of other pamphlets and printouts from other attendees. There were some chortles. Oh god, I thought, this was *stupid.*

But we were *swarmed* after our brief presentation. Activists, comms people, everyone came up to us to drop business cards in our hands: a music video parody for their organization about Obamacare; maybe an original song for the Susan B. Anthony List[12] about the evils of abortion. We took their cards, promised to reach out for coffees, shook their hands, then exited the room and, once we were sure no one could see us, began giggling with delight. We were *college students.* And these grown-up, powerful people—this secret community that actually set the agenda for the Republican Party—treated us like their peers.

———

I took advantage of all my new Republican connections as graduation and the real world drew closer, getting those coffees and asking them as many questions as I could, and they were always happy to oblige. I hit up Grover for help on my college thesis on Asian American voting patterns, and he immediately set me up with a friend of his who'd worked on AAPI outreach for the Bush administration. Monty connected me with Elaine Chao, the former secretary of labor who now worked at the Mercatus Center[13] and, like her, had been a member of the Republican Women's Federal Forum, for said thesis. (The interview never took place, for some reason, but the fact that I got close to a former cabinet member as a college student was cool enough.) It was *much* harder to lock down Democrat sources, much less any of the caliber of America's top Republican activist and a former cabinet official, and I promised to send the Very Important People my thesis once it was done. I flew to more seminars and met more people: philosophy students, economists, up-and-coming writers, people hoping to build futures within the conservative movement—and tried to see John Elliott whenever he was in Los Angeles.

Graduation was approaching and I needed to hustle, hard. The economic forces that took down the Philadelphia *Bulletin* were rippling outside of the news industry, and full-time, entry-level jobs and postgrad fellowships were rarer in 2011 than they were in 2009. I worked my Republican connections for comms jobs—I even toyed with the extracurricular idea of joining the comms team for a conservative Senate candidate out of Maine until a CMC professor gently dissuaded me, after seeing that the candidate had a ponytail. With my mother's disapproving sigh echoing in my mind, I expanded my search and sent applications to places like Groupon and (a long shot) Google.

John Elliott, too, had his own network for me building in his head, and as graduation loomed, he had an idea. In April, he forwarded me an email from someone searching for a tech reporter for the Daily

Caller. "At the time I thought of you. You have the experience for this and it would get you to DC. Shall I tell Jon to contact you?"

I instantly said yes. I'd followed the launch of the Daily Caller for a few months now, and I'd been fascinated by the premise: it was pitched as the right's own version of the *New York Times*—the news from a conservative perspective, driven by heavy-hitting, factually driven journalism. It was staffed by people who'd worked at legitimate places. And it was a job. In journalism. That *paid me.*

And *I could work for Tucker Carlson.*

4

THE DAILY CALLER

So how would you describe yourself politically?"

Neil Patel was the publisher of the Daily Caller, running the business side to Tucker's editorial, and was looking at me intently. Prior to that, he was the chief policy advisor for Dick Cheney, acting as the gatekeeper for the most powerful vice president in history. Patel's time in the White House was chronicled all over the walls, in pictures and in letters signed by Cheney himself, and his office, with its leather couch and dark wood paneling, looked like a suburban lawyer's office (but with more Dick Cheney). It was a stubborn contrast to what I'd glimpsed outside in the Caller offices—a jumbled, start-upy mess of birch IKEA tables, red IKEA Jules swivel chairs, a Ping-Pong table, and a kegerator.

"I'd say libertarian," I said brightly, sitting up primly in a green seersucker J.Crew jacket with my ankles politely crossed. Years of Koch-funded intellectual and professional training had given me quick facility in all things involving libertarian ideology, as well as the ability to present professionally and navigate an interview. At least, I hoped it did: this was the first real-world test. "Free market. Freedom of speech. Inalienable rights. All that jazz. I love what you're doing here, by the way."

I was ushered into another office to talk to Tucker Carlson, and stepped into what seemed to be a parallel world to the start-up madness outside: overflowing bookcases, a massive couch, Persian rugs on the floor, and fly-fishing poles leaning on the walls, all well-worn from years of loving use; posters of old presidential campaigns, paintings of placid, remote lakes, and other wall art of the estate sale genre, covering as much generic gray paint as possible. There was something immediately familiar about the place. Neil's office was formal, an attempt to establish order; Tucker's domain looked like he'd simply teleported prep school English teacher's den into a bleak office building as a prank. And Tucker was there, too, in a pink oxford button-down, chinos, sans bow tie, dressed the way that other parents at Milton Academy would dress.

We ran through the perfunctory get-to-know-you questions: where are you from, where did you go to college. He paused when I told him I'd attended Milton. "Do you know Todd Bland?"

"Oh yeah," I said, surprised. "He became headmaster after I graduated. How do you know him?"

"I *hate* that guy."

I gawked. *This* was Tucker Carlson? I remembered him from the first viral political moment of my youth, the one that transfixed me as a fourteen-year-old: a much younger Tucker Carlson on CNN, getting his ass thoroughly handed to him by Jon Stewart as the *Daily Show* host called his show "partisan hackery." At the time, I thought CNN had just made a terrible programming error, and that Tucker was himself a conservative who'd been given a raw deal and understood the purpose of theater. But as I diligently researched his background prior to our interview, I learned that he had my dream job: *a magazine features writer.*

Long before he became a cable news figure—and even *while* he was reporting on television for CNN and MSNBC—Tucker was writing features for *Esquire,* the *New Republic,* the *Weekly Standard,* thousands and thousands of three-dollar words per assignment. The legendary editor Tina Brown, who'd run *Vanity Fair* and the *New Yorker,* had brought him on to write for her latest venture, *Talk.* He was coasting through the skies of Liberia on a rickety prop plane with Al Sharpton; he was a fly on the wall next to George W. Bush during his first campaign, so good at his job that he could get the future president to let his guard down enough to make a mocking imitation of a woman on death row, begging for clemency. He wrote odes to the Ingenuity of the potato cannon for a print issue of *GQ.* He sat at bars, long after he became sober, scribbling slice-of-life articles about the Palm's longtime maître'd', a steak house host for the ultra-wealthy, for the *New York Times.* The words he used to bring those episodes to life were also, undoubtedly, *his* words and his views—none of these magazines dared to impose an official House Voice on their famous writers—and most importantly, he got *paid* to do it. The TV thing, to my young eyes, seemed secondary.

So how did he know *Todd Bland?*

Tucker leaned forward with a puckish look. "We went to high school together at St. George's. I was dating this girl at our sister boarding school and he didn't like that. He kept trying to steal her from me." He smirked. "*Todd Bland.* Such a boring guy. If you have a name like that, you better be a spicy motherfucker."

A man who could lob a perfect insult at a moment's notice. I *loved* that. "So, who won?"

"I did," he said with a grin. "I married her."

And that was when I knew the kind of journalist I wanted to be.

Back in high school, when I was still sitting next to Charlie in Ms. Baker's nonfiction English class, we'd blitzed through numerous writing genres. The big fall semester assignment was a long-form features article (where I wrote about teen beauty pageants, even entering Miss Teen USA that year to get firsthand knowledge), the big spring assignment was a memoir (where I agonized over the absence of my Bad Dad), and in the meantime we'd turned in restaurant reviews and reported articles and personal essays. During my pipe dreams about Harvard, I thought about joining the *Lampoon.* My college writing years were equally scattered: I'd thought about going into op-eds, briefly becoming the Opinion section editor of the *Tulane Hullabaloo* and writing something cringingly earnest about people booing Ann Coulter. At Claremont, I'd taken over the News section of the *Claremont Independent,* drew cartoons for the online CMC Forum, and filled in for my friend Trevor as the restaurant critic for the *Student Life* when he went abroad for the semester. (The one time I tried to write a joke column for April Fools' Day, where I wrote a fake "review" of the local strip club, it did not go over well. April Fools' Day columns, apparently, are best run on April 1.) And of course, there was that summer internship with BroadbandCensus.com—decidedly the least sexy reporting gig one could put on a resume, and a job that made me swear off policy reporting if I had the chance. But before I started looking at Tucker's clip file, I had no idea that one could build an *actual career* where you could be a professional adventurer, hunting down and entering a crazy situation that only a crazy person could find compelling—maybe in a suburban Starbucks, maybe in Antarctica—to listen to people spill their souls and witness the spectacular, figure out the precise *right* words to turn your experience into a story so gripping that other people had to drop everything to listen, to care, to *get it,* to feel what you felt. *That was a career.* And this man in front of me—a hilarious establishment-hater dressed in WASP clothing, shaking my hand and promising to get in touch with me shortly, *could he be a mentor too?*—had pulled it off.

("Oh, he's on television?" Mom asked. "You should ask him to help you get on TV. I think you'd be good on TV, like Connie Chung.")

I left the office, floating on the promise that the Daily Caller had made me: we were doing hard-hitting journalism, yes, but it was published alongside hilarious advice columns from Matt Labash and Jim Treacher and Jeff Winkler (who had written a legendary Awl article about breaking his penis during sex), a sign that the Caller wouldn't take itself too seriously. There were Democrats on board, another sign that this wasn't going to be an ideology machine and that maybe, *maybe,* I'd be able to execute the leap from a conservative journalism job to reporting at a bigger outlet—a leap that wasn't *un*common for reporters at the time. And if I just picked up the correct lessons from Tucker, maybe even scored a few connections, I'd be able to achieve that life too.

I was so happy that I floated into the third interview days later, imagining the high-flying future I was building for myself, and into a storm of red flags.

Jon Henke, whom Elliott had connected me with back in March, insisted on meeting me in a Dunkin' Donuts—our first in-person conversation—in the shady part of town, and he kept furtively looking over his shoulder, as if someone was following him into the dingy old dining room. "I'm trying to make sure no one's listening in on us," he said. I nervously picked at my French cruller, surprised that people wanted to eavesdrop in the real world.

A mild-mannered ghost who could disappear into the crowd of a cocktail party if needed, Henke had been a new media coordinator for several Republicans in the Senate, did a stint in the Republican Communications Office, had run the Twitter account of Fred Thompson, now a presidential candidate, and now ran his own comms firm, Craft Digital Media. I'd found all of this online, but because I was twenty-two, there seemed to be absolutely nothing weird about the fact that a guy in charge of a communications firm was helping the Daily Caller hire a reporter.

"So what I'm looking for is a blogger who's interested in muckraking," he said in a whisper. "There are so many companies and liberals out there who are complete hypocrites in this field and I'm looking for people who really understand libertarian values to report on those." I nodded eagerly. I was in. "I'll introduce you to the people you need to know," he said, pleased. "There's a lot of libertarians here that want the same thing I do. But this seems good. Let me make sure the funding is there to hire you."

The funding? I might have just entered the job market, but I was *pretty* sure companies didn't hire people or post job listings if they didn't already have the money to do so. Where would said money come from? "Jon Henke said something about how he was 'going to make sure the funding was there' to hire me, and I have absolutely no idea what that means," I told Elliott in an email later that day. "Are they looking for funding from independent sources, or is it revenue-driven?"

Elliott's response was one sentence, and I could practically hear the tension in his voice: "Tina: The DC is funded by investors and the purpose is to make a profit."

I was twenty-three and that answer was satisfactory, but at that point I should have pressed: *So why is* Henke *in charge of getting the money?*

————

If you looked through all the early coverage about the Caller, you'd have no idea who this Henke dude was. Few people would. I don't know if even Tucker knew that he was so close to the Caller. In fact, you'd view the Caller—as everyone back then did—as a conservative media to the Huffington Post, minus the stilted gentility of most conservative organizations of the time. Neil and Tucker, roommates from college, had looked at the embryonic world of online media and noted that the ranks of journalists from most major media outlets had left the field altogether, largely to become flacks for corporations or (shudder) the Obama administration. With an exclusively digital operation, they could be more nimble and financially secure—the plan was to drive the revenue with web-based advertising, and the publishing schedule wouldn't be tied to the plodding process of print journalism. With a libertarian tilt, it could balance the sensational growth of Arianna Huffington and her new website, where she posted the op-eds of her innumerable liberal friends. With a seasoned reporter like Tucker at the helm it would be more than a Drudge Report–style news aggregator, or Andrew Breitbart's all-caps scream machine of a website. And since Tucker was so popular in Washington, he could get both Huffington and Breitbart to write articles for his site, welcoming the Caller to the nascent, optimistic world of online political reporting.

At the time, Tucker seemed committed to it. After all, he'd been famously booed a few years earlier at the Conservative Political Action Conference (CPAC) when he suggested something audacious: that the right needed its own version of the *New York Times*—something that may have reflected a conservative view of the world, but one that was aggressively facts-first. "The *New York Times* is a liberal paper, [but] it's also a paper that cares about whether they spell people's names right; it's a paper that cares about accuracy. Conservatives need to build institutions that mirror those institutions." That part of the quote didn't matter to the crowd—they just heard *New York Times* and that was enough to set them off—but it was enough for him to get $3 million from a wealthy investor and launch his dream website.

———————

I was back home in Boston when I learned that I had the job, and I was so excited that I had *something* that I didn't even negotiate the $25,000/year salary, to Neil's shock. I just needed to get out of my mother's basement. So I packed my bags immediately and flew down to Washington, began searching on Craigslist for a cheap room, and began my job.

Immediately, I was thrown in the *Insane Asylum*.

By the time I'd arrived at the Caller, I'd learned, two people had been identified as the most intense right-wingers of the company— Neil Munro and Matt Boyle—and now shared an office off the main room. The new person would inevitably be put in this room on the spare desk, since no one else could survive their presence for more than twenty minutes. The DC's brass loved them, but they were . . . A. Lot. Hence the name of my new office. Not that they were *cruel*—in fact, they were both exceedingly kind to me during and after my tenure at the Caller—but they were, well, insane. Munro was a middle-aged Irishman who'd formerly worked at *National Journal*, one of the policy papers on Capitol Hill, who'd lost his job in the recession and came to the Caller soon afterward. His soft Irish accent, combined with his intense, long-winded theories about the Obama administration's recent actions, made me think of him as a combination of J. Edgar Hoover and James Joyce. Boyle defied explanation altogether. Twenty-three and round, with a signature fedora, Boyle spent his days laser-focused on whatever investigation he could pursue into the Obama administration, fueling his loud calls to agitated officials with an ever-growing mountain of Mountain Dew cans on his desk.

The rest of the team, however, weren't as crazy of characters. There was our national politics team—Jonathan Strong, who was about to break a story about Michele Bachmann's frequent migraines; C. J. Ciaramella, the resident libertarian who focused on drug policy and marijuana legalization (a controversial topic back in 2011); Alex Pappas and Alexis Levinson and Amanda Carey, young reporters who were traveling the country that year, eagerly chasing scoops from the Republican primary candidates. There was talk of bringing on a video team, and Tucker had nabbed Michelle Fields, a recent college grad at the libertarian rival Reason.TV[1] who had gone viral for a clip of her confronting Matt Damon about tenured professorships. The hope was that she'd do the same here. There were numerous columnists from across the ideological spectrum who wrote for the Caller on a regular basis: Matt Lewis, a traditionalist blogger; Matt Labash, a humorist from the *Weekly Standard* obsessed with fly-fishing; Jim Treacher, a man whom no one had ever met (and was most definitely a pseudonym), but had become a scathingly funny internet talent; Mickey Kaus, our resident Iraq War–era anti-Bush liberal. And a middle-aged man named David Martosko had started the same day as me as executive editor. His hiring had drawn more attention than I had—he had, apparently, been hired from a PR firm to become an editor, despite having no experience in editing whatsoever.

Tucker's purpose, it seemed, was to be the editor/impish company mascot, frequently emerging from his office to pull some shenanigan—like practicing fly-fishing casts across the office or stealing my Capital Bikeshare vehicle after I was unable to park it in a dock outside, riding it around the office like a sugar-happy child on a tricycle. (I should have just walked to work that day, no matter how sweaty Washington was. But twenty-three-year-olds are pretty bad at commute logistics.)

For a company barely two years old, the site was punching well above its weight—not just accredited at the White House, but also attracting the skeptical notice of traditional media. Right around the time I'd joined, CNN's Anderson Cooper had run one of his segments called "The RidicuList"—his attempt to do a snarky segment à la Jon Stewart—that had made fun of a Daily Caller reporter for her erroneous reporting on some celebrity issue, and did so by name, for five minutes straight on national television. When I met Cooper's target, I'd wondered why he'd decided to pick on her: she was a sweet Arizona State University grad named Laura Donovan, just months into her first postcollege job. "You didn't deserve it," one staffer kindly told Laura, who was still upset weeks later.

Looming over it all, mounted onto a pillar in the center of the room, was a television screen that showed a live feed of how many people were on the site at any given moment: a graph showing how many people had visited the site that day, a needle that swung back and forth, indicating how many people were on the site right now, a real-time list of whose story was getting the most traffic. Whenever a story popped—whether it was a big scoop, or a cheeky slide show about bikini-clad models doing socialist things—we'd grin and high-five as the traffic surged.

Data companies providing this kind of real-time data, like industry leader Chartbeat and its knockoffs, would be the jittery, anxious amygdala of every other outlet I worked at, from the muckraking blogs at Mediaite, to *Politico*, where it was mounted on a massive television screen in the center of the newsroom. And it became the pulsating heart of my career. The more eye-catching or controversial my stories—the topic, the headline, the content that could send you into a seizure—the more traffic I brought. The more traffic I got, the more ad revenue would stream into the site. And with every hundreds of thousands of clicks, and the dollars the company scraped out of that traffic, I would buy myself one more day of survival.

————

There was still, however, the odd question of *who* was paying me.

Back in March, in the middle of my job hunting, John Elliott had forwarded an email from Henke, a man in his network, saying that he was trying to help an unnamed right-of-center news outlet find a technology reporter: "A background in tech policy is less important than some experience as a reporter, a pro-market pov, and the ability to do daily muckraking/reporting/blogging." It seemed a perfect fit: we had a mutual connection, I did an internship reporting on tech policy in Washington, I liked writing. I sent over my clips and resume in a polite introductory email.

The next day, Henke sent me a brief message: "Thanks. Have you done much POV journalism or blogging?"

"In terms of POV journalism, a few times for class assignments, and I was the op-ed editor for the *Tulane Hullaballoo*," I responded, adding that Broadband Census was essentially a blog.

It was enough to start the conversation. Henke and I had one conversation on the phone, and he told me that he was a consultant and helping Tucker and Neil scout talent for a gig at the Daily Caller. The next day, he sent me another email, asking if I had any particular viewpoints about a list of topics.

I mean, I guess they're looking for libertarian-oriented journalists, I thought, and sent over a few bullet points:

- Role of the FCC: Probably shouldn't be responsible for regulating the internet. I do enjoy its anarchy.
- Net neutrality: Do not want.
- Privacy: Tough one. Depends on how you define privacy, because that's a really loaded word. In terms of selling user information to advertisers like Facebook is doing, I tend to agree with Facebook—they have to make a profit somehow to support the hundreds of millions of users they have. In terms of, say, the government asking Google to spy on their users' search queries, I think that's bad, because of both its inefficacy in finding legitimate threats to the country AND as a matter of the extension of government power.

It was apparently a perfect answer. Henke put me in touch with Patel. Patel had introduced me to Tucker, a full-time job had come out of it, everything seemed good. I was a libertarianish reporter who wanted to report and put the reporting before . . . whatever it was I believed. It was all good. It was totally fine. I'd literally just gone through a journalism internship that said it was completely normal to be a journalist with activist tendencies. It was all *totally, totally fine.*

Right?

––––––––

Tucker immediately took the new kids under his wing and to his regular booth at the Palm, my first time at an expensive clubby steak house; he'd paid out of his own pocket, greeting the maître'd' from the *New York Times Magazine* article as we entered. (I had never eaten a steak in my life, much less a fifty-dollar one, and ordered fish instead.) Even though he was sober, Tucker had apparently splurged on a party bus last month, watching his staffers instead melt into a drunken oblivion with glee. He was the guy we wanted to throw into a swimming pool—which we did that summer during a party at Neil's place, after plotting some way to get his iPhone out of his pocket first—and the guy who stubbornly believed in giving people second chances. He used to be a chain smoker and alcoholic, and a drug user, and god knows what other substances—and had quit through sheer willpower, patience, and packs of Nicorette he'd devour on an hourly basis. It was why he'd immediately slapped down any backtalk over Martosko's character—Martosko had become sober recently, he argued, and deserved to start anew—and shrugged off Washington's official shock over his hiring of the twenty-seven-year-old Kurt Bardella as the Caller's comms director. Bardella was formerly the press secretary for the prestigious House Oversight Committee, but had recently courted controversy when it was revealed that he'd been sharing private emails between him and Capitol Hill reporters with *another* journalist. Normally, that was a career ender; doubly so for Bardella, a kid with no college degree who'd built a reputation as an aggressive self-promoter on the ladder up—the type of person, in other words, that most DC insiders would happily kick off said ladder. And yet Tucker hired him. If you were in Washington at the time, and you'd heard these stories, you would understand why Tucker had been so beloved, and why it was simply the *best* when he emerged from his office with his fly-fishing rod, practicing his casts as he gossiped with the rest of the staff. And we basked in his sunlight.

There was a certain level of gravitas that swept into the newsroom whenever Tucker emerged from his office, one where we almost felt like we were working at a print magazine, or at least someplace without a traffic needle ticker, logging clicks and highest-performing articles, looming over our heads like some horrible Edgar Allan Poe death trap. And when he'd disappear, that bleaker reality would set in. It was the place where people rolled their eyes that the slide shows of supermodels in bikinis were getting more traffic than a deeply reported story on the Obama administration's latest issues, but clicks were clicks and ad revenue was ad revenue, and the ad revenue would pay for our jobs, so more slide shows it was. It was the place where we'd be puzzled as to why Boyle's antiliberal fervor was so rewarded. And then we realized: his talent at pummeling the Obama administration led to his traffic spiking every single day.

Either way, if you were a politics reporter at the Daily Caller between 2010 and 2012, you probably had the time of your life. You'd be part of a fratty camaraderie of journalists within the creaky wreckage of IKEA furniture and scrawled jokes on whiteboards, whose libertarian-to-right-leaning ideology was carefully cultivated as a way to keep themselves honest, a lens that would ideally help them find stories that their peers at other outlets elsewhere wouldn't find. You'd develop a thrill in pissing off Obama officials and getting into Twitter fights, and you'd develop a taste for whiskey and cigars. And you wouldn't know then that being a journalist at an institution described as a "right-leaning outlet" would, with exceedingly few, carefully navigated exceptions, condemn you to what my colleague Matt Lewis called *the conservative media ghetto*. That fate was *several* years down the line, and in the meantime, there was free beer and free snacks and Ping-Pong.

———

But it only took a month before I realized that I was not part of the journalists' world, and that I'd been siloed elsewhere by some unknown power to do a different job. It happened when some of the reporters asked if I was around to grab lunch. "Ah, I can't join you guys," I said. "I'm waiting on edits from Jon Henke."

"Who's Jon Henke?" one asked.

I froze, and turned back to my laptop. As far as I knew, he was my editor and the man guiding me on this new beat, through this new town. Within my first week, Henke immediately sent me email introductions to dozens of lobbyists throughout DC, and I got lunch with all of them—the Verizon guy, the AT&T guy, the libertarian think tank guys. The biggest tech story of the summer was AT&T's attempted acquisition of T-Mobile, which was under investigation by the Department of Justice's antitrust division. If it was successful, AT&T would have a 42 percent share of the US telecom market, dwarfing any other competition from Sprint and Verizon. The flacks and sources insisted on paying for lunch and coffee, which I let them do, wide-eyed and naïve and *certain* that I was being taken care of, if Henke knew them. I'd also tried to hit up several other comms officials for organizations that opposed the merger, whom Henke had *not* supplied me. For some reason, they would not respond to my emails. *How weird*, I thought.

Henke himself seemed intent on making sure I stayed on message. One of our first meetings was at the town house of a business he'd founded called Craft Digital Media, a corporate branding and messaging firm on Capitol Hill, where we brainstormed targets for me to report on. He had an obsession with Aaron Swartz, a cofounder of Reddit, and kept asking if and when I'd ever write a piece about how he'd downloaded academic articles from the Massachusetts Institute of Technology without paying for them.[2] And he seemed very intent on getting me to report on the planned AT&T merger.

The more I thought about it, however, the odder it felt: Weren't libertarians *supposed* to be antimonopolistic and encourage competitive enterprise? Why was Henke so mad about a man who believed that information should be free? Why did he keep telling me to hit up certain PR flacks, and avoid mentioning others? And most importantly: Why was my editor working full-time at a corporate communications firm? Quitting for the sake of integrity wasn't an option, since there were no jobs, and even if there was a job, my resume looked like shit: *Recent college grad with a 3.0 GPA who could barely hack it as a technology reporter at the Daily Caller, and wants to leave after three months? What happened to* her? I wanted to ask my bosses what was happening, but I'd just been hired and couldn't challenge them. I wanted to ask John Elliott what was up, but he'd been the person who'd introduced me to Henke. And I wanted to ask my co-workers for their insight, but they had no idea that Henke even *existed*. I might as well have asked them about an imaginary monster in the wall.

I finally got a hold of a spokesman who'd been dodging me—sliding into someone's DMs, I learned, was a great reporting strategy—and we finally arranged time for coffee in late September. We chatted about various topics—me, earnest and trying to get to know someone; him, a seasoned comms official probably several decades my senior, cagily trying to assess me. After a while, he looked at me quizzically and seemed to relax. "Honestly, you seem like a good kid. I really didn't trust you at first."

"Um. Why? Was it because I work for a right-wing outlet?"

He didn't answer either of those questions. We continued our conversation, when I'd mentioned the article I'd published earlier that week. The Justice Department had announced that they would file

to prevent the merger, claiming that it was going to create a monopoly, and the quotes from unnamed sources that Henke had cultivated for me expressed shock and suspicion over the department's motives, claiming that they'd been blindsided by the DOJ's decision.

"I mean, I didn't see that ruling coming—did you?"

He looked at me intently. "We knew about it for *days* beforehand. A *Politico* reporter asked us for comment way before the DOJ announced their decision."

If *he'd* known about it, I thought, so did my sources; ergo, my sources lied to me. That wouldn't have been such a big deal on its own, were it not for the fact that *my very own editor* told me to write that story—"Call them right now, I just spoke to them and they're absolutely stunned," he'd told me when the motion dropped. I quickly excused myself, though I'm sure he could tell I was shaken, and went back to the office to panic, unsure of what was right or wrong anymore.

I never got to the bottom of it all, and never knew what was going on, but it made me feel very uncomfortable. I started ignoring Henke over the next several days, putting off his increasingly angry emails with other, less fraught assignments that I'd wanted to do instead ("There's a big cybersecurity hearing on the Hill, it seems important") while trying to get answers from my bosses over what was actually happening. Coincidentally, this was the week that Steve Jobs died; a monumentally tragic day for the tech world, and a great day for web traffic about Apple stories. "Look, Steve Jobs died, I have to cover that," I told Henke—he couldn't possibly ignore my logic—and tapped away at posts about what had happened to Apple stock.

But the stress was getting to me, and, feeling that I could not trust Henke, I went straight to the managing editor, David Martosko, and laid out my concerns. "Why is he editing my stories?" I asked, almost

crying. "He doesn't even work here! That's just *wrong*!" He, too, seemed to have no idea who Henke was, and promised to look into it.

That night, and the morning after, as Henke kept filling my inbox demanding updates, I kept rewatching and rereading the commencement speech Steve Jobs delivered at Stanford University in 2004. The weight of the past five years of bad decisions was collapsing on top of me, from dating Charlie to whatever I decided now, as well as the hopes and dreams of my mother, who would have told me to suck it up, finish a year, and build a track record, and told me a horror story about how it could be much worse. But it was still a time when tech billionaires and visionaries had wisdom to offer, and people would lap it up, and I fixated for hours on the third part of Jobs's speech: the part where he talked about his first brush with death. "For the past thirty-three years," he'd told the crowd, wearing crimson robes, "I have looked in the mirror every morning and asked myself: 'If today were the last day of my life, would I want to do what I am about to do today?' And whenever the answer has been 'No' for too many days in a row, I know I need to change something."

I went to the bathroom later that afternoon, dodging erstwhile Daily Caller contributor Ginni Thomas[3] as she left, and stared at myself in the mirror: haggard, puffy with too much free beer, a mass of zits on my forehead, on the verge of breaking. *Can I keep doing this?* The answer hit me so quickly that I almost questioned myself.

No. I think I'd rather die.

———

Thankfully, I was spared the agony of trying to figure out how to quit.

"I'm not looking forward to this conversation," Patel said with a grimace as I walked into his office the next day. Hours ago, he'd

sternly summoned my colleague Amanda into his office, and minutes later she stormed out of the newsroom with the contents of her desk. Though he looked much less angry than he did hours ago, doom still emanated from him as I sat down, puzzled. "This isn't working out for us," he began. "I'm sorry, but we're going to have to let you go."

My stomach dropped. *No,* I thought, *this can't be happening.* What had I done wrong? "It's only been three months," I stammered. "That's not enough time to build a completely new section. I literally just got out of college but I'm getting used to the beat—"

"That's our fault," he said quickly. "We didn't have much time to launch this section and we shouldn't have hired someone so inexperienced."

I could barely process the logic in his statement—would a more experienced reporter accept a $25K salary?—and I was freaking out over what my mother was going to say. Patel then put a sheet of paper in front of me. "We don't normally do this for people, but we feel bad, so we wanted to give you a month's salary"—$2,083—"as severance. We'd just need you to sign this." He handed over a sheet of paper that I barely understood. "You can take this to a lawyer and have them look over it, but we don't want to make this complicated with lawyers coming into it."

For someone whose professional career was barely three months old, getting a month of severance appeared to be a kind gesture. I took the sheet of paper and muttered my thanks, aware that my family couldn't afford a lawyer. "Tucker's also waiting for you, by the way," said Patel. "He wanted to talk to you after I did." I took Patel's cue and, with whatever dignity I had left in me, walked into Tucker's office, where I exploded into tears.

Tucker was waiting for me with a box of tissues. "I am *so, so sorry,*

Tina," he said. "Honestly, I'm a good editor when it comes to politics. I can tell a politics person who's pissed at our reporting to fuck off. I know nothing about technology."

"Wait, could I apply for another job here?"

He smile ruefully at my harebrained scheme. "Look, if you ever have another job interview in the future, let me know and I'll gladly recommend you. I'll let them know it wasn't your fault and that it was a bad fit."

"You would?"

"Of course," he said quickly, as if he wouldn't dare think otherwise. "Where's your family right now?"

"Um, in Boston. My mom's teaching in the South Shore."

"Was she a refugee?"

The Tucker Carlson face—squinting eyes, agape mouth—may look stupid on television, but it has a devastating effect in person, especially when your entire world has collapsed around you. It's the kind of look you only receive from someone who really, truly *must* know everything that's on your mind or else the world might end. So I told him what I knew about Mom—that she'd escaped Vietnam, that she left my father, that she was raising three girls on her own and I was the eldest.

"That's incredible," he said after a pause. "You know what? Give your mother my number. I'll tell her that it wasn't your fault."

Shock, sadness, elation, a smile and more tears must have flashed through my face in an instant. "You *would*?!"

"Yes, of course!" We exchanged a few more words about next steps, keeping in touch, and then I had to get out of his office before it got too awkward. "One last thing," Tucker added. "Don't get drunk tonight. It's going to make you feel worse."

I nodded, knowing that it was the best advice, and the advice I was promptly going to ignore.

The other journalists at the Caller immediately took me out to drinks, already about to process Amanda's firing and now adding my firing to the agenda. As I drank several beers and continued to ignore Tucker's advice, the rest of the table tried to figure out what had happened with Amanda. The next morning, extremely hungover, I read an article about my own firing from *FishbowlDC*, our local media gossip blog. Two people fired in one day at a start-up was bound to raise eyebrows in Washington, and of course, everyone still wanted to know why. I steeled myself and clicked it open: the author wrote one sentence about me—"Nguyen was in over her head"—and paragraphs upon scathing paragraphs about Amanda's complaints about Martosko.

As I read what was, essentially, like an obituary of Amanda's career in journalism, a sense of relief flooded through me, knotted, inexplicably, with fear and panic. I had been granted mercy, and all would be well for me—as long as I remained silent.

5

EXILE IN FRUMLAND

February 2012
Marriott Wardman Park Hotel, Main Ballroom, Washington, DC
39th Annual Conservative Political Action Conference (CPAC)

I was sitting on the floor up on the mezzanine level, hanging out with an eight-year-old child, watching Sarah Palin whip up a crowd into a frenzy below. Even among professional conservatives, CPAC held an interesting status in the right wing as a carnival of die-hards: crackpot academics with fringe ideas on how to rewrite the Constitution, awestruck gangly children from campus conservative groups wearing their best professional clothing, and an inordinate number of people dressed up like inhabitants of Colonial Williamsburg, cheerleading the concept of limited government and Tea Party patriotism. They were there to meet, listen to speeches, and brainstorm the future of the activist movement over sloppy well drinks hosted by various activist groups— parties that involved hot tubs and mariachi bands and other shenanigans. "Do I have to give you money for the wacko convention?" Mac Zimmerman, my new editor at the Colorado Observer, had asked me sardonically when I pitched him a report on the event.

Next to me was Bea Frum, my former babysitting charge, raptly paying attention to the weird crowd around her. Even though I was no longer freelancing with FrumForum, the struggling opinion website run by her father, David Frum—the former Bush speechwriter forever known as the man who coined the doomed phrase "axis of evil"—I liked hanging out with her: she was bossy, precocious, a growing sophisticate, and I was indulgent, adoring, and terrified of disappointing her parents, which made me a perfect chaperone for her strange adventures.

For some reason unbeknownst to me, David, or his wife, Danielle, Bea *loved* going to CPAC, even though she was far too young to hold any meaningful political opinions. "I think it's the circuslike atmosphere of the event," David, who once had a CPAC booth for Frum- Forum, hypothesized at one point over happy hour in their kitchen, a giant tiled affair where Danielle constructed the platonic ideal of a gin and tonic. Zimmerman had begrudgingly let me cover Palin's speech that year and once Bea had heard, she'd begged her parents to let me take her. They agreed, I gladly accepted, and on the day of Palin's speech, she sprinted into my arms outside the Wardman and immediately dragged me to the expo hall to sweep up the free merch.

"*Roooooomney, Rooooomney; Romney is the one for me,*" she sang, skipping through the lobby with a tote bag full of buttons and stickers and little toy elephants. I tried to keep up with her but got sidetracked by the groups where she was harvesting her swag. The American Legislative Exchange Council had pamphlets out, looking for the next generation of conservative state legislators. The Heritage Foundation had a booth with tons of free movie theater popcorn, its buttery scent wafting over the entire place, as did the American Israel Public Affairs Committee (where Bea had snagged her tote), *Reason* magazine, and a dozen other organizations and think tanks—including IHS. (John Elliott had been working the booth that CPAC, but was not there that day, and emailed that he was sad to have missed me.)

No wonder everyone thinks it's a circus, I thought, scribbling notes. I was there as the Colorado Observer's Washington "stringer," covering stories out of the capital with a press badge and business cards, but without the W-2 and benefits. John Elliott had connected the two of us a few weeks back, suggesting that we'd get along, and I was glad to be at a place where I *seemed* to be doing normal journalism. Zimmerman also understood that I had a second part-time job to pay the bills, too: I was now a hostess making twelve-fifty an hour at the dubiously named Ping Pong Dim Sum, splitting a shift with a woman with anger management issues who'd tattooed her husband's name on her inner finger. (They couldn't afford to buy rings before he went to prison, she'd told me.) Everything seemed copacetic: Zimmerman would get stories about Republicans, I'd get some bylines under my name as I job-hunted, and at night I'd get discounted dumplings and lychee martinis. I filed the piece, scheduled my next shift, kept checking my inbox for the next pitch from Zimmerman.

The next day, Zimmerman emailed: "You working on the Polis story?"

My stomach dropped. Though I appreciated his flexibility with me, Zimmerman, whom I'd never met in person, had hired me rather quickly considering that I'd known nothing about Colorado politics, and had been badgering me about writing a story about Jared Polis, a wealthy Democratic congressman from Colorado, for the first two weeks I'd worked there. He'd teed up sources for me to work with: several secretaries from Colorado Republican offices, several conservative interest groups, and a fairly strong thesis that Polis was engaged in insider trading that he'd expected me to write about without question. It felt like Henke all over again.

———

Nearly two years before, Bea's father, David, was a prominent figure in the Republican world: a staunch defender of Israel and all things neoconservative, a fellow at the American Enterprise Institute. Then, in 2010, he wrote a blog post for FrumForum that was so controversial that it drove entire news cycles and would eventually get its own Wikipedia page: the infamous "Waterloo" essay, in which he'd condemned the Republican Party for uniformly opposing the Affordable Care Act's passage through Congress—not even trying to negotiate. It was a good move to win elections, he had written furiously; it was a good argument to keep viewers' eyes on Fox News. But 53 percent of voters had supported Barack Obama, and it was clear that the American people wanted health care reform, and ignoring that would lead to the death of the Republican Party. "Today's defeat for free-market economics and Republican values is a huge win for the conservative entertainment industry," he'd written. "Their listeners and viewers will now be even more enraged, even more frustrated, even more disappointed in everybody except the responsibility-free talkers on television and radio. For them, it's mission accomplished. For the cause they purport to represent, it's Waterloo all right: ours." The next week, he lost his job at the think tank.

Sometime during the summer of Caller, and a year after they blew up their professional lives, Maxwell had invited me to a pool party at their home. The moment they'd heard that I lost my job, David and

Danielle offered me a freelance columnist contract with their website for $300 a week, apologizing that they couldn't offer more. The money was nice, but having a workplace outside my depression nest at home was better. And the Frum house was a world away from anything I'd ever known: lush gardens, immaculate couches, a bustling kitchen where Danielle was constantly testing recipes for a Polish cookbook she was coauthoring, with cocktail hour starting on the dot at 5 p.m. Bea would run up afterward, chattering about what she'd learned in school that day and whatever she'd noticed out of the most recent presidential debate and *Downton Abbey.*

There was something lonely about the house, however. David and Danielle had bought the once-dilapidated house as a young couple and Danielle, a fellow journalist and author with a knack for cooking, had transformed it into a manse fit for DC's best parties. The family still had a small group of powerful friends who'd visit the house: Arianna Huffington would send David baklava as thanks for attending a panel, Ted Olson appeared at their wake for Christopher Hitchens, who'd been a close family friend; Laura Ingraham would come over for happy hour, bringing her children along for me to supervise with Bea while she and Danielle caught up over white wine. (I never got to stay for their conversations.) They continued to host one of the best Hannukah parties in Washington, which came with a signature blue cocktail every year. But there was a specific, distinctive thing that David and Danielle knew that they'd lost: their place within the movement, an ideological home that David had belonged to since he was a college student. It was as if he'd blinked, and everyone he'd ever worked with in that tiny town had suddenly gone to a different party down the street, unwilling to wait for him to catch up, even warning themselves to *leave that traitor behind.*

"That article was my suicide note to the GOP," he'd told me once, making a small joke about selling his father's art collection to ensure Bea could go to college.

————

My network was in full throttle as I searched for my next gig: Neil Munro and Matt Boyle were sending me leads, David and Danielle were talking me up to their friends, but it was John Elliott who got me my first post-Caller interview: an internship at Accuracy in Academia. I immediately did some research: a branch of an old right-wing watchdog group called Accuracy in Media, which was founded in 1969 and served as the progenitor to hundreds of groups that work against liberal bias in the media.[1] The interview took place in their office, in a strip mall in the DC suburbs, the sort of place where you'd set up five folding tables and a series of extension cords and a printer and call it an office. Mal Kline, the carbuncular president of the group, laid out his expectations. "What we aim to do here, is to hold liberal universities accountable," he said. "I'm hoping that you can go to academic conferences and events and take notes on what they're saying there. It's a good opportunity to build your clip file," he added. He later sent me several emails, forwarded to him by allies, of progressive groups and academic conferences he wanted eyes on. "I need a lot of help covering their events," he said as he forwarded an email from the Center for American Progress. "They periodically blacklist me."

After years of tagging along with my mother to lectures and conferences, watching people freely discuss things without fear of punishment, this group's mission felt like a desecration. But still, I felt obligated to consider it, my mother's insistence on keeping my resume up-to-date ringing in my head. *Well, I guess Danielle's informed opinion* could *overrule Mom's here*, I thought, and emailed her: "Is it even right to take the internship if the values conflict with mine?"

Aware that I was in financial duress, Danielle wrote back suggesting to do so *if* I needed the money *that* badly. "Is your name going on it?" she added. "I might give that more pause, as it will be googlable."

My name would, indeed, be on it. So I turned it down, with some mealymouthed excuse about how I was too busy. Besides, Danielle had set me up with her connections at the Huffington Post, at that point one of the hottest outlets in new media. They were expanding their Washington bureau, and they needed interns, and I was ready to take it on and finally get a real job in journalism.

————

"This might be the best gig in town," Elliott said with his next email opportunity, days after I bombed my Huffington Post interview.[2] He'd set me up with a woman named Therese at the Franklin Center for Government and Public Integrity, who immediately set up an interview with me, and almost immediately after, offered me an internship with a $1,600/month stipend. Now *that* was an upside, I thought—HuffPo's internship was unpaid. The Wisconsin Reporter, in fact, went a step further: they would pay me to move to Madison, Wisconsin, and the stipend would allow me a decent apartment there, perhaps a one-bedroom downtown. I'd be writing again, I'd be reporting—but I'd be reporting on teachers unions. *Very specifically* on teachers unions. "Therese says Madison is a war zone," Elliott had told me.

It had been months since the Wisconsin teachers unions had staged a three-month-long occupation of the state capitol, with hundreds of lefty hippies taking over the rotunda with signs and a drumbeat. At that point, they'd been cleared out of the building, but their ruckus

had led to something tangible: the state was about to hold a recall election targeting Governor Scott Walker, as well as his Republican allies.
"The first thing we ask whenever we write a story is: How much will this
cost the taxpayer?" my potential bosses asked me.

I hung up, feeling uneasy. At this point, the Wisconsin Reporter
sure as hell did *not* feel like the best gig in town. And the Franklin
Center, from what little I found of it, was suspicious as well: months before, PR Watch had published an article pointing out that the Franklin
Center had launched in 2009 but suddenly had the capacity to fund,
in forty states, forty-three state news websites that had connections to
conservative think tanks but were masquerading as normal news outlets. They had connections to the Koch Foundation and the Bradley
Foundation,[3] and dozens of former Americans for Prosperity[4] staffers
were on its payroll. By the time I read the fifth paragraph, I was absolutely done with the place, were it not for the screaming fear lording
over every decision I'd ever made: *If I don't take this job, am I a failure?*

The slow gnaw of anxiety escalated, over the course of several days,
into a feeding frenzy. By mid-December, as they testily reminded me to
give them my decision, I had drafted an email telling them that I was
turning it down, but couldn't bring myself to send it. During my entire
day at the Frums' house with the other FrumForum writers, I stared at
my laptop, mind wandering away from the precocious ten-year-old girl
I was supposed to be babysitting.

At 4:55 p.m.—five minutes before I was supposed to give my
answer—Bea skipped over with a sandwich, country bread with aru-
gula and slices of bresaola she'd proudly assembled. She immediately
sensed that something was off. "Tina, why are you freaking out?" she
asked, clambering onto my lap.

"Is it that obvious?"

"Duh."

"Fine, Bea, I've been offered an internship."

"WOULD YOU HAVE TO LEAVE?!" she shrieked.

"Here's the thing!" I hastily added. "I don't know if I'd like what I'd be doing."

"So why go?" she asked, drawing on her child logic. "You don't want to do it." I was baffled. It was the first time that someone had *ever* told me that I didn't have to do something I didn't want to do, simply *because* I didn't want to do it.

That settles it, I thought, and quickly hit the "send" button before I could change my mind.[5]

I could not stop questioning my decision in the weeks afterward, fighting off constant anxiety attacks for nights on end and ignoring my mother's increasingly frantic calls for days. On the advice of a ten-year-old, I had chosen gut instincts over plugging the leaking holes in my career—and, apparently, basic survival.

A few weeks later, David sat me and the rest of the gang down and laid out some sad truths: he had been hired by the Daily Beast to write a column full-time, he'd been able to hire the editor to come along with him, and, in the meantime, he had to shut down FrumForum for good. Leaving their final happy hour and their house for the last time, I felt like I was on the verge of collapsing in on myself, again. Say what you will about their politics, but being in proximity to the Frum family had been my one last thread to the world of legitimacy, of mattering. And lately, I'd started discovering what Not Mattering in Washington felt like. I'd been invited to a few holiday parties throughout Washington, mostly by friends who thought I'd be able to network at them, and at every single one, I noticed that people would stop talking to me within approximately six sentences when it was clear that I didn't have a job, much less an official business card I could give them. By the middle of these parties, I was left standing there alone in a borrowed dress with a wineglass; but with a schedule full of corporate events, no reasonable person in Washington would spend their precious networking time talking to an unemployed person in a borrowed dress standing alone with a wineglass.

———

After I'd filed my CPAC story, Zimmerman seemed rather keen to highlight that Polis was worth $66 million and engaged in a technically legal but rather eyebrow-raising form of insider trading. In his next edit, Zimmerman seemed more interested in proving that Polis had done something wrong. "STOCK Act just passed the Senate, I think—but I don't think it has become law yet. So this insider trading stuff is still legal right now, yes? Or am I wrong?"

"[The act's] not legal until Obama signs it into law," I wrote back. "They've also passed two separate versions of the bill in both the House and Senate, but they need to pass it through a joint committee to reconcile the differences."

"Ok. So it's factually correct. Nice."

The next day, Zimmerman sent me his other ideas, all about some other Colorado Democrats. "[Senator Mark] Udall just proposed some kind of a total ban on earmarks, even though he was a prolific earmarker when in the house (he once got money for a 'wildlife bridge' for animals over an interstate). And [Senator Michael] Bennet has proposed a harsh set of restrictions on lobbyists to curb the power of so-called special interests, but he takes contributions from lobbyists.

A story on the inconsistency—some would say hypocrisy—of this new-found populism might make for a good story."

What? The Udall story was from last February. I did some basic research on the Bennet pitch and wrote back. "In my opinion, this isn't a swing towards populism—it's more of a cooling-off period that's attached to the STOCK act. In short, this is not really a story—especially since Bennet wasn't tied to any of the unethical behavior that's being addressed by the STOCK act."

"Hypocrisy is the angle," Zimmerman responded. "Bennet attacks lobbyists as a festering plague on our political system, even while he accepts tons of cash—more than $1.3m—from lobbying and law firms since 2007. They are the top donors to his war chest. That's like bashing the tobacco companies and then having [cigarette company] Philip Morris bankroll your re-election campaign. Its disingenuous and misleading. Imagine if he was a republican what kind of stories the [*Washington*] *Post* would be writing."

We went back and forth on the validity of the story, my position being *the facts are not conforming to your reality* and his position being *but they're Democrats*. By the end of our ninth email, I found my angle: *find out who Zimmerman worked for*.

I scrolled through the Google search results, and my stomach plummeted again. Not only had Zimmerman never worked in journalism, but his resume boasted a slew of political jobs before this one. He had come off a job at the Koch Network's Americans for Prosperity. In 2010, he was the chief of staff for a Republican gubernatorial candidate; prior to that, he was Tom Tancredo's chief of staff for five years. And the more I'd read about Tancredo, the more I'd cringed. A former Colorado congressman and fringe presidential candidate, Tancredo was known for speaking at events organized by hate groups—at one point, the Southern Poverty Law Center reported, he was literally at a barbecue organized by a local white supremacist group with a Confederate flag draped on the podium. And according to one article from 2010, Tancredo credited Zimmerman with helping him draft a potential civics literacy test needed so people could vote, with Tancredo suggesting that people had voted for Obama because they were ignorant: "People who could not even spell the word 'vote' or say it in English put a committed socialist ideologue in the White House.'"

I hadn't fathomed that I could get any lower than laundering right-wing talking points through a fake newspaper in Wisconsin. And at that point, I would have rather had Matt Boyle living in my house than work for an undercover neo-Confederate whom I'd never met in person. *I fucked up my life*, I thought, burrowing into my blankets, pillows, and three weeks' worth of laundry, hoping to sink into the bliss of nothing. *I've fucked up for four years straight.* I didn't leave bed for days, ignoring Zimmerman's repeated emails asking where I was and what was the status on my story. I kept calling in sick to the dim sum restaurant, scrolling through Facebook on my laptop, looking at people who had made the right decisions to become trusted journalists—people who went to journalism school and had the *right* career track, people who would one day look at my resume and throw it in the garbage. People who hadn't been so blindingly naïve to the difference between a benign interest in American politics and multifront ideological warfare; people who were sharp enough to realize that the conservative movement was not a land of *Schoolhouse Rock!* idealism; people who were wealthy enough to turn down sketchy paid internships for liberty-minded students and work for free at respectable publications.

People who could make better decisions than I had.

Zimmerman soon sent me a termination letter for failing to meet the terms of my contract. I didn't care about it anymore. I didn't care about *anything* anymore.

————————

"I'm worried about your drinking, miss," my mother told me as I knocked back my third lychee cocktail. She had come into town that week to do some tourism and check in on me, and had initially been pleased at the possibility of getting an employee discount at dinner. She arrived, however, to a daughter who had been fired *yet again*, and she was barely restraining herself from making comparisons between me and my father, except unlike my father, I drank a lot. "You're still on my health insurance, but I'm not paying for rehab."

"Mom, I'm *fine*. I swear. Restaurant people just drink a lot."

"Well, I think you should cut back," she said curtly, spearing a dumpling and switching the conversation back to the dreaded topic of my career track. "Have you talked to Tucker or David again?"

"Yeah, they're helping me out." That was technically true. I *had* been emailing them repeatedly, asking for a recommendation here, or an application to an open position there, and I'd gotten polite emails saying that they'd look into it, or that they didn't know that specific industry, and the conversations ended there. I'd gotten the hint. My socially inept immigrant mom wouldn't have.

We spent the next few days seeing museums and staring at monuments and taking way too many photos, and spent one afternoon in a sauna at my local gym. She filled me in on how my sisters were doing—one was applying to college, thinking about computer science; the other one was getting A's in everything and the college counselors were telling her to aim for the Ivy League. (Mom had only given them two options, listed on an index card placed on their desks: "Harvard/ Yale/Standfor [*sic*]", or "Bridgewater State College.") One afternoon, Mom insisted on going to a rooftop bar, and I immediately knew of a place: the W hotel, overlooking the White House, with a striped awning and lounge seating where day drinkers sprawled. As we passed by one table, with four tattooed men doing shots in broad daylight, I did a double take. "Mom," I whispered, "that guy was on *Top Chef.*"

Mom knew nothing about *Top Chef,* but her eyes lit up. "You should talk to him about getting a better job at his restaurant."

She immediately scampered over, introducing me to them ("She works at Ping Pong, she's a great hostess"), and perhaps charmed by a tiny, exuberant old Asian lady, they invited us to sit with them. As she happily knocked back lemon-drop shots with the cooks, forgetting completely that she'd *just* scolded me for drinking too much, it dawned on me that perhaps Mom had stopped caring about what my job was—whether it was prestigious, whether it was respectable—just as long as I was able to support myself. After all these years, had she given up on me, seeing how I'd failed too many times for her liking?

Fuck it, I thought after she left. *I'm going to torch my life and move to New York.*

6

ESCAPE FROM THE CONSERVATIVE GHETTO

I gave myself a month off to pull myself together. I took minimal shifts at the dim sum restaurant—lunchtime here, dinner service there, with my day off being either Wednesday or Tuesday—pushed myself back into the gym, got my hands on some antidepressants, and ate more salads for once. When April rolled around, I began networking like a woman possessed by the spirit of LinkedIn, spending every free hour hitting up every connection I had to New York City. It was a crapshoot anywhere I went, I figured: I had no experience as a copywriter or in anything related to sales, business, or advertising. I *knew* that a job at any news-gathering outlet was going to look down on my sporadic resume. And I had no idea whether Tucker's word would carry weight in New York, or anywhere outside of conservative media—except for one place, where a Daily Caller alum *had* landed. Laura Donovan had just moved to New York to work for a blog network that had launched a few years back, Abrams Media, run by one of Tucker's old colleagues from MSNBC, the legal correspondent Dan Abrams. It was more of a network of websites: the flagship was Mediaite, dedicated to clips on cable news and writing about journalists and the gossip of news. But there was a site for nerds (Geekosystem), a site for lady nerds (the Mary Sue), a site for female entrepreneurs (the Jane Dough), a site for normal sports (SportsGrid), and the Braiser. It was a new vertical that covered celebrity chefs like tabloid stars, and it was a full-time job that made absolutely no sense to anyone, but it was as good an exit strategy from right-wing journalism as anything else. I had an interview with Dan, sent Tucker a heads-up that Dan was going to reach out to him right afterward, and I . . . got the job that evening???

"What on earth did you say to them?!" I emailed.

"I said you were funny, smart and awesome, and also that you had major balls for being honest enough to say you got fired from here," he wrote back immediately. "I love that, and so did he."

"I don't suppose fruit baskets are your thing," I joked. And then a prank popped into my brain.

I immediately hopped on the Metro and made my way to the nearest Target, raiding the gifts section for discounted holiday products as well as the most obnoxious card I could find, then running over to the health section. Back home, I assembled my brilliant gift, decking it out with cascades of shiny pink ribbons and placing my *extremely* thoughtful card on the front. The next day, I came back to the Daily Caller offices, told Neil what I was doing (he cackled), and seeing that Tucker was not in the office, I left my gift on his desk: a giant, purple, two-dollar Easter basket filled with pastel green plastic straw, and resting atop the pile, a forty-pack of Nicorette gum.

It was funny at the time.

————

I was no longer a DC burnout engaged in right-wing shenanigans. I was now a member of the New York City millennial creative class, with a cheap brick-walled apartment in Brooklyn and a Cool Job at a SoHo media company making $30,000 a year: the dream circa 2012. No one was going to know anything about my activities in college or the first year of my professional life—although, I realized, it was probably a good idea to find a therapist to help unpack that era. And according to literally every piece of pop culture I'd ever consumed, from *Seinfeld* to *Sex and the City*, having a therapist was a very New York City thing. (When I told Mom that I'd found a nice one, an older lady named Minerva who liked astrology and specialized in treating PTSD, Mom simply asked whether she was covered by her government employer's state-sponsored health insurance. "Therapists are for weak people," she sighed, "but maybe *you* need one.")

But that feeling of complete freedom didn't last long: to my surprise, I found *another* IHS alum at Abrams Media.

Andrew Kirell, a rebellious Long Island punk with a Nice Jewish Boy streak, had attended the seminar the year before I did. His libertarian-ness was of the *Reason* magazine[1] ethos—"Free Minds and Free Markets"—along with a healthy dose of *leave me alone and let me smoke weed in peace.* John Elliott had placed him at Fox News as a TV producer after he graduated, where he quickly realized that a darker world existed outside the little libertarian bubble he occupied with anchor John Stossel. Within two years he'd quit and moved to Mediaite starting a few months before I had. Like me, he had a problem with the pomposity of cable news and delighted in cutting down the blowhards a few pegs; unlike me, he'd done it all without lighting his world on fire.

There weren't many hobbies we had in common outside of work. I'd been bitten by the comedy bug and started taking sketch-writing classes at Upright Citizens Brigade; he was writing country music and collecting vinyls and cats with his wife. But we instantly connected over our missions to find the best Asian food in New York City, and shared traumas from Conservatism Inc. He, too, had started off optimistic in human nature and the free market—his fascination with libertarianism was of the economic sort rather than the political—then quickly became disillusioned by what committing to the ideology after college, as an adult in the real world, actually *meant*. Apparently, New York and Washington were littered with young journalists just like us: they'd taken the internship money out of desperation, got slightly weirded out by the seminars, and tried to move on. The easiest thing to do was become nihilistic about the ideology.

Most of us, however, weren't able to leap out like we had. "We didn't have anyone *really* weird in my year," Kirell told me during a lunch break at a nearby Chinatown restaurant. "But I got invited to the other private debates and I *definitely* remember Kat Timpf. What's she doing right now?"

"I think traffic reports? Or stand-up. No, wait. I think she goes on Fox News sometimes."[2]

"Dang. She's talented. She got into Columbia's journalism program. Had to turn it down because she couldn't afford it."

"Honestly, I don't blame her. J-school is expensive."

"Sorta wish there were better options," he mumbled. "I had to sit through IHS debates with Mollie Hemingway." I sighed, wondering what she might have been like inside a hotel conference room with a dozen other pundits-in-training.

It was, indeed, lean times for journalism, and the industry problems I saw in DC were magnified tenfold here. New York was the land of blogs, covering everything under the sun, serving, at the very least, as resume fodder. Blogging was less about reporting and more about cranking out content, even at the wee hours of the night, *even* as a food writer. But blogging was the only thing available that paid people to write for a living.

There was, however, a worse option for me and Kirell, other than hanging on to these blogs by our fingernails: to drop so low that we'd have to go to someplace like Breitbart. Technically, *all* of conservative media was a career life sentence. There were too many people we'd both known who had joined a conservative outlet in their first job outside of college, gained valuable skills, and then learned they could never again be hired in the mainstream press because of the toxicity of their resume, regardless if they were conservatives or not. "It's called the *conservative ghetto*," Matt Lewis, my old colleague at the Daily Caller, had once told me. "If you're not careful, you'll get pigeonholed. Then, you'll be stuck writing at conservative outlets. And then, the mainstream will never hire you—except, maybe, as the token conservative." The general options were either to accept one's fate and keep working at conservative outlets, go to a prestigious, slate-cleaning journalism graduate program to prove to editors that you were *really* an unbiased reporter (and taking on hundreds of thousands in debt), or leave the industry altogether. Kirell and I were maybe one of five people who'd managed to avoid any of those options, though we supposed it was due to luck: we applied for the right job openings at the right time, and we realized that Dan, our boss, cared more about cheap labor than he did about partisanship.

Breitbart, however, was a rare form of journalistic imprisonment, even in right-wing media. True, there were talented journalists who'd been brought over in the final years of Breitbart's life—Jonathan Strong, my colleague from the Daily Caller, was one of them. But my old office mates from the Insane Asylum, Matt Boyle and Neil Munro, had gone there in recent months. And ever since a guy named Steve Bannon[3] had taken over after Breitbart's death, noncompetes had been issued to even the entry-level hires. Any full-time staff who left before a four-year period expired couldn't write anywhere else—no new job, no freelancing—for six months. Of course, one could hire a lawyer and attempt to challenge the noncompete. But if you were desperate enough for a $30K-a-year writing job that came with *that* stipulation, it was highly unlikely you could afford such a lawyer in the first place. And what could young, underpaid journalists at a right-wing outlet do in response, *unionize?*

———

Eventually I learned that a career in food writing can actually *suck.*

It didn't seem that way at first. It was the boom years of the swaggering, hard-drinking Celebrity Chef Culture, and I spent my evenings hitting up events and trying the menus at new restaurants in Brooklyn and Manhattan, visiting food festivals, downing bespoke cocktails, running every so often into Anthony Bourdain, who would grumpily call me his archnemesis (I beamed), and becoming the target of a certain *Top Chef* personality who screamed at me at the Four Seasons for being too mean. It is fun to do that for a short period of time. It is *not* fun, however, to do that five nights a week for two years, coming home nauseous at 1:30 a.m. most nights after taking a bite of everything and downing at least four cocktails to be polite to the PR folks, and *then* being online by 7:30 a.m. the next day to write five blog posts about whatever there is to write about food culture, sometimes on a Saturday, because the content machine needed to be fed. Even getting nominated for a James Beard Award in 2014, the highest honor for writing in food media, didn't make me feel any better: the morning after the awards after-party, a night of bourbon and fried chicken and champagne and cupcakes, I woke up feeling dehydrated and artery-clogged and bloated and miserable. *I think I get why Gluttony is a circle of Hell,* I thought, and promptly threw up.

The easiest way out of the Braiser was the Mediaite mother ship, and I immediately put in for a transfer when I heard that one of their most-read writers was leaving. ("It's going to take you about two months to find someone to replace him after he leaves, and probably another month to train that person to meet Noah's old output, *if* they can at all," I argued to our CEO, who was shocked I would willingly stop writing about ham and wine.) Politics and current events were draws, but the biggest traffic magnet at Mediaite (a portmanteau Dan had made up to describe a media socialite) was coverage of the media itself: the journalists, the cable news hosts, and live breaking events. Which meant that at all hours of the day, *someone* had to be watching cable news. We didn't want to miss a single thing that happened: dignified journalists making horrible gaffes, anchors going on sudden tirades, and guests having screaming matches with each other, which we'd publish with words in the headline like "SHUTS DOWN," "RIPS APART," or "EVISCERATES," a word I hadn't used since a high school term paper describing Genghis Khan's torture methods.

I wasn't the best person at finding shocking cable news moments, but I'd watched the Mediaite team seize on an errant tweet from Donald Trump demanding Barack Obama's birth certificate, turning his obsession into dozens of high-performing news stories on our own internal Chartbeat and helping drive a multiweek news cycle about an obviously silly conspiracy surrounding Obama's citizenship. I decided to focus on every single trend that took over Political Twitter over the next year and a half, rapidly blowing itself out of proportion through the vectors of the internet, dive after it like a hawk hunting for clicks, write it up, slap on a headline, ship over to Kirell, now the editor in chief, and hit "publish" as soon as possible. By September, Dan was thrilled by the traffic my stories were pulling in. "I'm so happy you're on board," he said, and I breathed a sigh of relief. I had earned my keep as a blogging urchin, producing content like some twenty-first-century Oliver Twist at a digital workhouse,[4] and though it was thankless and grueling, it was *way* better than the alternative: pretending to be a conservative who was pretending to be a journalist.

————

"So where do you go with your career next, miss?" Mom, thinner than ever but still sharp after two years of fighting ovarian cancer, patted the pillow next to her, a sign that she wanted me to sit with her in bed. Ever since her chemo started in mid-2013, she'd installed a television in her bedroom, where she would binge cable news and send me photos of David Frum and Tucker Carlson whenever they were on. She loved the scant few times that I had appeared on cable news, taking photos of me on the screen and posting happy little captions on her Facebook page. She was thrilled I had a career track again, though she wasn't quite sure exactly how to define my career, and was already scheming up ways for me to have a more secure job, in the way that only Mom could. "Can Dan get you to go on television more?"

I sighed. She still didn't understand how these people operated. "That's not how it works, Mom."

"Why not? They should pay you to be on TV."

"They don't. I'm just gonna be making thirty-four thousand dollars a year."

"Maybe it's time for you to get a new job. I think they make you work too hard." She'd seen me typing furiously while watching *Saturday Night Live* to get blog posts up at 2 a.m. on a Sunday, grumbling that I needed to get on a better sleep schedule, and had been sending me *Forbes* web articles about work-life balance (a shock, coming from her). "Where do you think you can find jobs that fit your track record? Do people in your network have any leads?"

Not really, I thought later in my childhood bedroom, *at least nowhere that's* not *another right-wing thing*, and began madly googling all the job postings at every publication with a New York office. There was nothing suitable for my expertise at the *New York Times*, *Wall Street Journal*, or Gawker. Even going through the Condé Nast jobs board seemed like a pipe dream—those magazines were places for *real journalists*, I thought, not grubby little ex-libertarian blog monkeys banging on typewriters—until I hit one posting. It was looking for a blogger to aggregate news for their website. In other words: they needed someone to do *exactly* what I was doing right now, except at the most exclusive magazine in the world.

I immediately sent an email to an old editor, John Vorwald, who had been an editor at Mediaite for a year or so and by now was running digital operations for *Details* magazine, one of Condé's publications. We met at a bar in the West Village, and as I babbled my hellos and how-have-you-beens, Vorwald could see that I was doing too much small talk and cut to the chase. "So what is it that you want?"

I pulled the latest edition of *Vanity Fair* out of my bag. "How do I get to work here?"

––––––––

Vorwald told me to send my emails directly to the editors, instead of relying on the job application portals—"If Condé only relied on HR to find talent, *no one* would ever get hired," he said—and during a meeting with his counterparts across the company, approached *Vanity Fair*'s digital director and mentioned briefly that I'd applied for the job. To my shock, they responded, pushing me through a gamut of two phone interviews, one writing test, and one meeting with HR. In what felt like the blink of an eye, I found myself standing in the gleaming marble lobby of the newly rebuilt One World Trade Center, in an outfit that I'd anxiously purchased the week before: a J.Crew suit and a pair of questionably fitting heels, toting a briefcase my mother had given me, hoping upon hope that I looked the part of a *Vanity Fair* writer. This was the land of Graydon Carter, the man who threw the hottest party at the Oscars; David Remnick, the man who embodied the brilliance of the *The New Yorker*; Anna Wintour, the iconic, icy editor of *Vogue* magazine—I knew, at the very least, that famous and powerful people would hurl themselves at their feet for their approval. I had to stop myself from ruminating about *The Devil Wears Prada* as I walked into their offices, past beer-keg-sized floral arrangements and a larger-than-life photo of Tina Fey slyly saluting everyone who passed by her while doffing an Uncle Sam hat. On a friend's advice, I'd left the Daily Caller off my resume. *You were only there for four months, it doesn't count,* they'd pointed out, and

I'd wondered briefly if I would have been let into the building at *all* if they'd known.

As the interview started, I took a breath to banish my libertarian urchin Impostor Syndrome, went through some biographical details and small talk, and got to the heart of my pitch. "I can write three to five posts about the news every day," I said, running once again through the talking points I had memorized in advance. "My content's drawn the most traffic on Mediaite, and I personally draw an average of 1.1 million unique visitors to my posts a month. My most-read story received over one million views and was cited in the *New York Times*."

They nodded thoughtfully. "Where were you before Mediaite?" Mike Hogan, the director, asked.

"Oh, I was at this food blog where I got nominated for a James Beard Award. And, uh, right out of college, I was, um, freelancing in Washington."

It was technically true. And it worked.

On day one, I entered the office, trembling with anticipation over my shiny new life. I had my own desk, bathed in light from the massive windows that caught the sunset over New York Harbor every single day, and my own work computer for the first time. I'd said goodbye to being a grody content orphan on the outside of respectability: I'd had my farewell dinner with my old Mediaite sweatshop writers, held at the Hooters near Penn Station, and had already processed my disappointment that my mother was not more excited about this accomplishment. ("What's *Vanity Fair*?" she'd asked. "Are you making better money?") I had on a fresh new outfit and was eyeing the purchase of a real work purse instead of a threadbare tote bag. By the end of the day I had gotten the hang of the production cycle fast enough to write my first article—something dumb and snarky about Jeb Bush and the exclamation point in his campaign logo. On day two, the most *hilarious* news item popped up on Twitter, and I wrote it up with glee: "Donald Trump Announces Run for President."

Then I promptly forgot about it and moved on to the next piece. I was at *Vanity* Freaking *Fair*, I thought happily, and I never, ever, *ever* had to worry about fringe right-wing bullshit, EVER again.

7

THE NEW LEADERS COUNCIL

One World Trade Center
Condé Nast Cafeteria
December 3, 2015

I fumbled with my recorder as we sat in the empty cafeteria, trying to get used to doing interviews with real people again. "Just for the sake of me not being confused two days from now, do you mind saying your name to the recorder?"

"Sure. Mark Riddle."

"Matt Tompkins."

"Matti Miranda."

I'd met a chapter leader at someone's birthday at a bar, when the host dragged her over to me—"This is Tina, she works at *Vanity Fair*, you guys should talk"—and she'd begun telling me about her nonprofit, the New Leaders Council. Now that I worked at *VF*, this phenomenon had started where people would just come up and lob a thousand story ideas at me. Complex ones, ones with depth and oddity, and every single time, *you should write this up.* I'd brushed a few of them off, unsure whether they were Important Enough for *Vanity* Freaking *Fair*, or frankly had no idea how to handle them—I was the digital news blogger, for lord's sake, my job was basically the same as my Mediaite one—but the one Heather had told gnawed at me. Her group was a progressive leadership training incubator founded in 2005 that worked on identifying the next generation of Democrat talent, and the way she described it—revolutionary, unique, and new—made it sound like it was an anomaly. *Weird*, I thought. *I thought the Democrats* had *the resources my old team did.*

Though I wasn't on the right anymore, I retained a healthy skepticism of the Democrats, and the story, as I'd heard it so far, made sense: back in 2008, in the midst of his historic run for president, Barack Obama had been blindsided by the Democratic National Committee as they threw in for his rival, Hillary Clinton. He'd leaned into his massive grassroots organization, Obama for America, scraping his way past her and winning the party nomination, and eventually, the presidency. Still deeply suspicious of the DNC, he'd neglected the party's growth, fobbing it off to the incompetent Debbie Wasserman Schultz, and instead focused his fundraising efforts on what was now renamed Organizing for America (to keep the OFA acronym).

The party quickly realized, however, that the members of OFA had joined explicitly for Obama and hadn't cared about much else. The problem compounded quickly: over the course of Obama's presidency, the Democrats had lost a thousand State House seats, thirteen governors' mansions, a supermajority in the Senate, and eventually, both wings of Congress—an utter decimation, as the Republicans rode the Tea Party wave into a rabble-rousing, populist, and increasingly manic dominance.

But Heather had been telling me that the problem on the left went deeper than Obama's neglect, and I was interested in getting to the bottom of it—the problem she'd told me pinged something that I'd thought I'd buried the moment I joined *Vanity Fair* and tried to go legit. I'd pitched the story to my editor, Kia; he'd agreed to let me pursue it as long as I kept to my daily blogging schedule, and I arranged for everyone to meet me at One World Trade.

"You know, in a lot of the country over the last eight years, we've seen the decimation of the progressive batch. It's easy to blame the president, if you just look at the statistics, but I think it's been a longer-term game," Riddle, a graying man with a mild Kentucky accent, began. "I think the obvious thing is [to say] 'oh, let's just blame the president for all this.' But the conservative movement has been planning for forty or fifty years, and spending hundreds of millions of dollars and investing in their farm team and their bench, and working on school board races and city council seats and state legislative seats, which ended up drawing the lines, which puts Congress in an interesting place, where they can control the policy agenda. So while the quick, simple thing— too simple—is oh, let's just blame President Obama, because he's African American, and all these things, if you take a wider lens of this, it's really been since the fifties and sixties when the modern conservative movement started, they're seeing the results today.

"There was an article today in *Politico* about Joni Ernst—it's another in a series of articles about young conservative leaders who have kind of grown up in their farm team. There's an *Atlantic Monthly* piece last year on Tom Cotton. There's been any number of pieces. And so what you've seen is you've got conservative leaders like Marco Rubio, who has been groomed and gone up through the system. Paul Ryan, who is part of the think tank system in Washington, DC. They're in their forties. The leadership on our side in Congress are very old. Our presidential candidates are old, except for Governor Martin O'Malley"— the Maryland governor who, at that moment, had launched an ill-fated campaign against Hillary Clinton.

"He didn't come up through a farm system, right?" I asked.

"No. Well, he did," Riddle recalled. "He was very involved in the Democratic Leadership Council in the eighties and nineties. So I guess, really the nineties. And so he was part of that group of folks who grew up through the DLC, which was the centrist think tank in Washington, DC."

Was? "What happened to the DLC?"

"It ended up folding in 2010 officially. It was really a split in the Democratic Party then. You had centrist leaders like Evan Bayh and Joe Lieberman, who were really the leadership of the DLC and of the New Democrats in Washington." But Senator Lieberman of Connecticut, he continued, had been primaried out of his party in 2006 when he lost against Ned Lamont, a progressive, antiwar candidate who was backed by an activist group called Netroots Nation and had accused him of being too moderate. (Lieberman eventually ran as an independent, won, and kept his seat.) "That was really the first political divide between what had been a governing coalition under Bill Clinton—the moderate centrist Democrats and moderate Republicans, and then the extreme kind of the liberals and very conservative folks."

The Republicans, Riddle said, had come to terms with their very conservative folks, entering into a tenuous alliance with the Tea Party.

The Democrats had not—but it wasn't for lack of a good-faith discussion. "A lot of the moderates are gone, because of the way the lines are drawn in the states, which is in direct correlation to years and years and years of funding and infrastructure building through ALEC[1] and other conservative organizations, to draw [district] lines and create legislation locally. Now, that's a federal thing." And now the Democrats were increasingly shut out, due to being out-organized and out-benched.

"So you'd say the DLC was definitely the last effort to bench-build before you guys came along?"

"I wouldn't say the DLC was the last effort. They were very focused on state and local elected officials, and networking them and promoting them through the system. As far as grassroots things, there's been some training things like Wellstone Action and others, but there hasn't been a sustained training program on our side, like the Leadership Institute. So I would say the DLC was the closest. But what the Leadership Institute does is takes care of next-generation leaders, whereas the DLC was cultivating folks who were already in the system. We've gone back two steps into younger leaders—who will be running for those school board seats, or state reps, or running races or running nonprofits—starting them at a younger age, then being a member of Congress, or a mayor of a major city and then go to higher office."

My dormant right-wing brain began to churn. "So why do you think that most of the resources have been geared towards activism versus bench building?" I asked. Riddle paused in thought. "I mean, George Soros is putting his money somewhere," I joked.

"The moneyed leadership of the progressive side seems to like instant gratification, and goes from cycle to cycle, instead of a longer-term, almost business view of how to build essentially a company," he said with a hint of frustration. "It's like, 'Oh, what's the latest shiny object? Let's go fund that.' Whether it goes good or bad, you do a postmortem, and then move on to the next shiny object out there. Sometimes it served its purpose well, and sometimes it doesn't." Riddle was getting more animated. "You know, we're still a pretty young, modern progressive movement. We're probably less than ten years old. On the whole, across the board, a lot of these organizations are still relatively young compared to things like the Heritage Foundation and Leadership Institute—"

"AEI, Cato—"

"Cato, the whole thing. Those have been around forty or fifty years; we're still within a decade, or just over a decade on a lot of things."

"So in comparison, how big is the network at the Leadership Institute?"

"I don't know. I know their budget's $15 million."

"Yeah. And they've trained over 161,000 [activists]."

"And their model is, they bring people to Washington. They put them up in dorms. If you hear a young conservative talk about American exceptionalism, they've probably gone through Heritage or the Leadership Institute. It's like a little army of them out there that all are on the same message. Now some of them are running for president, which is the interesting thing. Marco Rubio. Ted Cruz. Scott Walker—"

"*He* was Leadership Institute?"

"I'm sure. Mitch McConnell's face is on their website. Ralph Reed."

"Grover Norquist."

"The regular talking heads on Fox are part of that group." Riddle shook his head. "I mean, Paul Ryan grew up through the think tanks. Now he's the Speaker. Marco Rubio was a commissioner down in Florida. He got recognized: state House Speaker, senator, presidential candidate, groomed up through the system on their side."

They kept speaking about the New Leaders Council, and how they'd be sprinting to catch up with the right, but my mind was lost in a hole. I'd taken the ideological balance of power for granted as a twenty-two-year-old. I was now twenty-six, and had barely thought about the conservative movement since 2013, save for the various random happy hours John Elliott had thrown before getting let go from IHS in 2013. (He was now at the Franklin Center.) And this was the first time I'd heard someone speak, in fear, of the things I considered background scenery.

I said goodbye to the members of the New Leaders Council at the elevator, promising to schedule interviews with some of their most promising candidates—two city council members of middling-sized American cities, hardly the stature of a would-be Paul Ryan or Mitch McConnell—and kept turning over the story in my brain over several insomniac nights. They had built something that looked like the merest shadow of what I'd grown up with, which was ever so mildly concerning. My new life had been predicated on a belief that the political universe, as I knew it at the age of twenty-six, was in balance: the Republicans had just as much power as the Democrats, and the left was just as good at protecting its interests as the right was. I knew that the Center for American Progress existed—that was *a* thing, I guess—but I'd lived my life thinking that there had been more of them. The left *must* have had summer camps and happy hours and think tank internships, and stacks and stacks and stacks of alumni ready to help young Democrats find jobs and careers. Surely they had their own version of the Franklin Center? Or ALEC? Or their own journalism programs with an alumni network, sending their trainees into newsrooms across the country? The right had *at least three* that I knew of. But behind the shining glamour of the Obama years, if the NLC had described it correctly, was a frail Democratic Party, to say little of a movement. And if the NLC was trying to plug up tiny holes in *city council* races, was the right already working down at that level?

Trump's name hadn't come up in that prescient interview, but it began popping up again. I first had an inkling in September 2015 that something was off, as I saw more people attend Trump rallies, seeing that he'd nabbed 25 percent of support in a recent poll. I'd watched Trump's speeches and TV appearances, and saw his tweets fly across my screen. The rest of my office found them funny—*Vanity Fair*'s editor, Graydon Carter, cheerfully recounted their feuds in 1980s New York City, involving Trump's tiny hands and propensity for tweeting about Graydon's "bad food restaurant"—but a tiny, gnawing feeling of recognition was not going away, as foolish as it felt.

My therapist, Minerva, who'd been seeing me for three years at this point, shook her head when I told her that Trump's loud, bullying ways and Twitter-amplified, dubiously true statements reminded me of Charlie. He'd just been banned from Twitter after he tweeted that he would "take out" DeRay Mckesson, one of the first founders of the Black Lives Matter movement, a post that was widely viewed as a physical threat—but he was still, somehow, getting funding and meeting with right-wing congressmen. All the while his name kept popping up in stories about the men financing the fringes of the movement: Blackwater founder Erik Prince, who had been running training camps for Project Veritas secret-camera moles, and billionaire Peter Thiel, whom Charlie likely met through the Claremont Institute.

"Is it just because Trump's acting like Charlie on Twitter?" she asked. "On the *internet*?"

It's not that, I thought. *It's that Trump is* better *than him.* Though they both shared the same beliefs and talent at Twitter, as well as the same desire to break any rule that got in their way, Charlie had purportedly

grown volatile and unpleasant in person over the years, prone to conflict with benefactors and friends for perceived disloyalty, and seemed
barely able to speak in public. Trump, on the other hand, was wealthy
and charismatic—good on camera, charming in person, and *brilliant*
in front of a crowd. Trump could ignite the latent anger that Charlie
never could, channeling it to . . . I still couldn't find the words to artic-
ulate my paranoia.

Minerva sighed. "Tina, what did I say about catastrophizing?"

She's right. Besides, it's early on, I told myself. *Poll respondents are most
likely to gravitate to the novelty candidates; that's what Ezra Klein said.* But
my mind couldn't stop pinging like a pinball, calculating its bouncing
trajectory through the machine: *Trump getting the nomination means he
has access to the activist network. The ones that supported Charlie. Some of
them won't help him. Some of them will fall over themselves trying to help him.
And the left is not going to be able to balance it out.*

Ugh. Stop it, Tina. You're at Vanity Fair *now, act like it.*

———

The New Leaders Council connected me with their most prominent
trainees, many of whom had been successfully elected to office, so I
could interview and profile them for their piece: a city councilman
named Ian Cain, whom I visited when I went home to the South Shore,
and Bill Moen, on the Camden County Board of Freeholders in New
Jersey. I began trying to draft brief profiles of them, though I could
not figure out how to make the story any bigger: they seemed so lost
and small compared to the Leadership Institute's Hall of Fame–level
alumni. Ian Cain was certainly no Marco Rubio. *This story seems so important, though,* I thought with some frustration. *How do I pull it together?
How do I make people* care *about it?*

But I never figured out the answer to that question, because my life suddenly upended itself: one day, without any warning, I got a new job with a new editor.

He'd told me to meet him in the elevator bank so we could grab coffee at the cafeteria downstairs, and I was scanning the lobby, searching for someone graying and tweedy, who likely collected jazz records and biked to work—a magazine editor, in my head, probably had some wacky ideas about what the internet was like. I nearly overlooked the guy in the corner, thinking he was a finance bro on the wrong floor, until he quickly pivoted to me—"Hey, Tina?"—and stuck out his hand.

It took a second for my brain to process it. "Wait. *You're* Jon Kelly?"

Gimlet-eyed, Irish-Jewish, sandy-haired, and thirty-four, Kelly walked faster than I did and spoke more quickly than he could think, and before I knew it, we were downstairs, halfway through our coffees, volleying quip after quip at each other while the ESPN *SportsCenter* alert kept going off on his phone. We quickly bonded over our shared fascination and loathing of the uberrich, and Jon was stunned to find out that billionaire investor Henry Kravis was a CMC alum (he had never heard of the college). After fifteen minutes, I was sold, loving the way he described things and people: witty, punchy, and slightly too close to the bone. ("There are two things you shouldn't be doing when a person in your life dies," he told me at one point. "Don't operate heavy machinery, and don't write about people who can sue us.")

The conversation turned to the GOP primaries, where Donald Trump was still stubbornly in the race. Jon had told me about his time at *Vanity Fair* in the early 2010s, when he interviewed Sarah Palin's son-in-law, Levi Johnston, as his closest brush with the Tea Party. And Trump's existence as an avatar of the blue-collar worker baffled him. "Do you think he could win the Republican nomination?" he asked.

At this point in 2015, it was socially perilous to be someone who wrote about politics, simply because it would derail what would have been a pleasant night out. But it was more reputationally dangerous at *Vanity Fair*: I'd learned that my opinion was quite unusual at Condé Nast, and verged on ignorant and uninformed. I had even been told once, by a snotty new coworker, that I was too *poor* to understand how things worked: "I heard that scholarship kids don't perform very well in college," she once told me, and continued to roll her eyes whenever I talked about the rise of Trump. (Claremont, she once told me, was worse than a state school.) I'd learned not to speak out loud in my office, a hard task since I was naturally talkative. But I couldn't *lie* to my new boss.

"I think he could actually win the *general*," I said, and his eyebrows shot up. "There is . . . a lot of anger in the base about the left and the establishment and he's hit that nerve. And if he does win, it's going to be a dark time."

He stared at me, and I immediately felt stupid. Though he'd done stints at Bloomberg and the *New York Times Magazine*, Kelly had started his professional life, at the age of twenty-two, as Graydon Carter's assistant, the catbird seat of first jobs out of college. Graydon, one of those Famous Magazine Editors with distinctive hair and the ability to throw the Best Parties,[2] had watched Trump scheme his way through New York's upper class for decades. He'd even *feuded* with Trump since the 1980s: Graydon kept calling Trump a "short-fingered vulgarian" in the pages of his magazine *Spy*, and Trump in turn kept sending Graydon photos of his hands circled in gold Sharpie while tweeting endless insults about Graydon's West Village restaurant, the Waverly Inn. From what Jon and Graydon knew of him—and to be fair, it was several decades' worth of intel—Trump was *hardly* the kind of man whom working-class populists in Real America would gravitate toward. If my therapist of three years thought I was having a psychological trauma response to Trump, what was this well-connected insider who'd just met me thinking?

Whatever he thought, he set that aside, and laid out my new responsibilities. He was launching a new web vertical at *Vanity Fair* called the Hive and wanted me on as a political reporter, doing quick-hit posts and original reporting on the side. That, I thought, was a *big* jump for a web monkey—or maybe I was just a different, fancier type of web monkey. And if Kelly didn't believe me about Trump, at least working with him would be fun.

————

I quickly adjusted to the perks of being a *Vanity Fair* political reporter, leveraging the coolness of my outlet into the strangest access: I wrote a feature on Bernie Sanders's Brooklyn headquarters, convincing my editors into paying for a photographer to shoot candids at their warehouse on the Gowanus Canal, then quickly persuaded them to let me write an article about Jeb Bush's increasingly desperate attempts to save his candidacy. If Jon Kelly started laughing at a pitch, I'd succeeded, and I knew I'd enjoy writing it too. The presidential race was winnowing down from sixteen candidates, to five, to two, everyone else trying valiantly to stop Trump from winning the nomination. My wariness was ameliorated by everyone constantly reminding me that Hillary was more likely going to win than not, and I soon forgot about the Democrat farm school story. I was having too much fun in the chaos of it all.

But everything changed during the Michelle Fields incident in May 2015.

At this point, Michelle—the old coworker at the Daily Caller who'd confronted Matt Damon on camera—had a major glow-up, became a Fox News contributor, and was a politics reporter for Breitbart. She had been assigned to cover the pile of Republican candidates who were trying to stop Trump from being the nominee, but one day, when she was filling in for a colleague at Trump's Mar-a-Lago residence in Palm Beach, Florida, she was forcibly shoved by Corey Lewandowski, his then campaign manager. The incident had blown up across the internet, the media was bearing down on the Trump campaign to apologize, and I knew the backstory—about Breitbart, about Michelle's career, even some of the Trump stuff. "Oh my god, I *know* her," I said, looking up at Jon. "Should I write about it?"

Jon was dismissive at first. "Who cares about some fringe website?"

A familiar sense of shame fell over me. Once again, I'd mentioned something from back in my right-wing days and was met with blank stares at best, and *you're a classless fringe lunatic and how did you get through security* stares at worst. I'd told the snotty new writer, who'd interned at the White House, that Trump could be the nominee back in September 2015, and she started moving her computer away from mine within days. I huddled back into my computer to do my web monkey work, banishing foolish thoughts from my mind.

But within days, and I will never know why, Jon's mind had changed. "Go write about it. I wanna know more about these people," he told me, popping up above my desk. "And really dig *deep* into it. I want this fully reported."

Hmm. I sat down to brainstorm leads. *I could easily DM Michelle. I worked with Michelle's current boyfriend, so I could talk to him too. I could email Tucker.* The list suddenly grew longer, ideas bursting through a dam full of repressed memories. *I think she worked for Young Americans for Liberty.*[3] *I remember she became known for accosting Matt Damon at some event. I could talk to her boss at* Reason *magazine. Matt Boyle went to Breit-*

bart. Still can't believe that someone made him Washington editor. Oh gosh, and Jeff went to Breitbart, and Jonathan went to Breitbart, and Kurt went, too—everyone's there now, huh? And that guy Steve Bannon runs it now, right?

It felt odd, I thought as I executed my reporting plan, as if I were looking at my former colleagues through a thick glass pane. It had only been four years since I'd run into Michelle on the Metro in DC, she in a perfect tweed suit asking kindly how I'd been and if I was doing all right, me, smelling like cooking oil and sadness and nodding that I was okay. But whatever warmth and camaraderie had existed between my old crew and me had become strained, and in a way that likely wouldn't have existed if I'd stayed in right-wing reporting. (If I was a right-wing reporter, I later realized, I wouldn't have written about Michelle at *all*.) And it was odder when the people in Trumpworld whom I *didn't* know (and who, I was sure, didn't know *me*) started bringing up an article about Michelle from a site called GotNews, with negative information they suggested I should cite in whatever I published about her, written by one Chuck Johnson.

"How interesting," I'd say, but there was absolutely no way that I'd use that information. Sure, after college, Chuck had won the Collegiate Network's Breindel Prize, as well as a six-month internship at the *Wall Street Journal*, with a full stipend that included a free apartment in Midtown Manhattan, mere blocks away. But for some reason, that was the best he could do. First, he stopped being published at the *Wall Street Journal* or any other Murdoch publication, and his byline started appearing at the Daily Caller and Breitbart. Then it stopped appearing *there*. I'd heard through the ex-libertarian grapevine that Breitbart had stopped accepting Chuck's pitches, finding them to be too much trouble to be worth it, and a *Washington Post* article hinted what had happened at the Caller. He and Matt Boyle had written a story claiming that a New Jersey senator had been soliciting prostitutes; it later emerged that they had been fed the intel by Cuban counterintelligence.

Informally blacklisted at all other conservative outlets, he started his own crowdfunded site called GotNews, setting up a digital fundraising page and begging everyone around him for money to get it going. Somehow he strung together a livable wage by writing rightwing dross: one day, he'd be publishing a student claiming that he'd been subjected to liberal bias, ignoring that the student was also known for being physically disruptive (and was later arrested for groping a random woman on the street while on acid); the next, he'd be rewriting someone's resume to point out their clear and obvious links to pro-Palestinian groups. There was one particularly brutal incident in 2014, when he published the name of the woman at the center of *Rolling Stone*'s story about an alleged gang rape at the University of Virginia, and threatened to publish her photo and address, too, unless she recanted her story—and then promptly published the photo of the wrong woman. He was not even good at a hit job.

But it didn't matter whether or not I'd brought up their talking points. *Well, then,* I thought, stomach turning, when I saw that Trump's campaign manager had tweeted the anti-Fields post. *They're allies.*

8

THE LOWEST CLASS

S o wait," I said to Jon Kelly. "You want me to cover . . . the *right?*"
"Yeah." He was sitting *on* his desk, feet dangling, like an Elf on a
Shelf about to go to a parent-teacher conference. "I want you to cover
the Bannons and the Breitbarts and all those people who made it into
the White House." He'd been up for weeks straight ever since Trump
was elected, trying to figure out who to cover and how to meet the
sudden surge of interest in reading about the incoming administration. Personal dramas and feuds were beginning to form, the establishment was about to run up against the Jivankas, and there was this
odd man from the internet who was now Trump's political advisor.
And to the rest of the media establishment, the odd man with the two
polos seemed like the *least* important figure in that room—a terrifying
presence *too* close to the president, sure, but obviously not one with
more sway than Jared Kushner.

"I mean . . . are you sure? I just had a giant score." I'd recently written a snarky little article reviewing Trump's steak house at the base of Trump Tower, and was so blunt about my dystopian power lunch—bad steaks, bad desserts, cocktails that could cause depressive symptoms—that Trump had tweeted a negative comment about Graydon in response. The article went viral; we received a huge traffic increase and made roughly $1 million off subscriptions alone. I'd already received pitches in the office for other things to review: Trump Wine, Trump golf courses, Trump spa products. Surely *that* was a successful formula. "Couldn't we just repeat the Trump Grill thing again?"

"It's derivative and stunty and we're better than that," Jon said. "We're going to approach this administration as seriously as possible. And *you* were ahead of the curve on all this. You know these guys better than anyone."

For some reason, that piece of insight, from a man who worked at the top of the industry and signed my paychecks, and whom I actually *liked*, felt like a gut punch: *Did he think I was one of them?*

It felt strange, at first, to revisit the material of my adolescent years. Everyone I'd known from back then had, somehow, fallen into some new category: Maxwell was now reputedly hanging out with Richard Spencer and his white nationalist cadre. My old office mate, Matt Boyle, was now the Washington editor of Breitbart and the subject of curious magazine articles. I picked up on small details in various people's backgrounds, saving myself hours of laborious research. (*Oh dang, Stephen Miller was David Horowitz's protégé.*[1] Now *his "Western civilization is under attack" thing makes sense.*) I even recognized the names of others whom I'd read in various publications ages ago in the context of their rising profiles. (*Whoa, wait, when did* Ben Shapiro[2] *become a nationally popular podcaster?*) But it wasn't so much the *knowledge* that felt weird—it was how quickly I slipped back into a persona I'd tried to bury in 2012. I could instantly make myself smaller, gigglier, happy to be in a crowd of far too many red, white, and blue outfits. I found casual ways to drop my background into conversation ("Back when I was at the Daily Caller" or "For real, I smoked cigars with Andrew Breitbart"), or nerd out about various Christian denominations, or the minutiae of Ronald Reagan's biography, or what I saw on RedPill87's latest broadcast on whatever the new MAGA social media platform is these days. I started referencing old memes in conversation, a thing I had tried to stop doing when I moved to New York, and quickly realized that my frame of meme reference was increasingly outdated. (I immediately went back online to get acquainted with the new memes.) I easily fell back into my un-PC patter, learning the difference between "things that win sources over" and "things that they can record, publish online, and get you canceled if you eventually piss them off." I even figured out the wardrobe, which ranged from "Banana Republic Red Sheath Dress with Ruffly Bell Sleeves" to "What Mom Wore to Costco on the Weekends." No blazers and jeans, *never* blazers and jeans, especially with a lanyard dangling a press badge—that was *such* a "fake news media" look. I became more bristly, more chaotic, more classless—something that did not go unnoticed in the polished world of *Vanity Fair.*

It was easy to slip into a crowd of activists—one year at CPAC, I ran into at least twelve other women, and a toddler, wearing the exact same red dress with bell sleeves as me—and people appreciated that I had a grasp of the shorthand, though they never *quite* liked it when I wrote frankly in my voice. (The word *snarky* kept popping up in my reputation, even as they knew that I'd probably write about the left in the same way, given the opportunity.) And sometimes, the cross-cultural fascination went both ways. In April 2018, I met a conservative publisher at the launch party for Geraldo Rivera's memoir who was equally rapt when I mentioned my bizarre resume. "And now you're at *Vanity Fair*. My goodness." He leaned into my ear, making sure that none of the dozen-or-so media reporters in attendance, milling about the Midtown Manhattan Del Frisco's Double Eagle Steakhouse, could hear us. "Say, would you ever be interested in writing a book? I think that the story of a young, right-leaning person going inside the mainstream media would be so compelling to conservative readers."

———

At one point I met Ali Alexander, the man who would go on to organize the January 6 "Stop the Steal" rally, who would run Kanye West's presidential campaign and stuck with him as he spiraled into an antisemitic haze, in the most unusual of spaces: a shitty, bare-bones Airbnb in a walk-up apartment somewhere in lower Manhattan in January 2018. He was showing off a pair of goldenrod-colored patent-leather dress shoes, wrapped neatly in tissue paper and still in its original box. Over in the corner, Gateway Pundit's[3] White House correspondent Lucian Wintrich was changing into a suit; another friend was taking a shower, and I was chugging a ludicrously expensive, cold-pressed juice, fretting about what I would wear for the party that night. "Those are damn good shoes," I acknowledged. (One of the tricks about working at *Vanity Fair*, I learned earlier, is that I could compliment anyone's outfit and instantly make them feel validated about their lives. Guys in particular loved it when I joked about putting them on next month's cover: "I'm seeing you now in Zac Posen, probably a gold, mermaid-cut ballgown.")

They were about to pile in a taxicab and go to Hell's Kitchen, helping prepare for a giant party hosted by compulsive internet theorist

Mike Cernovich and held at, of all places, an EDM nightclub called FREQ. There had been some drama in the days leading up to "A Night of Freedom," which was designed to be the kind of Cool Kid Rager that the right could never quite pull off. Venue after venue in New York City had canceled on "Cerno" after they learned what sort of people were attending: Proud Boys, Pizzagate conspiracy theorists, anarcho-capitalists, bitcoin millionaires, men's rights activists. He could not risk the embarrassment of canceling the event, since several far-right celebrities were slated to attend—Stefan Molyneux, Jack Posobiec, populist-nationalist DJ duo Milk N Cooks, Proud Boys founder Gavin McInnes—and the media would have raked him over the coals of failure if he couldn't follow through, so at the last minute he withdrew $30,000 in cash from the nearest Wells Fargo and deposited it in the hands of some unscrupulous nightclub owners. I was simply an invited member of the press who enjoyed shit shows and a good dive bar.

One of the party attendees was griping about a particular reporter who used to work for the Leadership Institute's news site Campus Reform, digging up dirt on college professors and publishing them for the world to see. "Oliver Darcy's a traitor," he said viciously. "He used to be one of us and now he works with the enemy. Not that you're one," he said hurriedly, as I raised my eyebrows and gestured to myself. "Like, I get why you have to be snarky. You work for the media but you're at least fair to us. Lachlan too. He gets us." (Lachlan Markay, who'd attended the IHS seminar with me, had been working for the Washington Free Beacon before jumping to the Daily Beast, where he now covered the Trump administration.) But Darcy's path out of the right took him on an "unforgivable" path: to CNN, where he now nodded along to *Reliable Sources* host Brian Stelter as their least favorite reporter pontificated about liars in the White House. "He flipped on us."

It was specifically the CNN thing that must have been so offensive, I thought later once I arrived at FREQ in a proper outfit and walked past a long line of young guys scrounging for dollars at the coat check line. (There was a firm dress code for all the attendees: suits and ties for men, cocktail dress for the women who showed up, no MAGA hats.) Of course, Trump and his supporters disliked the media, save for Fox News, a handful of blogs and Twitter personalities, and a few little-known cable outlets at the time, such as OAN and Newsmax. And I seemed to have an aura of acceptability in this world thanks to my resume: "You're a *Claremonster*?!" a drunk partygoer told me that night, with a look of sheer delight that there was someone in the MSM who Got It. But there was a hierarchy of media loathing, and except for Fox, the television news outlets were always on top, followed by the *New York Times* and the *Washington Post*. Which made sense, since I'd learned about one month into the administration that the right had its own completely different set of newsworthy priorities in the world.

The *aha* moment came around the beginning of February, when I asked a source what she thought about the latest twist in the investigation into James Comey's firing as FBI director, for one of those "what does the right think about X news story" pieces. She was smarter than me, more accomplished, with a degree from a much better college than mine, and yet she just shrugged. "Oh, do people care about that?" she asked, with absolutely no malice. "The Seth Rich thing seems more important."[4]

———

We published the story about the Night for Freedom on the *Vanity Fair* home page, trying to capture the event in all of its absurdities: drink tickets, hordes of Proud Boys chatting up secret bitcoin millionaires who refused to give me their names, WikiLeaks whistleblower Chelsea

Manning showing up and then realizing that politics had somewhat *changed* from the days when she was on the left, old women in American flag dresses partying alongside young men with American flag ties in an electronica club—a strange bar mitzvah for the far right in its gangly, awkward years. A few other outlets had attended the event— more than I'd been told would come, to be quite honest—and had published their own stories. And as I sat down at my computer at work to click through my toxic river of Twitter feeds, I caught an alert: Cernovich was livestreaming on Periscope right now.

Cernovich, the author of a self-help book called *Gorilla Mindset* who'd briefly been a lawyer before settling into the far less stressful world of right-wing internet punditry, was reading the articles out loud in his basement on a live stream: " '*The thing about the movement formerly known as the alt right—a far-right subculture whose anarchic ideology is inseparable from the Internet—is that its inhabitants are, by and large, painfully, haltingly awkward.*' Now see, that's just them being snarky," he said immediately, as I realized he was reading my article aloud. "They're just trying to make it seem like we're losers. Trying to diminish our movement." He went through other articles from the Huffington Post and BuzzFeed, stopping in between sentences—"See, that's what they do to us, they're trying to set a narrative"—declaring that they were all trying to make their burgeoning movement look bad. A few thousand people were watching him spin our coverage in real time, aggressively reclaiming the narrative: the event was actually a success, more successful than you could imagine, and the media elites didn't want you to know about it.

————

Despite them publicly dismissing my article as "snarky," the Night for Freedom folks ended up pulling back, somewhat, from their attempted rebrand as the Party Hardy MAGA Right. The next Night for Freedom was held in a basement restaurant in an office building in Washington—*during* CPAC, the "boring" event that Cernovich had mocked during my interviews with him—and people were less likely to get drunk with me, unless we were in the sacred environs of the Trump Hotel lobby bar in DC, where nearly every patron was a gossipy MAGA power broker with a beefy expense account and a roving eye for who was sitting where. But over twenty-five-dollar martinis and eventual late-night phone calls, I still gleaned plenty: they were frequently in touch with Don Jr.'s subordinates, the name Peter Thiel fell from their lips more than once, they increasingly mentioned conservative internet personalities who had created pro-MAGA memes. Sometimes they'd roll their eyes at Steve Bannon's latest shenanigans but admitted that he was *quite* effective. (The right certainly had their internal disagreements, verging on petty bitchiness, but they always adhered to Ronald Reagan's famous Eleventh Commandment: "Thou shalt not speak ill of any other Republican." Even if that Republican was a raging demagogue who wore multiple polos at once and tried to replace Republican establishment elected officials by running populist candidates against them in the primaries—the kind who couldn't win general elections but would almost certainly be victorious in a referendum run by the Republican base.)

I'd started mapping out a loosely connected confederation of people in the current MAGA movement, something that almost paralleled the conservative movement of my youth. Members of the Claremont Mafia had started detaching themselves internally from their more staid peers and created their own publications to parallel *National Review,* like the new website American Greatness, which took the hard-line nature of the Flight 93 essay[5] and spinning it into their own intellectual interpretation of American history and politics, positing that American morals and values were *so* under attack that institutions could be thrown by the wayside. (*Claremont gonna Claremont,* I sighed.) Turning Point USA, a student organization founded by a young man named Charlie Kirk, had started opening chapters at colleges and universities nationwide, differentiating themselves from groups like Young Americans for Liberty and the Young America's Foundation in their trollish ferocity in opposition to the supposed spread of socialism on campuses. I never imagined the heirs of Ronald Reagan costuming themselves in diapers as some sort of commentary on Obamacare, but that was a stunt TPUSA pulled in their early days. They were fascinated with a growing group calling themselves the Intellectual Dark Web— Joe Rogan, Jordan Peterson, Ben Shapiro—who had begun growing massive audiences on their respective podcasts with screeds against liberal academia and the media's interpretation of sociopolitical phenomena, the Trump administration included.

This is when QAnon popped up, too, though at the time it was too embarrassing to acknowledge publicly. After an armed, Q-brained man showed up at a DC pizza parlor with an AR-15, convinced that there were child sex-trafficking victims in the basement, the higher-level MAGA movement learned there was a limit for what sort of anti-Democrat messages they could attach to their names. To that end, they frequently told me that they believed QAnon—the theory that a high-level government operative in Trump's White House was dropping Nostradamus-esque "crumbs" on the internet predicting a mass purge of Satan-worshipping elites from the perches of power—was probably foreign psyops. Back then, they seemed to take debunking QAnon seriously: I'd even see Alex Jones, of all people, openly having fights with QAnon promoters on his show.

"So I want to do a piece about the Claremont Institute," I told one of my editors, a genius with a degree in intellectual history. "It's super fascinating how the Straussian ethos has woven its way into the Peter Thiel segment of the Republican Party." He gazed at me blankly, and I realized something, as jarring as a record scratch. "Wait. How do the Ivies teach people about Strauss?"

"I'm not familiar with him," he said with a shrug. "He wasn't central to the program. Though I think he may have been part of a conservative theory seminar my senior year."

It was one of the nicer ways my *Vanity Fair* colleagues saw my beat. Most of the time, my stories would get shot down with "That's too fringe for our readership," or "What the actual fuck," or "Isn't that too weedsy?" But it was less about what was said to me than what was happening to my career within *Vanity Fair*. Had I not written the Trump Grill article, I realized, the print magazine staff would not have known who I was. And now that I wrote about right-wingers, my potential growth inside the magazine had ground to a halt. I watched my work colleagues maneuver into positions and worlds of prestige: red-carpet events at the Cannes Film Festival and after-parties at the Oscars, with designer ballgowns on the company dime; reporting trips to the Hamptons and Bahamas; invitations to host high-profile panels at the Vanity Fair New Establishment Summit. It was even more prestigious to get your work *printed* in the magazine, and only the best web writers would be deemed worthy to even write blurbs, much less get their articles published on glossy paper. *Is my beat too low-class to let me into the magazine?* I wondered. *Or am I the one who's too low-class?*

True, there were higher-profile writers at the Hive who'd already built their reputations over decades, and I didn't fault them for moderating panels or getting five-thousand-word print articles. But there was a cohort of writers my age, and we'd all started off as news writers and bloggers. Our Trump-era beats were rewarded differently: Abby, who'd started digging into the Mueller investigation, was now going on Ari Melber all the time; Emily, who had a direct line into the mon-eyed worlds of Jared, Ivanka, and Melania, soon signed a contract on CNN. Once, I walked into work and realized they'd all dyed their hair blond—a better color for television. The woman I went to for haircuts later told me that it would cost hundreds of dollars for a full head of highlights. "Your hair *does* wash you out, though," she sighed with understanding.

By now I owned a real leather work purse, had learned how to properly do my makeup, and had pulled together a wardrobe of better clothes (I was a consignment store beast). But I still rolled with pigs in the populist muck. Every pitch was received with confusion like I was shilling them a wacky pyramid scheme that would never be taken seriously. I would go back to my cheap group house in Brooklyn—"You live with *four other people*?" Emily, who lived by herself in the South Vil-lage, once gasped—trying to tamp down the memory of my parents pitching Melaleuca products to the Taylors and Kennedys. I was born to rubes, studied with rubes, took jobs with rubes, and still talked like a rube. And that was why I was covering rubes.

There was another editor who saw value in what I wrote: John Homans, a towering, legendary magazine editor in his sixties who had supervised the first feature profile of Steve Bannon for *Bloomberg Businessweek* in 2015, and had been the first editor, back at *New York* magazine, to turn reporters on to investigating Fox News. He already knew some of the background of the right, though not all, and he constantly reminded me of it. "Why should I care about these fringe freaks?" he'd asked in his booming voice whenever I came to him with a pitch, though eventually I realized he was trying to provoke me: if I could tell the story clearly to *him*, like Odysseus shooting an arrow through twenty axe heads, I could tell the story to the world. But Homans was only one man at the institution—a crusty, legendary island unto himself, the kind of guy who could get away with saying "HIYA, ANNA" to Anna Wintour on the elevator. I always felt safest in his spartan office, devoid of any of the designer frippery that littered *Vanity Fair.*

"I want to write about the Daily Wire," I told him in 2018. "Fox News is the most powerful voice in conservative media, yes, but they haven't conquered the digital frontier yet. This company is good at it. Ben Shapiro's got the top podcast in the country. They're more professionalized than any conservative media company I've ever seen. I visited their studios. Ben's set looks better than *Bill O'Reilly's.*"

Homans put me under a battery of questioning: Who were the characters I'd follow? What was their business strategy? How did their ideology turn into virality? Why should *he* care? Why should *anybody* care? I answered them as best as I could, interviewed dozens of conservative activists and writers and artists, and eventually put out my first, best profile: "Let Me Make You Famous: How Hollywood Made Ben Shapiro." It was a dive into the burgeoning conservative entertainment complex—a professionalized form of activism that, unusually for a conservative media project, was focused on getting clicks, gaining influence, and making gobs of cash.

Homans and I hammered out each paragraph, refined each sentence—I was flowery, he was direct—and wrought the story into shape. We sent a photographer out to shoot the Wire's offices. It was my best article, one that I thought illustrated a rising trend.

"It's not going in the magazine," he said after we'd submitted it, as disappointed as I was. "They think it's too small-potatoes."

We both knew exactly what that meant.

9

THE PROGRESSIVE SNOWFLAKE POWER HOUR

T he first mistake is that I tend to think that we as a party compromise before we even get to the table, which to me, I don't think, is
a good negotiating position," Alexandria Ocasio-Cortez—a new congresswoman, barely six months younger than me, who had just toppled
a powerful Democratic congressman in her primary and was the talk of
American politics—told me in a trailer, as her young staffers hovered
nearby. "Like, they start off where they want to end up, where, when
you're dealing with just these insane people that are kind of holding
the country hostage on the right, you can't go in with your endpoint.
You have to go in with a strong position, because they're trying to end
Planned Parenthood."

For once, I'd been assigned to do something technically cool by *Vanity Fair* office standards: I was interviewing her for the New Establishment issue, at a photo shoot in her Bronx home district, with the fashion department trying to figure out which designers in their closets would suit her best. She arrived to the shoot with her staff as a normal woman in a plain black suit and flats who had just been saying hi to her neighbors, nothing unusual about her save for the fact that a besotted campaign volunteer was following her with a sign. But as soon as she sat in the makeup chair in the trailer, and the fashion people swooped in with the Calvin Klein suits and the Manolo Blahnik heels, AOC—the trailblazer, the insurgent, the *future*—emerged. "She's *gorgeous*," the volunteer, a young teenage girl, sighed.

"So I don't think we don't go in with *let's keep Planned Parenthood*," she continued, gratefully accepting a water bottle. "I think we go in with, *let's expand women's rights to health care and guarantee it in every state*. For me, I think we can compromise in our tactics and how we get there. But I don't think we compromise on where we're going, for me personally."

Eh, I watch a bunch of right-wing activists say the same thing on a regular basis, I thought. "Are the party elders receptive to that?" I asked instead. "One of the big things that the right has been, you know, doing their weird little happy dance over"—*Oh god, that was a bad phrase*—"is the fact that Obama hasn't endorsed you yet."

"But he's only endorsing red to blue," she said, frustrated. She had only been in the national spotlight for less than a month, not enough time for a twentysomething-year-old community organizer, especially one without the money for media training sessions, to learn how to sit for an interview with a national outlet without saying *like* or *um*. "So like, there's no reason for him—like, that's why they're doing this happy dance, because like, they invent these fantasies, they invent crises, that then everyone else responds to. And to me, sometimes it's like, we give up so much power by doing that. Because they create a crisis, and then the reasonable press responds to the crisis that is more hysterical, kind of, [than] more hysterical outlets or pundits can create. So just go over Benghazi, Solyndra—"

"Solyndra! What a throwback."[1]

Ocasio-Cortez laughed. "Yeah. Like, they make up things to be faux outraged about, and then the problem is that we get dragged onto their court. So for this Obama thing, like all of those were Democratic Congressional Campaign Committee–target red-to-blue districts. And when we have limited resources between now and November, we need to focus on what we can win. You know, for me, I get involved in primaries because that is our opportunity to select the best Democrats. But after these primaries are through, we need to buckle down and flip every district that we can flip and I think there are probably even more that are close than we probably realize. So yeah, it's like not a big thing, because what he did was the practical big-picture thing to do."

We wrapped up the interview and she stepped out to be photographed, swiftly transitioning from the city sidewalk to a blank white studio backdrop *Vanity Fair* had set up next to a bodega. She *did* have a point, I thought. It was quite possible that the Democrats would retake the House in the upcoming midterm, and Obama really didn't have a reason for interfering in the primary process, unless he wanted to piss off hundreds of local power brokers across the nation. But for all intents and purposes, Ocasio-Cortez was an outsider who wanted to change things on the inside, with a die-hard progressive mandate from her voters that she needed to match. She talked a big game about changing the establishment—she was, after all, a Bernie Sanders supporter, and he had shaken the foundations of the Democratic Party in 2016. Her words, I realized, didn't seem much different from Ali Alexander telling me that they planned to hold the RINO establishment accountable.

I wonder if there were parallels between her world and mine, I thought, watching Ocasio-Cortez say hello to a child who'd wandered up to her on the sidewalk. I had a hard time imagining a Proud Boy, or Steve Bannon, or Trump himself kneeling down to meet that child at eye level.

I came back from the Bronx and beelined straight to Jon in his office. "What if I covered the progressive movement like I did the right?" I asked. "It's a force trying to flex outsider power on Washington and the Democrats. Given the upheaval on the right, I'd bet there's a similar dynamic going on in the left."

"I mean, go for it," he said, relieved I had come up with this on my own. It was a good beat, covering what looked like a new power center, and it solved a second problem for him: I was burned-out, and he knew it.

———

My mother's death the year before had been abrupt, even though I'd known her cancer was likely terminal. But the indomitable Thanh Nguyen seemed incapable, almost unwilling, to acknowledge the possibility of her death, and we'd begun to believe her fantasy. She was still driving and working, laughing and fussing, micromanaging our Costco runs, even threatening a weed supplier on the internet with an FBI investigation for selling her fake CBD. At one point she even started planning a trip to Portugal. But when she was told she had two months left, her spirit broke. She died in six days.

Logistically unprepared, I suddenly found myself dealing with wills, estates, funeral planning in a foreign language,[2] legal battles; how to keep my younger sister in college, how to ensure my long-absent father didn't get his hands on the life insurance, where the remains of my mother, a magnificent woman turned to dust in a porcelain jar, should go. The process went on for months, and months, and months, and with every email to every new lawyer I met, I gritted my teeth. *Yes, it's very sad that Mom died, but there are things you have to take care of, just solve them. You get five minutes to cry about it.*

Although Jon had given me time off to get her affairs in order, I eventually needed to come back to the office, where I'd shelved *another* emotional quandary. I had proven my ability to speak fluent right-wing activist—few mainstream journalists could say that they'd worked at the Daily Caller, much less knew every obscure think tank under the sun—I suddenly started feeling something I should not have felt as a journalist at all: a painful sense of *disloyalty*, like I'd sold out my old friends and old life, somehow, in the pursuit of journalistic success.

It didn't matter that the beat had found me, or that the MAGA phenomenon had happened *after* I went to *Vanity Fair*, or even that my break from the movement had occurred years before Trump descended the golden escalator of Trump Tower to announce his candidacy in 2015. It didn't matter that I hadn't pulled an Oliver Darcy and gone full Resistance Journalist. And my experience should, ideally, have been an asset. "It only makes your reporting better," Jon had told me when I'd first expressed doubt over whether it was okay to cover the right as a former student activist, even an accidental one. Bill Cohan and Michael Lewis, two of *Vanity Fair*'s best financial journalists, used to be bankers on Wall Street—Cohan for years at Lazard Frères. Dominick Dunne had become the best reporter on the judicial system, famously covering the trial of O. J. Simpson, and had gotten his start by writing about the miscarriages of justice during his own daughter's murder trial.

It was all well and fine that Michael Lewis had burned his bridge when he wrote Liar's Poker, *I thought* bitterly, *but the bankers weren't going to take their blackmail material from college straight to the president to unleash anonymous cyber-stalkers against him.* No one understood why I compulsively kept searching internet records for my personal information to delete, or barely tweeted out my own stories, or spent my evenings burning my mail in the fire pit in the backyard, to the concern of the artsy New Yorkers whom I now lived with. I was unwilling to weave my own rope with which to eventually hang myself. But the bad metaphor didn't end there: one could be a banker without having to swear unshakable, ideological loyalty to Wall Street as if it were the Illuminati. On the other hand, the very act of reporting on the right was like breaking a vow of omertà: The movement had raised me. They had let me into their networks, they had given me money, they had built my resume, and now I was betraying them. I was their judge, not their soldier. I was writing *about* them, not *for* them.

But that stance, that internal tension, flew over the heads of my new mainstream colleagues. The vast majority in New York saw me as a convert, and the moment they'd learned anything about my background, they immediately asked me if I knew how to change the minds of Trump voters. Even as I feebly protested *That's not my job, man, go get someone elected or something,* they kept prying, looking for that one moment when the scales had fallen from my eyes. "Are you a liberal now? How did you not become a Nazi?!" one potential book editor had asked me, sending me into a spiral of anxiety: Did my colleagues suspect that I sympathized with Trump's extremism? Was it immoral, awful, wrong, that I could continue to speak MAGA and not get angry about it? By associating with Charlie in high school and the Claremont schools and the Daily Caller, had I been a *bigot*?

Even the act of capturing the subtleties of the MAGA movement—trying, in other words, to do journalism—offended my peers. Early on in the Trump years, I saw that a prime-time anchor I'd idolized from my youth had sent me a Twitter DM. But he was, apparently, unhappy that I wrote about Mike Cernovich, and all too happy to tell me so: "I think you're giving him a benefit of the doubt and affording him a nuance he does not deserve." My excitement immediately turned to deep shame, along with an impotent confusion. What was I supposed to do? Forget everything I knew about the movement and call him a Nazi, even if his brand of nationalism and antiliberalism was definitionally different,[3] because it would make my colleagues feel better? Spend my days trying to upend the Trump administration for the sake of goodness? The entirety of my industry, it seemed, had an impulsive need to condemn my subjects, and was hell-bent on using me, the person with the most insider knowledge, as their avenging angel to destroy the movement. Anything less than that, a TV producer screamed at me once when I refused to help him work on an antifascism film, was complicity. Normally I would distract myself with piles of work, but it wasn't a pleasant option at the bitchy, backstabbing, social-climbing Thunderdome known as a Condé Nast office, worse now that there were rumors Graydon Carter would retire. Everyone wanted to survive the inevitable layoffs, and if they could knife the weirdo street rat who covered fascists, it might save their jobs.

In Vietnamese culture, the grieving period lasts a year, a chance for the family to properly process the absence of the deceased. I took that to mean that I needed to hold myself together for that period of time to let the absence of my mother settle. *Just make it to July, everything will be good*, I told myself, *and you'll have the emotional bandwidth to deal with that reporting problem then.*

I'm not sure I could pinpoint a moment that led to me breaking, though. Maybe it was when I tried to attend a dinner at the Claremont Institute, only to be told by their comms director that I would be unable to hang out with my old friends. Maybe it was when I heard that Peter Thiel was both Chuck Johnson's new benefactor *and* a growing donor in the Republican Party. Maybe it was Mother's Day, when I overheard people in the office groaning over scheduling brunch. But eventually I found myself curled into a ball under a table in an office that had once been a video editing bay but was now a storage room, and realized that I'd been bawling my eyes out for an hour behind a high pile of expensive Knoll Generation chairs—chairs that once belonged to nearly two dozen former *Vanity Fair* staffers, nearly all senior editors hired by Graydon who'd been there for decades, and who'd all been laid off that Valentine's Day due to budget cuts from his replacement. I am not sure how I managed to wedge myself in there, but the moment a coworker saw me through the window, I realized that something was deeply, deeply wrong.

———

After Jon gave me the green light to start reporting on progressives— at least I had no weird emotional hang-ups reporting *there*—I tried to be as expansive as I could during this period. I met people across New York City and traveled across the country—attended Sean McElwee's Socialist Happy Hour in the East Village, called donors and operatives and politicians, traveled to Representative Jim Clyburn's annual fish fry in South Carolina to meet approximately nine hundred different Democrat candidates vying for the presidential nomination. But every single one of my pieces felt inconsequential. Sure, the people I spoke to were nicer to me, and weren't as hell-bent on anti-establishment vengeance as my old set of sources were, but it seemed like they were working on much smaller projects that would barely cause a ripple once launched. Was the Socialist Happy Hour going to birth any new advocacy groups, for instance, or ensure that people weren't going to be sour over certain donors getting tapped first? Would a college student be personally mentored by the founder of the Center for American Progress, one of the left's biggest think tanks, after meeting them at a campus event? Or was it simply a marketing ploy for journalists to interact with various progressive influencers? I kept grinding. Was I just unable to map the left as well as I could the right?

I need to find a billionaire, I realized.

I soon found one in Reid Hoffman, the founder of LinkedIn. He had been a member of the PayPal Mafia, the infamous group of young programmers who'd built the online transaction site and then went off to found their own mega corporations, including Elon Musk to Tesla and SpaceX, Peter Thiel to Palantir and Facebook. The tech billionaire, putting on his Silicon Valley venture capitalist hat, had launched a fund called "Investing in US" (as in, the collective "us," and also the United States) that was already irritating Democratic Party organizers. Both entities concurred that they *had* to work together: Investing in US had poured hundreds of millions of dollars into local races and election groups, nearly flipping the Virginia state legislature to the Dems in 2017 and funding several of the anti-Trump ("#Resistance" in Twitter parlance) groups that were instrumental in the Blue Wave of 2018. They'd pledged to donate hundreds of millions more into ousting Trump in 2020. But they still had a rocky relationship with the Democratic Party overall, and several state party chairs were willing to tell me why.

"They think that they know the answer better than people who are working at the state and national level on a daily basis," Jane Kleeb, the state party chair of Nebraska, told me over the phone. Nebraska had been written off as a lost cause. From the local level to the national committee, she argued, the Democrats had been getting their people into office through decades of work identifying talent, building up voter files, and establishing turnout operations—the kinds of things that would support generations of Democrats, from the phone-banking volunteers who could activate voters, to control of state houses and Congress. "But instead, big donors think that we're not effective, that we don't know what we're doing. And they then throw money at shiny new objects when instead they should be funding the fundamental institutions that are always going to be here, which are party organizations—"

"—and not things that are going to possibly go out of business," I added.

It was worse for her, since Kleeb was in a state that had been largely neglected: when she came on as chair, she told me, her budget was a paltry $30,000—which would be barely enough to pay for a Hell's Kitchen nightclub party for the Proud Boys—and under Obama, the Democratic National Committee sent her $2,500 a month. "The office desks were literally held up with duct tape," she fumed. The party leadership had not just failed to keep wealthy donors invested in their organizations—they'd *incentivized* them to take their resources elsewhere, and the billionaire technocrats with their super PACs were in constant warfare with the locals on the ground. And no sign of disunity on the left was more apparent than the fact that Kleeb had given me an on-the-record apoplectic burn of Reid Hoffman—something that a conservative, always aware of the Eleventh Amendment—*thou shalt not speak ill of your fellow Republican*—would never do to an ideologically aligned billionaire benefactor, unless it was to declare open warfare and forever enmity.

Mark Riddle's comment from years ago—"The moneyed leadership of the progressive side seems to like instant gratification"—kept ringing in my head. If this had been my world, I thought, the Nebraska Democratic Party would have spent a decade with thirty times that amount, or with shadow groups at the ready to step in when necessary. There would have been comms officials from Washington on speed dial, activists in every town ready to muster up a hundred door knockers at any given moment for any purpose. If they hadn't, someone else in town would have had it. Reid Hoffman, as well as the other tech billionaires who'd worked with him, would have easily surrendered their money to any of a hundred organizations who could, with just $200,000, win a state house seat and staff the new lawmaker with an entire office, thanks to people who knew people. Everyone would have met in a room once a week in Washington, or a secret online chat room, making sure that they weren't stepping on each other's toes, that the money was going somewhere efficiently, that everyone was getting along as smoothly as they possibly could, given the circumstances. No one would ever speak ill of any other Democrat—especially to a reporter.

It wasn't that I couldn't map the left, I realized. It was that the left had, relatively speaking, nothing to map. Sure, they performed well in 2018, winning the House and barely flipping the Senate, coasting off a wave of anti-Trump hatred. But how long would that advantage last?

I was in the middle of scrolling Twitter for work once again when Andrew Kirell, my old Mediaite coworker, texted me a link—"You need to read this right now"—from a news site called Splinter: "Leaked Emails Show How White Nationalists Have Infiltrated Conservative Media."

How is this surprising? I thought, and opened the link. The story, written by Hannah Gais, was about a private email group called Morning Hate, where up-and-coming conservative writers would secretly brainstorm ways to push racist ideologies into right-leaning publications. Within seconds, though, my intrigue had plummeted to horror: John Elliott, our mentor from the beginning of our journalism careers, was at the center of the group.

> *Elliott was among the most prolific and undoubtedly the most well-connected of the "Morning Hate" group. He had been running internship programs meant to prepare journalists for work in print, broadcasting, or investigative reporting for years at a variety of think tanks in Washington, DC, and beyond. From 2008 to 2013, Elliott headed IHS's journalism program, helping libertarian and conservative journalists make their way into the media world by placing them at various affiliated media organizations for internships. (An archived page for the program boasts of placing people at outlets ranging from MSNBC, CNN, ABC, and Fox News to Breitbart and the Daily Caller.) But the "Morning Hate" emails show that Elliott was leading something of a shadow life, and that there were some people he let his guard down for.*
>
> *According to one former mentee, Elliott opened up to those he deemed "red-pilled"—a term used by white nationalists and so-called men's rights activists to refer to someone who has been awakened to their cause. (The same source noted that Elliott played a large role in their radicalization process.)*

What the fuck.

I stood up, ran my hands through my hair, and sped to the fire escape stairwell to process this gut punch. *What the ever-loving fuck.* I sank onto the hard concrete steps to catch my breath.

John Elliott hadn't been front and center of my mind for years, as I'd gotten absorbed into the world of prestige media and met new mentors, ready to push me onto a higher level of writing and journalism and career than Elliott could have ever provided. All I'd known was that Elliott had turned Trumpy—"Just read his Facebook," Kirell had warned me—and seemed to be jumping between conservative journalist organizations. First he left IHS, the program where I'd met him, when the journalism program got shuttered in 2013; then he went to the Franklin Institute, the home of that sketchy Wisconsin "reporting" internship he'd tried to hook me up with; now he was at the Charlemagne Institute,[4] running a ten-week internship program that tutored students in journalism, business presentation, professionalism, and the intellectual framework necessary to fight the Americans who "have largely rejected our Judeo-Christian heritage."[5] I'd seen his name pop up earlier that year when he appeared in a BuzzFeed article about Katie McHugh, a young former Breitbart writer and Elliott mentee, also an alum of his internship program, who'd been radicalized into white supremacy. She blamed him for setting her down that path. At the time, he'd denied everything, blaming her for going down "the dark path of those fringe groups" and saying he had nothing to do with them.

But according to Splinter, he had been actively setting up networking meetings between the interns he'd identified with an inclination toward hatred, and prominent ethnonationalists—the kind that had entire entries in the databases of the Southern Poverty Law Center, the

Anti-Defamation League, or any other nonprofit research institution that tracked full-fledged hate groups. And even for the majority of the MAGA sources I spoke to, full-throated ethnonationalism of the type that Elliott expressed was, publicly, a step too far.

Elliott had used the group, full of mentees now at think tanks and publications like the Daily Caller and Breitbart (and, apparently, quite by accident, *Vanity Fair*), to workshop his most racist ideas, such as limiting population growth for minorities (I blanched). The group had debated intensely how to slowly slip their ideas into publications like the Caller, without anyone noticing, in the hopes that they could turn them mainstream. And they'd taken advantage of the Caller's weakness: the content machine had to be fed, the slide shows had to be published, the publication needed to be staffed by people who'd willingly be paid pennies, and what was one or two ultra-right-wing op-eds in the giant churn of page views? To Elliott and the group, this was ideal—the infinite fringe was perfect for them. "No one owns the commons of conservatism, and so it's extremely vulnerable to outside subversion," one member, Daily Caller employee Jonah Bennett, observed. "This subversion would not have been able to occur without the Internet. Praise be."

All of these thoughts were blurring together in the background, and all I could think of was my mentor's double life. John Elliott, the representative of a program that espoused the equality of humankind across race and creed and believed in meritocracy, dabbled in racial science. John Elliott, kindly and old and white-haired, had used a secret code to disguise ethnic slurs and pro-Hitler slogans with ironic labels. (As Splinter put it: " 'Hawaiians' was a stand-in for 'Hebes,' an antisemitic slur referring to Jews; 'Alaskans' for 'N's' (the n-word); 'our good friend' for 'AH' (Adolf Hitler); and 'our good friend's son' for

Trump." He later compared Trump to "our friend" who made "no mistakes" from 1932 to 1934.) My mentor, who had offered to guide my career along the right path during breakfast coffees at IHOP, going in the morning to take advantage of the senior special discount, was taking other IHS students to dinner with famous white nationalists, having drinks with them during in-person meetups he called "hateups." My mentor, who had written recommendations for jobs, and given me my first internship and (I thought, I *hoped*) applauded my rise in the mainstream media, had apparently referred to some of my fellow IHS interns as "homos" and asked the group for recommended readings for his newest crop of interns at the Charlemagne Institute. (The institute fired Elliott after the story was published.) This evidence stretched even to the days where he was listening to me hyperventilating on the phone about my lack of a career. I was a young, Asian American woman he had taken under his wing, whom he promoted as a promising young person—and *John Elliott had thought these things the entire time.*[6]

I was talking to a Democrat source days later, trying to explain the concept of a conservative training camp for student journalists—a concept light-years ahead of his baby-level plans to identify candidates for state office—and how a sworn white nationalist could have lived in the conservative establishment, nurturing extremists under the nose of the Koch brothers. "We never *knew* him as a racist," I said. "None of us knew." But I couldn't let go of a sentence from the BuzzFeed article. Elliott noticed that in McHugh's application—sent to him in 2010, the year after I'd applied—she'd mentioned Joe Sobran, a hypernationalist, paleoconservative, Holocaust-denying columnist who opposed the very idea of constitutional democracy. "You are the first applicant to ever list Joe Sobran as an influence," Elliott wrote back to McHugh, according to BuzzFeed. "Joe was a friend. He had the same influence on me. I was delighted to find a young journalist who has profited from his work." He would later go on to introduce her to numerous other famed white nationalist thinkers, placing her at the Daily Caller, and then at Breitbart, where he thought she'd fit best.[7]

"The way I read the story, it was like he was trying to find specific people in my cohort to take down that path with him," I explained.

"Huh," said the source after a pause. "It sounds like he was sifting for zealots."

I suddenly remembered how Elliott once told me that he'd rejected Harvard students from the journalism program because their intellectual influences were "incorrect." *Katie McHugh had given him the correct answer,* I realized.

I kept trying to focus on the original topic, but I couldn't stop thinking about what Elliott had sowed years ago, how soon the harvest would arrive, and whether it was futile for me to continue to run away from covering that movement. And the more I tried to explain John Elliott and IHS to this source, the more I realized: I was more invested in explaining the conservative movement to this man than I was invested in writing about literally anything else.

Well, suck it up, snowflake, I thought. *Time to get out of the snow globe.*

10

THE YEAR OF THE STORM

January 6, 2021
US Capitol, South Entrance, Dirksen Senate Office Building
10:27 a.m. EST

The premise of the story would be that people of all stripes had gone to Washington to heckle and intimidate lawmakers as they entered the building to certify the 2020 election of Joe Biden as president. I was to get a few interviews with the die-hard MAGA types who'd come to the Capitol, write it up as quickly as possible, sprinkle it with some color, file it to my *Politico* editors before 1 p.m., and then call it a day as the Congress team took over.

But over the course of the 2020 pandemic, I'd become close to groups of researchers from think tanks and universities who'd anonymously embedded themselves in the private chat rooms of extremists' online communities. They had warned me that a different brand of MAGA was on-site today—groups that didn't see their activity as playacting, or clean fun. Proud Boys (street fighters, black and yellow polo shirts, obsessed with masculinity, reactionary movement seeking to get into brawls with liberal protesters), Oath Keepers (militia, non-identifiable, obsessed with protecting the Constitution), and the Three Percenters (militia, marked with the Roman numeral for three, obsessed with their Second Amendment rights, antigovernment and anti-leftist). *Why* those groups were coming, they could only hypothesize at that point. And quietly. "I always feel like a psycho street heckler when I'm outlining potential threats," one researcher, Jared Holt, told me at one point as we brainstormed two days before. "And you know I am not into scaremongering." The "normies" were definitely a little more agitated than usual ("There's more of us than there are them," a MAGA-aligned pastor told me that morning, pointing to the Capitol Hill Police, a sign of what was to come), but I'd become used to that specific type of Trump supporter. Even if they loved to boo CNN, the *New York Times,* or any other mentions of the "fake news," they'd happily chat with reporters if asked, give us quotes, and send us on our way with a sincere entreaty to just *tell the truth to the American people and do your job,* which I promised I would.

But it was not yet noon, and I'd already seen three people in full-fledged body armor. *That* was different. And despite this sudden new knot twisting in my stomach—*Am I . . . nervous?*—this was a detail that needed to be in my story.

I spotted a man in a black bulletproof vest next to a giant speaker, near the Capitol's north entrance near Constitution Avenue. *Chin up, maybe he's just an overzealous MAGA paramilitary cosplayer who thinks antifa is behind every corner,* I thought, and asked if I could interview him. His name was Asher—Colombian, Jewish, from South Florida, perfect skin, and no last name given, though I prodded. "We're Proud Boys."

This was the first time I'd ever met one in the wild, and I hadn't expected to run into one so early in the day, much less be surrounded by them. "I *heard* the Proud Boys weren't wearing the shirts," I blurted out, as if utterly charmed by this pleasant surprise. It was true. Enrique Tarrio, their leader, had suggested on Twitter that the Proud Boys would not be in their distinctive regalia: $100 Fred Perry polo T-shirts, with black and yellow trim on the collar and arm bands, and a laurel embroidered on the breast. "Why are you wearing black? That's antifa colors."

"Because we wanted to blend in a little more," he said, seemingly impressed that I'd followed the Proud Boy chatter. "It's not just black. There's some of us wearing patriotic gear. Trump hats. That's what the order that came down from leadership was. That's what they wanted to do and they have, I guess, a bigger plan in mind that I'm unaware of."

We kept talking as my *Politico* coworker Daniel Lippman joined us, having wrapped up other interviews. It was the first time that I started speaking in Proud Boy lingo, and I'd asked where Tarrio was. "He's out of the city right now. He's not allowed within DC so he's gonna sit this one out," said Asher. (The real story, apparently, was that Tarrio had been detained by DC Police for attempting to bring guns into the gun-free zone of the Capitol.) "But we have a second in command today. They have a plan."

"You're confident?"

"Confident? We really have to see what the day brings." He paused, realizing he might have said too much. "We're really a reactionary movement. We react to groups like antifa terrorizing patriots walking to their cars."

———

Yes, I had moved back to DC. Yes, I got trapped there during the pandemic. No, I wasn't happy about it.

Right around the time I'd learned that my first mentor was a white supremacist, a cataclysm erupted in the leadership of *Vanity Fair*. Jon Kelly abruptly left, John Homans was suddenly editing twice as many posts, and the powers that were put me back on daily blogging. My stories on Democrats were, apparently, not performing very well on web traffic, and I was already the poor kid who should have still been grateful to even be allowed in Condé Nast's lobby. It was a kick down from my already low place on the *Vanity Fair* career totem pole, meaning that I was back to mining Twitter for blog posts. But I still had my MAGA influencer feeds intact, and one day in July, as I was half-mulling the thought of quitting *Vanity Fair*, I saw my timeline erupt. Diamond and Silk. Carpe Donktum. James O'Keefe. Ali Alexander. Charlie Kirk, Bill Mitchell, Lucian Wintrich, Tim Pool, Benny Johnson, Ryan Fournier, Will Chamberlain—a slew of accounts, run by people whom I'd met over the years,[1] were all posting photos of themselves in the White House, sitting in the Rose Garden, listening to Trump ramble, alongside fellows from the Heritage Foundation and congressmen like Matt Gaetz and Marsha Blackburn. They were paraded in front of a shocked press corps, preening and picking fights with certain offended reporters. They were tweeting about meetings lined up with the White House press secretary and Trump's social media guru Dan Scavino.

My internet people, of *all people*, were inside the White House.

The mainstream coverage of the event made note to point out that for something ostensibly called a Social Media Summit, no one from Facebook, Google, or Twitter was invited. The right-wing coverage depicted it as a defiant stand against those Big Tech overlords. It turned out that some brilliant comms person had, apparently, decided to host a "Social Media Summit," selecting a host of important MAGA influencers and inviting them to spend time with the Trump administration to vent about online censorship against conservatives in Big Tech.

I would like to state for the record that I was into multiverses long before they became a cinematic box-office crutch. Chalk it up to my lonely childhood days of reading online fan fiction, where young authors could imagine their own version of beloved books and franchises and write stories about how they wanted things to end up. (Somewhere, in my sad youth, I wrote a crossover of *Monty Python and the Holy Grail* with characters from an anime called *Card Captor Sakura*.) Or maybe it was when I read Ray Bradbury's "A Sound of Thunder" in fifth grade and had nightmares for weeks, horrified about a time traveler who stepped on a butterfly a million years ago and accidentally turned his home timeline into a fascist dystopia. In any case, I have a special fondness for speculative fiction: alternate histories, parallel universes, multiversal crossovers where the laws of physics are tweaked *ever* so slightly and one minor event changes the course of history forever, or establishes an alternate reality. And there's one special trope in this genre: when two parallel universes collide—the MAGA world and the real world, for instance—things can get really, really bad.

I'd been fixated on the implications of this officially sanctioned crossover event when Blake Hounshell, a hilarious magazine editor whom I'd been on DM terms with, sent me a text out of nowhere asking if I'd be interested in joining *Politico*'s White House team. The thought of leaving my prestigious, orchid-scented office and returning to Washington, home of my earliest mistakes, was agonizing—but so too was the thought of not being able to report this story out in 2020. Within days, I'd pulled together a memo describing the beat I'd cover: how Trumpworld interacted with the outside, non-Washingtonian, nonpolitical elite forces that now had pipelines directly into the Oval Office, where once only Big Money or big titles could venture. "With their ability to somehow burst the quietest rooms of power through technology and social media, outsiders are now an institution in and of themselves," I wrote.

Little did I know exactly how true that would be.

————————

Technically, according to the job description, I was a member of the White House Correspondents Association, with all the prestige and responsibilities that membership entailed: international flights on Air Force One; nationally televised showboating in the Briefing Room; black-tie galas and off-the-record dinners with mysterious Senior Administration Officials. They would be good, clean, *normal* Washington stories, reported out of the tiny White House James Brady Press Briefing Room, which had looked much bigger on camera. But COVID-19 had emerged four months after I'd joined, and with my ability to meet new people severely curtailed, I started covering the people farthest away from the building pulling inspiration out of the dregs of my internet-poisoned brain: vaccine crackpots, QAnon conspiracy theorists, internet influencers, and militias. I'd never met the Senior Administration Officials in person, and I didn't particularly care for whatever spin they'd have on whatever Trump tweeted: every time Trump reposted their content or repeated their claims on television, mainlining it into the minds of a massive voting base that trusted nobody except for him, it was an official statement from the president of the United States. And I was now a White House reporter.

There was the time that Trump retweeted a post that said #Fire-Fauci, sparking a media frenzy suggesting that Trump was mad over

Dr. Anthony Fauci's media appearances contradicting his COVID messaging—until I discovered that the tweet had, in fact, been written by anti-vaccine activists, who were infuriated that Fauci was proposing Bill Gates–funded jabs as a potential cure, and now believed that Trump agreed with their message. There was the time that Elon Musk and Trump were exchanging pleasantries on Twitter, when Joe Rogan—the comedian and podcaster my former MMA-obsessed Brooklyn roommate had introduced me to—had become a main source of COVID information. There was one of the first stories *Politico* ever published about QAnon: how numerous congressional candidates had been promoting theories claiming that Trump was about to purge Washington of Satan-worshipping pedophiles, based on posts from an online figure known as "Q," and one of those candidates, Marjorie Taylor Greene, was most likely to become a congresswoman. (I guarantee no one else at *Politico* had written the phrase "Satan-worshipping pedophiles" before I did.) There were stories about MAGA people champing at the bit for a new alternative to Twitter, flocking to a MAGA Facebook alternative called Parler; stories about militia members showing up at rallies and falling into denial about coronavirus.

Tweets and retweets became action: one influencer's question of "Why does BLM have signs about abolishing the police?" snowballed over time into a larger frenzy of "They want to abolish the police!" and from *then* into militia groups taking over small towns and suburbs, jacked up over the possibility of lawless antifa looters[2] swooping in and destroying property, while the police were unable to act; pleas for Trump to use the Insurrection Act to come and save the day went unheard. One random internet person's suggestion that hydroxychloroquine might be a useful adjunct therapy for a COVID patient turned into a Trumpian miracle cure frenzy.[3] And thanks to four years of an alternate news world being built around Trump supporters, including their own alternate interpretations of what the Constitution could and could not do, or how many people did or did not support Trump, it was fairly obvious to me that they would never accept a Biden victory.

The street-brawling Proud Boys being upset were one thing. I'd met several of them, as well as their founder Gavin McInnes, at the 2018 Night for Freedom, and for all their tendencies to pick fistfights with their ideological counterparts, they could still claim that they were an *unarmed* protest group. The militias, on the other hand, were a new factor. When I was younger, the militia ideology was the wackiest of the wacko infinite fringe—more than CPAC, more than whatever Chuck Johnson or Peter Thiel had been doing, so radioactive that even my normal right-wing activist sources wouldn't go near them. Prior to Trump, they'd spent decades off in the woods of eastern Oregon and Idaho, howling about vaccines and prepping defensively for the fall of the government and the anarchy that would likely ensue.[4] Occasionally they'd break into mainstream coverage, but mostly as sideshow rubes: I remembered Stephen Colbert singing a parody country song about Ammon and Cliven Bundy, the ranchers-turned-founders of the People's Rights militia, when they'd tried occupying federal land in Oregon in 2016. But something about Trump had emboldened them—possibly the thought that he would upend the political system that had oppressed them so and cleanse Washington of corruption—and the chaos of 2020, a truly apocalyptic situation where the government was seizing control of everything, had sent them on a holy mission to save America. The COVID lockdowns, the mask mandates, the increasing chatter about a vaccine cure, had spooked them out of hiding and brought Ammon Bundy out in armed protest against state government buildings. The QAnon-related online content that had made up the bulk of their independent newspapers—Redoubt News, InfoWars—had jacked them up to the possibility that Joe Biden, along with his son and the Chinese government, were about to steal the election. And the possibility of a future where Anthony Fauci and an army of BLM-antifa supersoldiers would jab them all and smash their homes was so horrifying that they could not hold back their forces for long. The best part was that in 2020, Trump had endorsed them as "very good people" who were simply "angry," and they were taking orders from him as if he were *their* commander in chief: compulsively joining the police during the summer of antifa protests throughout the Midwest to guard storefronts, chatting about watching polling locations on Election Day, speculation on what they might do if Biden won.

I woke up bleary-eyed in my apartment on Wednesday, November 4, 2020, after a fitful three hours of sleep. A winner hadn't been declared yet, since hundreds of thousands of mail-in ballots were being counted across the country, and at least four states—Pennsylvania, Georgia, Wisconsin, and Michigan—were still uncalled by most of the news networks. The last time I'd covered an election night, back at *Vanity Fair* in 2016, we were all in the same conference room eating pizza and cranking out content. This year we were all confined to our homes, and my war room had been Fox News on the television, Twitter on my computer screen, and a lavender-scented candle burning on my table in a futile attempt at stress management. I'd been so jittery and unfocused the entire night that I'd made myself go to bed early, partly because I knew the election wouldn't be decided at 4 a.m., and partly because my *Politico* future was uncertain: if Biden won, I learned recently, it was widely expected that the people covering his campaign would replace the current White House team, having built the connections needed to report on the new administration. I had barely any time to meet people face-to-face before the lockdowns started—I could hear my mother panicking about networking from the grave, or rather, her urn—and "digital insanity" did not seem like a viable beat in the allegedly sane Biden administration.

But speaking of "digital insanity," there was something going on in my Twitter feed: the influencers whom I'd seen in the Rose Garden last July were now reposting photos of a government building in Maricopa County, Arizona, with MAGA supporters swarming around the entrances yelling about miscounted ballots, and they were all yelling about . . . Sharpies. I made a few calls, searched a few Twitter trends, and pulled up reams and reams of audio of Jay Sekulow, Trump's lawyer during last year's impeachment hearings, gamely listening to MAGA callers on a radio show who were frantic about what had happened to their ballots. The theory, it seemed, was that election officials had thrown out ballots because they were written in Sharpie (hence #SharpieGate). Every allegation of Sharpie shenanigans was also tagged with #stopthesteal, and within days, which had started sprouting tendrils throughout the internet as all my old sources from my MAGA days tweeted it out.

But no sooner did I hit "publish" on that story on Wednesday than my feed morphed again. Suddenly, the influencers started tweeting out a new event in November: *something* was going to happen in Washington, DC—Freedom Plaza downtown, next to the White House, specifically—on the weekend of November 14 and 15. It was either going to be called the Million MAGA March, or Stop the Steal DC, or the March for Trump.

Whenever there were too many coincidences in MAGA world,

there was one source I would always reach out to, and I pinged him immediately.

By that time, Jared Holt and I had known each other for four years. He had gone from being a journalist for Right Wing Watch, chronicling fringe movements in right-wing media, to a research fellow at the Atlantic Council with an incredible array of digital forensic tools at his disposal to track their obscure online activities. With the new gig, he'd introduced me to dozens of his colleagues in the burgeoning disinformation and extremist research spaces—think tankers, academics, and independent operators—who'd uncovered darker corners than even I could imagine existed. They'd become my best sources, able to counterbalance the pure ideology of the people I'd covered with the evidence of what that ideology led to. I started seeing how the tweets and messages from my online influencer sources were colliding into the real world, the kinetic impact of the digital rhetoric disrupting spaces—classrooms, churches, and now the US Capitol—far beyond the reaches of Twitter. I sent him the tweets and the phrases I'd heard. "Have you heard about these?" I asked Jared.

In response, he sent me something more disturbing: several posters advertising the same informal gathering that had started circulating inside militia chat groups and white nationalist websites like the Daily Stormer and Stormfront. "[W]e will rally in DC this weekend. GROYPERS WILL STOP THIS COUP," declared white nationalist influencer Nick Fuentes on Telegram.[5] Stewart Rhodes, whom I'd covered in the past for another story on militias, was now telling people that he was staging armed members outside the District of Columbia for reasons unknown.[6]

Normally I'd check for permits for rallies like this, except this time,

I couldn't find any. And it seemed like Rhodes was taking a caravan of Oath Keepers and their hangers-on to Freedom Plaza.

"Soooo basically it's just gonna be chaos," I texted Jared. "GREAT."

I hit up Ali Alexander immediately, who was now the point person organizing Stop the Steal rallies nationwide, thinking about his strange trajectory over the past year: less than ten months before, he was texting me about Kanye West's presidential campaign and trying to get me to cover the rapper's weird rally. Now his march was attracting actual Nazis, like flies to honey. "Lots of people are going to come up with different names and hashtags because they are excited," he texted back. For some reason, it felt like a shrug: *We can't control this crowd and we're not particularly inclined to.*

Thus began my first proper article on the Stop the Steal movement, and its first public gathering; several thousands of supporters in tow:

> *The disparate tribes of MAGA Nation—Oath Keepers, Three Percenters, Infowars fanatics, Groypers, Proud Boys, white nationalists, neo-Nazis and the people who would simply call themselves die-hard MAGA—have declared that they are simply going to show up in Washington en masse over the weekend to rally together, with the marquee event on Saturday.*

———

For months leading to the election, the Trump team had been blowing flirty little e-kisses to QAnon, the online conspiracy movement that had managed to stay deeply and nearly exclusively online for so long. From son Eric Trump posting a giant *Q* on Instagram (the White House had no comment) to President Trump going on an Independence Day retweeting spree when he platformed fourteen tweets linked to QAnon-promoting accounts, the "digital soldiers" of the movement had received just enough sustenance from Donald—leader of the free world at this point, mind you—to "know" that their movement was working.

It was hard to justify to editors and Trump sources that QAnon stories should be covered by a White House reporter. But the movement, which began on an online message board in 2017 and went into turbo mode during lockdown, had hyped itself into believing that Trump was the only man in Washington who could pull off the Storm: an apocalyptic Judgment Day scenario, obliquely prophesized by "Q," where the Satan-worshipping Deep State pedophiles of Washington would be tried and summarily executed en masse in a military tribunal. In campaigning terms, Trump barely had to do anything to win them over—in fact, it was better that he *not* acknowledge them at all, since the movement would read their own messianic meaning into his rhetoric. Literally, Trump once waved his finger in a circle during a speech, and his followers thought he'd drawn a *Q* in the air. (The closest Trump ever got to praising QAnon directly came in the form of a verbal shrug around August 2020: "I don't know anything about it other than that they do supposedly like me.") But after Election Day, when the QAnon crowd believed that the Deep State Satanists had stolen the election from Trump, the nods to their beliefs were more overt from Trump's team: there were now people inside Donald Trump's world who started to attach their names and reputations to QAnon theories.

General Michael Flynn, Trump's former national security advisor who had been ejected for lying about meeting with his Russian counterpart, was now unofficially a member of the movement, having tweeted a grainy video of himself reciting the QAnon Oath ("Where we go one, we go all") over the July Fourth weekend—the weekend, *coincidentally*, that tens of thousands of other QAnon believers were up-loading #TakeTheOath videos. Sidney Powell, a former federal pros-ecutor now on Trump's election fraud team, was all over the media, claiming that a voting machine company called Dominion Voting Sys-tems was the front of a conspiracy run by George Soros, the Chinese government, the (very dead) Venezuelan dictator Hugo Chávez, and more. (The campaign distanced themselves from her, but Trump still listened to her counsel.) Mike Lindell, the MyPillow CEO, and Patrick Byrne, the Overstock.com founder, were constantly in Trump's ear too. QAnon had treated these figures like intercessional saints, able to get their theories up to the Big Guy, and they could tell every time Trump tweeted about stolen elections that their prayers had worked.

My spirit finally broke in mid-December, when I pulled up News-max and saw Flynn, appearing remotely via Skype, demand that Trump use the military to seize all the election machines and redo the election. All the data I'd gathered over the past several months suddenly organized themselves into a machine, each factor bouncing off each other, passing ahead the energy like Newton's cradle, headed toward disaster: *QAnon thinks the election was stolen. Militias think the elec-tion was stolen. Their famous go-betweens are telling Trump all these theories, or at least, Trump is watching Michael Flynn say this on television. They are all hanging out now.*

FUCK.

The f-word on its own does not constitute a full, publishable story, so I went off and gathered the evidence, spoke to some researchers who were watching the same thing as me, and wrote up the story. In that extraordinary period of time, that was the only way the story could have been written: the die-hards would have never spoken to me ("WE

DON'T SPEAK TO LIBERAL JOURNALISTS!" one rally organizer had texted me, promptly before blocking me), the people around Trump would have instantly downplayed the threat as *not serious* or *too fringe and unserious*, and Trump himself would have airily brushed it off into a confused garble: *Well, these people, they like me very much, but they are angry, BOY they are angry, there's tremendous anger at Sleepy Joe Biden and the tremendous theft in our elections.* The only people I could cite at this point, who could make any sense of it at all, were the experts—people like Jared Holt, living inside the morass, and Brian Levin, a professor at California State University, San Bernardino who had studied right-wing extremism for decades. "What is the heart of the Second Amendment, pro-militia, anti-government patriot movement? It's the insurrectionist theory of the Second Amendment," he'd told me. "It says people can rise up against a tyrannical government. To me, this looks like the last exit on the Jersey Turnpike before we get to that spot."

The next day, Maggie Haberman of the *New York Times* reported that Trump had indeed asked Powell, his legal advisor and Flynn's lawyer, whether he could, actually, declare martial law—and my story absolutely *exploded* on *Politico*'s front page, taking up the A1 spot with a giant bold headline, racking up millions of views.

This was now, officially, a Washington story.

———

There was now a *new* D-Day for the MAGA movement, drawn from the obscure sections of the Constitution and blown into apocalyptic significance: January 6, 2021, the day that Congress and the vice president would convene and ceremonially count each state's Electoral College results, then declare the winner of the presidential election. In modern times, the day was supposed to be ceremonial—America had long moved past conveying the states' electoral decisions to Washington via messengers on horseback, and everyone knew who'd won by now—but several dozen MAGA legal scholars had reached into the dustiest corners of election law to try to assemble a response. One man who'd been gaining traction was John Eastman, a California law professor affiliated with the Claremont Institute, who had been going all over the airwaves promoting a radical theory that had been cobbled together from various internet blog posts and Twitter threads: using a *very* creative interpretation of the Constitution, Mike Pence, in his capacity as vice president and president of the Senate, was not only responsible for certifying the results of the Electoral College, but could *reject* the results of the college altogether, declaring certain votes as fraudulent and handing the election to Trump.[7]

I'd become close with Mac Bishop, a former war correspondent who'd covered riots in Hong Kong, and he'd given me drills about covering civil unrest and what to do if a crowd turned violent. (We would both be covering January 6th and he hinted that he was *not* going to rescue me.) I was saving copies of maps to my phone, and plotting my route back to my apartment if things went south. Days spent studying old inauguration stories had prepared me for what would happen—typically—when it became clear that Biden won. But the pro-Trump congressmen had already seeded the idea that Black Lives Matter and antifa protesters would come to drown out and attack Trump-loving patriots—and those patriots had a right to self-defense. The Proud Boys, the right-wing street brawlers known for picking fights with leftists in the streets, would likely try to beat up counterprotesters under the pretense of protecting MAGA supporters. And the militias—

Wait, I thought. I'd never dealt with a militia up close before. *What would militias do here? They can't bring guns into DC. So if they were to protest, where would they want to fight?*

I texted Jared. "Is there a natural target for militia members, if things go south?"

"The Capitol for them. Militias do less street fighting," he responded. "If big fights break out at the events we might see them act up, but generally their ire is at the government. They're not typically street prowlers."

Of course, I thought. The past year had proven that militias would absolutely confront police if they felt threatened, and that they had this absolute mania for occupying state capitol buildings under the pretense that those places belonged to "We the People"—a phrase from the Constitution that had been warped into their declaration of entitlement. That summer, armed militia members had appeared at anti-COVID lockdown protests in front of state capitol buildings across the country—Salem, Oregon; Lansing, Michigan, where they actually *entered the building with guns*—and by the time of the George Floyd protests, it seemed like they *wanted* a BLM activist or antifa saboteur to confront them in the streets. In recent months, they had started congregating around government buildings—courthouses, polling centers—in the states where the Steal needed to be Stopped. And Representative Louie Gohmert, a proudly far-right Republican congressman out of Texas, had gone on Newsmax days before, warning that certifying Biden's victory would "mean the end of the republic," and that Trump supporters had to "go to the streets and be as violent as antifa and BLM"—not that he was advocating violence, of course, but warning that antifa or BLM supporters would show up and be violent against *them* as well.

"Makes sense that Gohmert and everyone are hoping that BLM or antifa show up," I responded. "Because the cost of attacking the Capitol is too high."

"It's also costly for protesters," Jared replied. "That's the ultimate shit hitting the fan situation."

We knew what would happen if it got that far, but didn't want to think about it. We were running on fumes, barely propped up by coffee, photos of his new Pomeranian (a fluffy little boy named Pierre Turbo), and a mounting frustration about the number of militia groups we'd observed organizing trips to attend a January 6th rally. Few were taking us seriously, though I could understand why. I had learned so many new things about the fringiest of the fringe over the past several months, and I didn't know whether I would need to retain them after Biden's inauguration. Right-wingers don't like acknowledging that extremist groups exist even if they're part of the movement, if they're deemed unnecessary,[8] so it seemed possible—if not likely—these activists would go the way of right-wing has-beens Sarah Palin, Ammon Bundy, or Lyndon LaRouche. But the well-meaning part of me wondered why they didn't take the guys with guns seriously.

————

It was finally noon on January 6. Congress was about to start counting the votes, and we had to get our story up before then, so Daniel and I ducked into a Senate cafeteria to grab lunch and whip up our story illustrating the sorry state of the protesters. He sent his quotes to me and I dropped them in a Google document, the two of us tapping out descriptions and names at lightning speed while scarfing down sandwiches and chugging Snapples. Daniel went outside to get some more quotes while I wrapped things up, and was about to hit "send" when our editor sent me a message with a link: "Can you check this out? Looks like some people are trying to break into the Capitol."

It was a tweet containing a video of several dozen people in orange hats bum-rushing the gates at the north entrance. I rolled my eyes. It was probably a bunch of meme-obsessed hooligans trying to Naruto-run past the guards, and nothing would come of it, because there was most *certainly* top-notch security at the Capitol that would take care of it. (There *was*, right?) But colorful details were colorful details, so I crammed the rest of my sandwich in my mouth and left the building.

"I'll be able to get back inside in case things get crazy, right?" I asked a member of the Capitol Police as I exited the building.

"Oh, of course, miss," he said with a textbook professional smile.

As I left the building, I kept running through the war correspondent's lessons in my head. There were stupid things a journalist could do while covering civil unrest—he once saw a journalist put on a helmet *before* a tear gas mask, for instance—but the most important thing was to keep aware of the crowd's mood.

"Is the crowd obeying the directive of law enforcement?"

Not really, I thought to myself, which is the equivalent of a no, as I stepped outside, running into a vastly larger crowd, gazing across the city as they awaited thousands of flag-waving demonstrators marching in their direction. Though the police were trying to gently guide the crowd away from the building and across the street, there were murmurs running through the people, wondering why the cops were keeping them away from *their* building.

"When does it make sense for you to be easily identifiable as press? When does it endanger you?"

I asked another police officer if I could reenter the building. The crowd might be unruly, but the Capitol was safe. "I'm with *Politico*," I said, flashing my badge. He waved me through, but then another cop turned me back, saying they were no longer letting anyone on the Capitol grounds. Meanwhile, the people near me were getting amped about how awesome the guys who'd broken through the fence were, and increasingly getting enraged by the cops trying to get them, very nicely, to cross the street. "Just disobey!" one man said, to everyone's glee.

"The most important thing: when you feel unsafe, you need to know when to leave. Stay near solid things if the crowd stampedes. Don't be dumb."

I turned around. Without any protective equipment on, the safest thing right now seemed to be getting *away* from the Capitol. But perhaps walking down Constitution Avenue would be productive and help us get a sense of how big the crowd was. "Put your badge away," I hissed to Lippman. We walked toward the crowd, phones held out in front of us to shoot footage, blending in as well as we could: a tall white man in a blue dad hat incapable of expressing fear, and a tiny figure in a white parka of indeterminate ethnicity, looking for all the world like activists taking photos for social media.

There was supposed to be a rally stage set in front of the Capitol, though that seemed a moot point by now. I pulled up my Twitter feed for updates. "Well, shit," I said, and showed my phone to Lippman. It was filled with images of MAGA fans storming through the Capitol Rotunda and upending desks—and suddenly, video footage of the Capitol Police inside the Senate chamber, blocking the doors inside and pointing guns at the entrance.

Lippman looked at it, puzzled. "That's not good," he said, then his head shot up. A Department of Homeland Security car was whizzing by him. "This is bad," he said. "Homeland Security never comes out."

He instantly sprinted away from me to tail the car, like a golden retriever chasing the news, back to the Capitol, and I chased after him, trying to run and text my sources who'd organized the rally at the same time. (The rally, I was told, was now called off.)

Lippman and I sprinted furiously past ranting men accusing the police of betrayal, old Asian grannies carrying South Vietnam flags and signs in Mandarin about the Chinese Communist Party's chokehold on Joe and Hunter Biden, middle-aged women in sparkly pink MAGA hats, people bearing twenty-foot-high flagpoles with TRUMP 2020, people blaring "YMCA" on giant boom boxes. I started picking out the flags that I'd seen all over the internet in the past year: the Gadsen, the Thin Blue Line, Come and Take It, a big *Q* with the Stars and Stripes. "Everyone's running to the Capitol!" I heard a man scream, clambered atop a statue honoring Ulysses S. Grant. There was, I suddenly felt, no difference between the militia men in army surplus bulletproof vests and the MAGA troll men in the Party City American flag suits—they had the same aura of exhilaration, the same undercurrent of rage. They had mounted the security trucks I'd long avoided, up the staircases I'd frequently been shooed off, smashing the windows of offices I'd been forbidden to enter, even as a registered member of the press.

A member of the press. I stopped. *Right. I'm here to report.*

Soaking in everything around me, my thumbs flying, I began pouring words into my phone:

Hundreds of people—and soon thousands—started pressing forward, forward, forward, past the barricade, trampling over the abandoned structure erected for Biden's inauguration on Jan. 20. They broke up and swarmed around the sides, where the Capitol police had been trying to keep out reporters, confronting officers who tried to hold them back. They fantasized about breaking into the building itself.

The small contingent of Capitol police—once cheerfully guarding the entrance and politely pointing Trump supporters to the bathrooms—was soon overwhelmed by waves of flag-bearing protesters. Though they'd earlier thanked the officers for their service, the crowd began to turn on the police. Crowds began gathering around officers, demanding that they let them into the streets, up the lawn, onto the balconies.

Angry rumors ripped through the protesters—several of them waving Blue Lives Matter flags—that the police had tear gas, which officers later deployed inside the Capitol rotunda. Outside, one tattooed man ripped his shirt off and told a small group of people that he had been hit in the head. "I don't care who they were, but they got the badge," he said resentfully.

I pressed the "send" button, hoping that there was enough reception for the text to go through to my editors. Around me, hundreds of people were screaming into their phones, streaming their location or calling their friends ("Everyone's going into the Capitol!"); screaming at the police on-site, people "wearing the blue" who had hit them with gas canisters. I burrowed deeper into my parka, following Lippman as he plowed ahead closer to the Capitol. I wasn't sure whether the Stop the Steal activists had planned for this—they'd stopped responding to my texts—and I had no idea if Trump was going to do anything about this.

My phone flashed—the first notification I'd gotten in nearly a half hour—and I pulled it up immediately. It was the war correspondent, who had somehow made his way to the Capitol balcony and was interviewing Trump supporters.

Supporter shot by plainclothes cop he said
Everyone here saying it
They are yelling at the cops and calling them traitors

I leaned into Lippman's ear. "We're leaving," I told him quietly, as he looked up at the thousands of Trump supporters crawling over the stage that was supposed to host Biden's inauguration in mere weeks, with thousands of tiny, dark figures off in the distance, stark against the white marble of the Capitol. From this vantage point, it looked like a swarm of termites were eating the building from the ground up. I wondered briefly what Asher and the Proud Boys' plan had been, before turning north and heading home.[9]

"Well, I don't feel so alarmist now," Jared texted me later.

11

THE ROAD TRIP

Somewhere in America

Over the next few months, I turned into an AAPI version of Alexis de Tocqueville, trawling through America to poke and prod at parts of the country I'd never visited before. Jon Kelly, my old boss from *Vanity Fair*, had appeared out of nowhere to lure me to his new start-up, an online magazine-newsletter-reporting format called Puck, and as he tried to woo me, told me that I could work from wherever I wanted, as long as I turned my articles in on time. Freed from the shackles of Washington, I used the salary bump for a down payment on a zippy little white Honda hybrid, itching to go somewhere, *anywhere*, for as long as I could. I named her Jules, in honor of my mother's old car (a Toyota Highlander we called Judith), and gunned it out of Washington the day after I quit *Politico*, because I had someplace to be: Mike Lindell's Cyber Symposium, a three-days' drive away in Sioux Falls, South Dakota.

The first time I wrote about Lindell was in March 2020, after a friend of mine at *Politico* offhandedly mentioned that he'd heard Trump was encouraging him to run for governor of Minnesota in 2022. At the time, I'd cackled: *The MyPillow dude?! We* have *to write this up.* I certainly knew Lindell and his life story, having read innumerable profiles of him: Lindell was a former crack addict who had discovered Jesus, sobered up, and created a billion-dollar company built on the perfect pillow and a glut of ads on Fox News. To put it lightly, a lot had changed by the time I'd caught up with Lindell over a year later: he was now an A-tier election denier who believed that China and the Democrats and Hunter Biden had conspired with the voting machines to steal the election from Trump. And thanks to all that talk, he now faced a billion-dollar defamation lawsuit from Dominion Voting Systems—a challenge that he was willing to accept. In Lindell's mind, he was an apostle of QAnon, preaching its gospel to the nonbelievers at the risk of persecution by the elites. (Not that he'd ever use the phrase "QAnon" to describe his beliefs regarding the election: like nearly every MAGA A-lister, he believed that the entity known as QAnon, pretending to be an inside mole in the Trump administration, was a Chinese psyop.) All the eccentricities of being a wealthy pillow maven who had pulled himself out of a crack addiction through sheer force of will were now fully in service to his quest to prove the election was stolen. And when I'd spoken to him in July, Lindell was hell-bent on a new plan that would get Trump back into the West Wing by September. "I'm now doing a Cyber Symposium," he told me, insistent that he'd gotten his hands on a data set that proved that China had secretly sent packets of code to certain voting machines, with the goal of electing Joe Biden.

He was inviting politicians, cyber experts, and the media to Sioux Falls in August, and he offered a plum prize: $5 million for anyone who could prove that his data was *not* legitimate. And as for me, well, Sioux Falls was on the way to Mount Rushmore.

As I entered the South Dakota Military Heritage Alliance center—a giant community center and event space, specifically for veterans, with a twenty-foot-tall American flag draped on the wall—I walked into something I hadn't expected: a room full of cyber experts, QAnon streamers, conservative journalists, politicians, and Lindell, maskless heads bent down in prayer. I peeked at the balcony. Steve Bannon was there, too, praying as well.

"We give You all the glory, God; we ask for You to order all this today. Order it according to Your will," a blond woman named Kit said onstage. "Let Your will be done and Your kingdom come, God, to our lives on earth as in heaven. Everything involved with the technology and getting Your word out, God, and getting the truth out, God, who says that 'we will know the truth and the truth will set us free.' I'm asking for the truth to be revealed today, God."

Puzzled, I wove through the crowds silently, taking a seat next to Khaya Himmelman from the Dispatch, whose masked face had earned her the stink-eye from everyone else around her in the room. (For some reason, MAGA folks only got mad at the *white* journalists whom they saw in masks—never me.) I had steeled myself for three days of Lindell talking in loud circles about data and George Soros and Hunter Biden and the Chinese Communist Party and how much he hated Fox News and Ben Shapiro and the whole lot of them. I'd been prepared for QAnon podcasters rubbing elbows with Bannon, and for my buddy Zach Petrizzo, a wispy young reporter working for *Salon* at the time, to get verbally assaulted by everyone. I had plans already to go to a tiki bar afterward. But this was completely different, even by my standards.

"In the next three days, Lord, I'm asking You to uncover—I'm asking to bring forth *anything*, God—that we need to see more," Kit said louder, more emphatically. "And we just want Your truth, God. You are Truth. Now we worship You, we praise You, God. We thank You, God, for this nation that You founded. This nation, God, with religious freedom. We acknowledge that we are one nation under God. We give You the glory."

Amen, the crowd rumbled, and then, unprompted, broke out with "The Star-Spangled Banner."

I left the Cyber Symposium three days later with a massive headache, peeling off in the general direction of Ernest Hemingway's house in Ketchum, Idaho, passing by thousands of bikers on their way to the Sturgis Motorcycle Rally. News-wise, nothing came of the event, other than the MyPillow guy having a viral meltdown when the data was proven to be fake. I had a sense that the serious data scientists and politicians would have bailed early (which they did by the end of day two, except for a few people whose flights could not be moved). I'd suspected that I'd see big MAGA trucks with giant Blue Lives Matter flags and shirts depicting Trump as Rambo.

But I hadn't expected two things. One, that Lindell and his crowd saw Fox News as an arm of Satan: a New York–based media corporation run by elites, so craven in protecting their billions that they'd censor Lindell to prevent lawsuits, so sneering of their viewership that they'd propped up *Tucker* as a fake populist. ("He knows which way the wind blows," said one speaker, an anti-vax MAGA influencer known as Dr. Shiva.) Two, that as the hours passed and no election fraud was proven, the belief, and prayers, deepened. There were people preaching gospel in the parking lot, blessing the security members in tongues; dozens of protesters on the road nearby proclaiming that Biden was Satan, screaming at me, Himmelman, and Petrizzo. Off in the distance, a man dressed in a tunic climbed out of a white pickup, dragging a massive cross down the side of the highway toward us.

"Is that Jesus?" Petrizzo asked, pointing to the man.

"Are you *blaspheming*?!" a woman yelled at us. "You snake media!"[1]

————

God, for a political journalist from the media bubble, this is one step slightly above the laziness of "hanging out at a diner," I kept thinking to myself as I drove across the country, wandering as the spirit took me. But then again, none of my peers were doing it, either.

There was the time I went into the remnants of a charred town with Caitlyn Jenner, the groundbreaking trans athlete adjacent to the Kardashians, who was mounting a futile run for governor of California at the time. Virtually no one had shown up to her campaign event in what remained of Greenville, a once-thriving town still covered by the haze of the Dixie Fire—the largest wildfire in California's history. But the ones who came to meet her told me that they'd barely seen Governor Gavin Newsom, the Democrat whose push for prison reform threatened to gut their community of vital resources. The California Correctional Center in Susanville employed nearly half of their adult residents, and it was still suing the state to remain open. "Guess what they train there? Firefighters," a local resident, Chris Gallagher, told me next to the charred remains of a bank, as Jenner intently listened to some other locals nearby. "So they're going to close down the prison that trains firefighters badly needed, especially on this fire. And what are we going to do? Where are the firefighters going to come from?" Because, he added, they certainly were not coming from the federal government, or the state, to help douse the fire or rebuild the town. And they were *definitely* voting to recall Newsom.[2]

There was the time I flew to Tulsa, Oklahoma, at the invitation of a source, to attend a rally for Jackson Lahmeyer, a pastor mounting a Republican primary challenge against James Lankford, a Republican Oklahoma senator who'd voted to certify Joe Biden's election. The crowd was full of anti-vax, pro-Trump superfans of Lahmeyer, who'd come to see local favorites and MAGA influencers, and I was introduced to the chair of the state party: John Bennett, a beefy former marine, local pastor, and former state legislator who hated Muslims and loathed Lankford. "I was preaching the sermon after on January 6, and telling my congregation, 'You have a biblical and civic duty to get involved in sending the right people to office and represent us. And if you don't, you can't complain,'" he told me after the rally was over. "So I told them, 'You need to get off your bottoms and get out there and do something.' Well, I was overwhelmed with convictions. Like the Lord was telling me to stop griping at them and lead by example. Well, I did." He won with 56 percent of the vote, and now he was backing Lahmeyer. "I checked all the rules, regulations, all that stuff. There was nothing saying that I *couldn't* endorse anybody in the primary. Which is the reason we're in the mess we're in today, because the counties, the precincts, and the prior state party chairs didn't have the backbone and wouldn't vet the right candidates."

There were infinite people I met in infinite locations—bars, museums, airports, lines for giant telescopes at observatories—who, upon learning I was a political journalist and was duty-bound not to judge them, spilled their pent-up feelings about politics to me: their anger over capricious COVID regulations, their genuine confusion about whether the election was stolen or not, their fury over rising gas prices, their not-unfounded fear that the southern border was overrun by cartel violence, telling me horrifying stories off the record, for fear of reprisal from gangs. (They lived there. I trusted them.) One man anxiously asked me if Russia was going to destroy Texas's power grid, a system isolated from the rest of the country, and pointed out that the CCP had been buying up parcels of farmland nearby; another woman grilled me about whether there were sex perverts at CNN; a random judge placed reams of paper in front of me explaining why masks didn't work when he saw me with one on. None of these problems, they emphasized, had happened under President Trump, and now they were getting worse under Joe Biden. How had *he* let everything fall into such disorder?

And there was a *lot* of Christianity, which I'd learned to expect after I'd met a woman named Amanda Moore, a former DC event planner with a permanently sardonic look on her face. Amanda was regarded in the researcher circles as a valuable asset: for some unknown reason, after her business got shut down during the pandemic, she'd been going undercover at QAnon conferences and revivals, pretending that she was a true believer in the MAGA gospel. She warned me against wearing masks in certain crowds and to take down my vaccine selfies on Instagram. ("They think you can shed vaccine and cause infertility to everyone around you.") And free of the strict ethics I followed as a journalist, she got to experience *far* more of the movement than I could have. For one, she could surreptitiously record conversations with MAGA supporters without disclosing it; for another, she could simply pretend that she was an ideological ally. And there was one more advantage she had over me: "I grew up in a fundamentalist church," she said when we met at an outdoor bar, stabbing her straw (awkwardly, her right arm was in a hard cast) into a frozen Aperol Spritz. "So I can speak Jesus pretty damn well."

"Wait, is the Christian part important?" I took a sip of mine and winced as the brain freeze hit me. "Because I thought I was pretty good at speaking MAGA. Like, if someone starts ranting about the Fifteenth Amendment, I'm just here smiling and nodding, because I've heard it all before." I waved my hands in a fluttery circle.

"Oh my god, you do not under*stand*, Tina," Amanda gasped. "They *literally* think that *Satan* stole the election from Trump. Hold on a sec. I have to show you something." She rustled around in her bag and pulled out her phone. "So I was hanging out with the CloutHub[3] guys at the media center—which, can you believe, was about two miles away from the church. Yeah. The pastors didn't allow even *right-wing media* in," she added as I gawped. "This crowd *haaaaaates* Fox News because it's corporate. Don't get me started on how they think *Breitbart* is cucks. Anyways, they saw my cast and they started, like, praying over it. In *tongues*." I took the phone from her and played the video: four white, middle-aged women stood over Amanda, passionately babbling over her cast, channeling the spirit of the Lord into her broken wrist.

It's the little things that help you blend in when reporting on the fringes of the MAGA movement, I'd learned over time. My prerequisite set of red dresses and USA gear made me look unassuming in a Trump rally, as did going ash blond after binge-watching a lot of Korean pop music videos during the pandemic. Rereading *The Shadow University* and glancing through the latest copies of the *Claremont Review of Books* and checking out the latest tweets from a specific group of influencers kept me apace with the movement. But I was raised Buddhist—a tiny 0.5 percent sliver of the American population—and it was the first time I ran headlong into a reportorial wall.

My family, like a healthy majority of Vietnamese people, had practiced Pure Land Buddhism for hundreds of years (we were *not* aging white hippies desperately grasping for meaning, thank you very much) and regarded Christianity as an academic curiosity of Western civilization, which only intersected with their lives whenever Mormons had tried to convert them back in Utah. Over the years, my curiosity over Christianity grew: I went with my friends to Mass, joined my Catholic roommates at their reading groups to discuss G. K. Chesterton and frequently fell into Wikipedia rabbit holes reading articles about the history of the Vatican, or binge-watching *The Chosen*, at 3 a.m. I compiled note cards on Southern Baptists and charismatics and Pentecostals and mainline Protestants and the seemingly infinite different subcategories of Catholicism for class. But it was the type of knowledge that could get me through, say, a round of *Jeopardy!*—not something that had been the cornerstone of my family or community. On the one hand, psychologically unburdened from America's eternal Judeo-Christian angst over the role of religion in public life, I actually *enjoyed* talking to people about their Christian faith. Everyone, in turn, found my descriptions of being a "lapsed Buddhist" rather intriguing—there are so few Buddhists in America that harmful stereotypes aren't particularly commonplace—and had always been gentle in their attempts to convert me.

On the other hand, my MAGA fluency now had a massive weak spot. The Claremont view of the world, after all, treated Western philosophy and Judeo-Christian values as so fundamental to their world view that in the process of inducting me into conservative activism, they'd skipped over the part where they tested my actual working knowledge of the Bible, much less any Abrahamic religion. It perhaps had weakened my attachment to conservatism: I had approached their ideas academically, treating its views on morality and good governance as a series of interesting pros and cons like a dweeby rationalist would, instead of attaching it to a two-thousand-year-old religion that had formed the core of my moral, spiritual, and cultural identity.

"So . . . does saying that I worked for Tucker Carlson help here?" I asked futilely.

"They might not even like *that*," said Amanda.

————

Over the summer, I had read about Ammon Bundy and the People's Rights militias protesting mask and vaccine mandates outside of hospitals in eastern Washington State and had immediately booked an Airbnb in Spokane. But by the time I made it up there in November, the violent militias and neo-Nazis were in hibernation. Daniel Walters, an investigative reporter at the *Inlander* whom I'd met through another researcher, told me bemusedly that the ones who were known more prominently nationwide—Patriot Front, Oath Keepers, Patriot Prayer, and so forth—were more active from the spring through the summer, marching *outside* town halls and school boards and hospitals handing out the vaccine and harassing nurses trying to get to work. Obviously, it was too cold to protest in November. Spokane was blissfully cheap compared to California, however, so I decided to stick it out for a few weeks to see what I could catch.

Which was how I found myself in a rec hall in Colville, a speck of a town of three thousand people built around a railroad depot about three hours away from Spokane, watching a January 6th attendee preach the gospel of the Patriot Church to a rapturous crowd.

"I want to draw a few potential possible parallels tonight between the story of Elijah and what is happening with America," said Josh Feuerstein, a hulking mountain of a man dressed in a friendly gray fisherman's sweater and a friendlier beard, pacing up and down the aisle, to a captive audience of roughly fifty locals, their faces rapt. "Because as we see Israel in Scripture, that Israel would backslide away from God, when they would tear down the altars and begin to worship false gods. You will see that God would allow phantoms to come into the land, and for evil dictators to take over."

I sat in the back, trying to make myself unnoticed, still unused to going maskless. Walters had passed along a social media posting advertising this Friday night sermon of the Patriot Church, and I'd driven out to Colville to see for myself. The moment I hopped out of my car at the Walmart Supercenter to pick up a quick dinner, I knew this was the hardest of hard-core Trump country, the likes of which I'd never seen: TRUMP WON, GET OVER IT bumper stickers; TRUMP 2024 decals, "Let's Go Brandon" shirts as I walked down the aisles for peanut butter. *It's super rural and open carry is legal here*, I reminded myself when I checked in at the Comfort Inn, walking past several otherwise polite hunters in camo carrying high-caliber rifles in the lobby. I tried not to stare at one man in a T-shirt depicting the Punisher skull overlaid with the Blue Lives Matter flag. My normal reportorial superpower in MAGA environs—being an invisible, nonthreatening Asian woman—was far less effective here. Being blond now was a bigger mistake. *Man*, I kept thinking, *I hope they think I have a Caucasian husband who's running late.*

"Now, there is a particular time in Israel's history that they backslide away from God," Feuerstein continued, as two people, both fans of his, recorded him on their phones. "And now God puts two evil dictators in the proverbial White House. I want you to see who they were. One was King Ahab, and the other was Jezebel. Ahab was a senile, weak old man, and Jezebel was a seductress who slept her way to the top. I don't know if that sounds familiar or not," he added, to chuckles.

"But they then get into power. And the first thing that they do is . . ." He paused for dramatic effect. "They go after the church. Because they understood that the church was going to be the enemy of whatever it was that they wanted to enact in Israel. I can draw a few more parallels tonight, because Ahab and Jezebel loved to steal things that they would not own. In fact, the Bible—read this, okay, I'm not making this up—the Bible says that they looked at Naboth's vineyard, and they *wanted* Naboth's vineyard, but they did not have legal access to it. And so what do they do? They literally got elders of the city to vote, signing fake ballots, that said that it was theirs. And they killed him and stole it from him. I don't know if that sounds familiar at all." I made a note to myself to look up the story of Naboth, and looked around the room. Over in the corner, Pastor Ken Peters, a bald man with a tight black T-shirt whose organization held sermons outside of Planned Parenthoods, nodded. This speck on the map, foggy and rainy and surrounded by deep woods, this town that already had twenty-three churches—this was where they would build their newest Patriot Church.

Feuerstein continued for nearly two hours with a spellbinding sermon, broken with the occasional hymn, pulling the new faithful into this tiny senior center on a Friday night, weaving a tale about the downfall of the American family to demonic forces unraveling their small community—social media, smartphones and televisions, Black Lives Matter and antifa. He drew a line from the division of church and state, accusing teachers of filling schools with "critical race theory and paganism." He brought up the nostalgia of the 1950s ("The Andy Griffith generation, wasn't it a lot better back then?"). He had a *killer* Donald Trump impression, and the congregation ate it up. He had flown to Washington on January 6, picked up on Mike Lindell's plane, to protest that "sissy" Mike Pence. He even had the FBI investigation into him to prove it. I quickly got the sense that in a certain adjacent conservative world that I wasn't fully aware of, Feuerstein was a *big deal*.

"Now, let me preface by saying, if you have a great church and your pastor has testosterone and is bold—because we don't need any more pastors that are tiptoeing around the issues, right?" said Feuerstein. "Black Lives Matter isn't going to save us. Antifa isn't going to save us. There's only one entity that's gonna save this land. That's the Holy Spirit–filled church of Jesus Christ, amen. And we almost have the power to do that. But in the next month or two or three, we are going to plant a Patriot Church right here in Colville. So once again, we won't want to pull anybody from good churches. But if your pastor is lame, get out. I'm serious. You don't want to stick around with a pastor that doesn't have a spine."

When the sermon ended, I walked up to Feuerstein, who smiled at me warmly. "You know, I'm always fascinated by the people I find all over the country," he said. "I'd never expect to find a Thai restaurant up in Colville but it was *delicious*."

"Um, actually—" I stuttered, too nervous to be offended, feeling like I'd intruded on something private, even though the event had been open to the public. "Please don't hate me, I'm very nervous you might, but I'm a reporter who heard about this event and wanted to come and see what was up . . . ?"

Everyone's heads turned toward me in shock and delight at this odd new stranger who had come to their door. They could not believe that I'd driven there all the way from Washington, DC, or that I'd worked for *Vanity Fair*. ("And you came all the way to *Colville*?") I joked that it would have been slightly more awkward if I were a *New York Times* reporter. No one called me *lib media*, to my pleasant surprise, and by the end of the night, I felt surprisingly warm and welcomed.

Maybe I've been too used to internet trolls, I thought. *I think these are just normal, good people.*

"Oh, we're fine with reporters as long as you write the truth," one woman said, with a deep sincerity. "And *thank you* for not wearing a mask here."

Peters and I spoke over the phone: in addition to his duties as the leader of the Church at Planned Parenthood, which stages prayer protests outside abortion clinics, he had opened several Patriot Churches across the country—one in Spokane, one in Moses Lake, one in Knoxville, Tennessee. I asked him whether he'd found that certain Patriots came from specific denominations of Christianity. "In every denomination of Christianity in America right now, there is an absolute split," he told me. "Now, they might still be worshipping together. But if you get into deep conversation, you'll find that in every denomination, there's a divide to those that are more woke, and to those that are more what I would say Trumpian, or Constitutional Patriot." Part of it had been over mandates, which had opened and closed churches with frightening irregularity; part of it had been over the sense that Biden had stolen the election and was leading America into ruin. "I think the future for our Patriot Church movement is really bright because I don't see the battle—the culture war battle—I don't see it lessening, I think it can only intensify," he said. "And so that bodes well for what we're doing. Because more and more people are going to be looking for churches and Christian communities like ours, where we boldly talk about it from the pulpit."

Feuerstein met me a few days later at the hotel he was staying at, a casino outside Spokane. He was getting ready to fly back to Dallas with his family, reading the Bible on his iPad while he waited for me to arrive, and was just as jocular and friendly as I remembered him—so friendly that his insistence that America was, at its core, a Christian nation seemed like the most obvious thing in the world, and that the left was getting its interpretation of the separation between church and state severely wrong. "I'm sure you're well aware of this: this whole idea of separation of church and state is a total misnomer in the society that we live in, because people want to say, 'Oh, the separation of church and state means that the two should never collide, ever, ever, ever,' " he told me. "When in fact, as we know, number one, it's not in the Constitution. It's not in any of the actual founding documents of our country. But when we see separation of church and state, it specifies that government is supposed to stay out of the church's business. That's what it actually specifies.[4]

"So if you actually read the writing and all of its context, and not just use this one little cherry-picked phrase, then now you understand it's actually meant to protect the freedom of religion, etc. So now I feel like people are realizing, 'Wait, if my faith doesn't affect my politics, then I'm doing something wrong, then we're never going to see change.' I don't believe that you can legislate righteousness. But I do believe that you can legislate protections in there that are righteous."

We slipped into our corresponding languages: he of the pulpit and I of the CMC research assistant from 2009, recalling Washington's letter to the Rhode Island synagogue, the Virginia Statute of Religious Freedom, Ben Franklin's secular deism and his love of listening to the evangelist George Whitefield, the fact that National Days of Prayer had been commonly declared by Congress, that entire legislative sessions would open with *hours* of prayer. Feuerstein had gone deep in his study of Scripture and the Founding and traced a sterling line between the elimination of Bible studies and religion from public schools, to the prevailing liberal belief that teaching anything about the Christian faith of the Founders was nothing short of white nationalism, all the way to the intense fear that government was encroaching even closer upon people's individual liberties.

"It's interesting to me that people don't realize this whole experiment that is America was founded on religious freedom," he said at one point. "It was founded by men that believed that our rights came from a creator. The Constitution was only a governing document meant to protect citizens' rights [given] from God. The Constitution doesn't give you rights. They said *God* gives you rights. And the Constitution protects those rights. It's literally our passport to freedom, our guarantee—as long as we enforce it. Our guarantee that we'll never be ruled again. And what are we doing? We're just freaking giving it away, one little piece at a time."

Feuerstein added that one day, he hoped to run for office—Congress, perhaps, or the presidency, even though he knew he was unlikely to win. "Essentially the function that I would want to serve, is just keep everyone on the debate stage honest," he said, adding that that was Trump's appeal the first time around: "I think I'd probably be like the super Christian version of Trump. As you witnessed the other night, I have no problem saying controversial stuff."

———

The snow fell gently over the next few days as I continued to write and research, punctuating my days with runs through the Riverfront Park and near Gonzaga University, and my nights hanging out with bartenders I'd met downtown. *There's a lot I still don't know,* I thought, jogging through the flurries as the Spokane River roared underneath the bridges. I hadn't had time to learn more about the Redoubt, the thing I'd come to Spokane to research. I hadn't spoken to more militias or watched them in action, soaking in the extremist parts of the antigovernment culture animating the most energetic parts of the right. I had literally stumbled across the heart of Christian nationalism, which I hadn't expected at all, and felt as if there was yet another universe I needed to learn more about. Spokane had unveiled a multitude of dimensions to the rise of populism, of which the MAGA movement now seemed a small part, and there was not enough time to learn more: I was supposed to fly back down to San Diego to see my family for Thanksgiving, pack up Jules, and begin a very long journey home.

Though I felt much smaller in a world that felt more precarious, I felt better. For too long, the personal and the professional had waged war inside me—editors and fellow reporters who'd known about my secret background; sources who'd learned that I was a former activist and immediately thought I was a traitor to the movement. On the road, I was simply known as a reporter, and I was talking to the people who'd existed outside the media arena I'd lived in for too long. *I guess I knew so little*, I thought, *and I'll never know enough.*

If I hadn't known about all this, however, what was the likelihood that my political influencer sources had? I pondered the question over more runs, over endless pourovers at the local coffeehouse, over several bowls of fried rice at the local gay bar. I'd been certain of my own knowledge about how the movement worked, but I'd rarely, if ever, seen how it had impacted everyone outside of my world. Either the activist movement had not told me everything they'd known, or they themselves didn't understand the scope of the forces they were dealing with.

But I imagined it would not take long for them all to coalesce.

12

FEELS BAD, MAN

March 18, 2021

When I visited my dentist for the first time since the pandemic began, he looked at my neglected teeth and immediately told me that I needed a gum graft. Thankfully, he offered an alternative to harvesting tissue from the roof of my mouth: they would just need to poke a hole in my gingiva, put some collagen strips inside, and push it over the exposed teeth roots (no biggie). Though way less barbaric, the operation still required several vials of lidocaine injected into my canines, and I was laid out on my couch afterward, swimming in an opiate haze with an ice pack on my numb, swollen face, when a friend texted me a massive article from the *New York Times* about Clearview AI.

Bleh, I thought, rolling over to look at my phone. It was a controversial, secretive facial recognition technology funded by Peter Thiel, the Claremont-affiliated PayPal billionaire-turned-MAGA-bankroller, which could match footage of rioters at the Capitol with any photos they'd ever taken of themselves online. I read that several Trumpworld associates were involved, the technology was being used to track down rally attendees, and—

Well, bleh.

Chuck Johnson's name was *everywhere* in this article.

Johnson had dropped from the headlines circa 2017, when he'd told another *Politico* reporter that he was going underground and deleting all his social media. For the duration of the Trump administration, I'd only heard bits and rumors about what he was up to, either from sources who'd randomly started complaining about his behavior, or old mutual friends who'd heard about a mysterious facial recognition technology he was involved with. Here he was now, breaking god knows how many nondisclosure agreements with a secretive, vengeful tech billionaire, to brag to the *New York Times* that *he* had come up with one of the most horrifying, privacy-smashing technologies of the modern era. It was *he* who had deserved the money, *he* who was responsible for the idea, *he* who was now horrified that Thiel had given the technology to the government. And it was he who had suddenly become screwed over by Thiel: according to the article, shortly after Chuck had started talking to the *Times* reporter, Clearview AI immediately diluted the value of his shares in the company, effectively flushing him out.

Well, I can't feel anything about this if I can't even feel my face, I thought, and rolled back onto the couch to binge-watch more YouTube cooking shows. It was a good day to be sedated.

———

My new Honda, Jules, was the first car I'd ever owned that was made after 1994, and among all of her innovative new features, such as air-conditioning and rearview cameras, I learned somewhere in Los Angeles that she could automatically read new text messages out loud in a pleasant robot voice, announced with a *ping*, even when I was driving.

PING. "David sent you a link from The Guardian dot Com and writes: *Did you see that Charles Johnson is now a Biden supporter? Wild!*"

I nearly swerved off the road.

It took all the discipline I had not to pick up my phone and read the article, but I couldn't help glancing at it at every single red light along Santa Monica Boulevard. Apparently he had started talking to journalists again, becoming a major source in a book that had just been published about Thiel, and was now described as a "Biden supporter." The link led to his new blog. A friend of mine read it for me. *He's supporting Biden because Biden's researching genetic engineering*, she reassured me.

The second post I received appeared to announce his break with the Claremont Institute, ostensibly for their support of the January 6th insurrection. Once again, I'd gotten the message while driving on the highway, and I finally had the chance to read it while at a coffee shop in Spokane. "I am very proud that Clearview, the facial recognition firm I cofounded, caught thousands of rioters during both the events of January 6th and the George Floyd riots in Summer 2020," he'd written, seemingly ignoring how he'd told the *Times* he was horrified that the government had used the tech to track said rioters.

But several grafs later, I nearly spat out my coffee:

"Larry Arnn was a founder of Claremont. Arnn's mentor was engaged in a similar odd political project—the Judeaization of Sir Winston

Churchill. Martin Gilbert, himself the son of a jeweler (and Churchill's official biographer), was engaged in a very Israeli project indeed. Arnn helped (Republican Senator Tom) Cotton find a wife. She's a neocon naturally. Or, perhaps, they'll do the coup with Governor Ron DeSantis, slated to give the Claremont Institute's statesmanship award later this month, whose sycophancy for the late Sheldon Adelson knows few limits. DeSantis is clearly compromised by Israeli intelligence."

For over five thousand confusing words, Chuck railed against the "Jewry" and "Eastern European Jewish" interests that had captured not just the Claremont Institute (?!) but also Facebook, Harvard, the Trump administration, and WASP-built cultural institutions. (To put it lightly, he was not a fan of Jared Kushner.) There were theories I'd never even heard of before, allegations novel even by the most creative white nationalist standards. There was talk about "Singaporization" and the "Chinese and Jewish pharmaceutical interests" that enabled Ronald Reagan to win the presidency. By the time he listed all the Jewish people associated with Facebook—founder Mark Zuckerberg was "the mob done good and gone to Harvard," CEO Sheryl Sandberg, he alleged, was "a child of Mossad and may be, in fact, an agent herself"—the list of conspiracies broke my brain. (*What is this, the Protocols of the Elders of Facebook*?!) There were other blog posts forswearing his connections with Alan Dershowitz, the Trump administration, his connections with the far right, and he accused nearly all of them of being puppets of the Jews. There were even posts attacking Thiel's friends as secret Jewish agents, though he'd still remained a supplicant to Thiel, who he claimed was still invested in one of his companies. The powerful right-wing operative I thought I'd known was now reduced to ranting and name-dropping in the dark. *Is he even powerful anymore?* I wondered.

But there was one telling glimpse of something I deeply recognized as the old bitter Charlie peeping through. He kept mentioning Harvard, over and over again, complaining about a "network of Eastern European Jewry" who had taken over the Ivy League to replace the "WASP elite," of which he proudly identified himself as a member. "[A]s we know the Clinton connections to Mega aka Israeli spy Jeffrey Epstein we might ask if the looting of Russia by Harvard connected Jews was itself a Mossad operation," he wrote. "We might even ask if the capture of Harvard's admissions department and the faux claims of meritocracy was itself a Mossad play."

Poor boy, I thought, despite myself.

13

THE PATRIOT ACADEMY

Every so often I find myself awake at 3 a.m. to play a game, imagining ways I could undermine democracy if I *really* felt like it. When I first met my therapist Minerva in 2012, she delicately called this habit *catastrophizing*: automatically coming up with the worst possible outcome, no matter how dubiously improbable and far-fetched, to some random story that comes across my desk, or some crazy *what-if* scenario I've imagined that day. But after years of marinating in right-wingerness, it's less of a neurotic complex and more like playing out games of chess on the ceiling. And the longer I worked in my beat, the more often I found I was right on the money. (Let's just say it feels good when you ask your therapist, two days after January 6th, if she thinks you're catastrophizing *now.*)

But even I was baffled when I learned what Ron DeSantis was involved with.

I was attending a conference in Florida, sipping wine on a balmy balcony near the ocean, talking to a Florida insider who'd followed DeSantis's career. Ever since I'd joined Puck and reunited with my beloved old boss Jon Kelly, I had gone back to circling the power brokers of the universe, and DeSantis was now one. For months, he'd posed a looming threat to Trump, gathering wealthy donor allies, building an online coalition of influential supporters, posing himself as a calm, sensible alternative to Trump. He refused to directly challenge the former president, either on or off the record, and none of his surrogates would ever crack, sharing his remarkable sense of discipline, always telling me that *the governor is focused on winning reelection in Florida.* He won, by a *lot*—a 19.6-point blowout over his Democratic rival—in a cycle where Trump's endorsed election-denying candidates went belly-up in Congress, costing the Republicans a handful of governors' mansions and control of the Senate, and giving them the barest of votes in the House. DeSantis's ascendancy was *supposed* to mark the end of Trumpism and MAGAism, of conspiratorial bullshit and norms-destroying politics. It was supposed to be the beginning of the restoration of sanity.

The insider shook his head. "Yeah, no. He's airing radio commercials in Idaho for the Convention of States."

The Convention?! It took every ounce of adulthood to prevent myself from spitting out my wine. "I'm sorry, *what*!?" I gasped instead.

Right-wing plots are either dramatic and drastic, but meant to cause a scene (see: January 6th), or extremely subtle and planned out years in advance (see: the Federalist Society's long-running plan to stack the Supreme Court with conservative justices[1]). The Convention of States is one of the few examples I've seen of something that's both, because this group wants to *rewrite the United States Constitution.*

Various versions of the legal theory behind the Convention of States' plot to rewrite the Constitution have been proposed by a handful of obscure conservative academics and pundits over the years. But generally, the premise—a perfectly constitutional one, though without any precedent whatsoever—is the same across the board. According to Article V of the Constitution, there are two ways to propose an amendment:

1. Two-thirds of each chamber of Congress votes to put forth a specific amendment to the states, which gets sent to the state legislatures for ratification, *or*

2. three-fourths of America's state legislatures vote on convening an amendatory convention, either nationally or within their own states, wherein they get together and vote on *any* amendment they'd like to propose—without any say from Congress whatsoever, or any input from their actual constituents. (*Technically,* the state legislatures are supposed to represent the people, but the Democrats, often packed into America's cities and gerrymandered into minority status, have been godawful at holding on to their seats.)

Currently, every amendment ever passed has come down via Congress, and no one has ever used state legislatures to independently push an amendment into the Constitution. But this process was concocted by Founding Father George Mason, who, during the Constitutional Convention of 1787, proposed a backup option to create amendments "if the Government should become oppressive, as he verily believed would be the case." Centuries later, as the conservative movement began turning on the idea of Big Government, its founder, Tea Party activist Mark Meckler, had a brainwave: if one were to seed enough representatives across the country who'd independently propose their own Constitutional Conventions, one could, with a bit of coordination, create a scenario where three-fourths of the states could spontaneously rewrite the Constitution without Congress having a say. All they'd need to do is propose one giant convention to discuss one superbroad topic: limiting the power of the federal government to do, well, whatever the federal government does these days.

Here's where the Convention of States, or the Convention, gets *extremely* intricate. In order to get enough states to call a convention, the Convention is trying to get the support of 40 states' legislatures (38 plus wiggle room), requiring Republican control of both state houses' chambers. (At the moment, the GOP has 21 states.) These 40 states have a total of 4,000 districts with 4,000 representatives, so in the aggregate, the Convention needs 3,000 representatives to support calling a convention. Over the past eight years, the Convention has started recruiting captains, one per district, to get one hundred volunteers to keep pushing on their representatives to support calling an Amendatory Convention.

Such a small number to change the lives of 270 million people overnight.

I first learned about the Convention of States in April 2020, when I was speaking to a researcher in Michigan who was telling me about various anti-lockdown groups he'd been tracking during the beginning of the pandemic. There was one group in particular, Citizens for Self-Governance, whose president had been actively coordinating their volunteers to drive around Lansing, endlessly honking their horns in protest. He'd seen their flyers at gun shows to recruit activists, and watched their president, Mark Meckler, appear on various talk radio shows and online streaming programs. But their group was based around a larger project called the Convention of States, and the researcher emailed me one of their flyers.

As I scanned through the brochures (he kept sending more and more), I saw dozens of names and organizations pop up that I'd recognized over the years. Citizens for Self-Governance had successfully sued the Internal Revenue Service for targeting conservative political groups, a lawsuit that had huge ramifications in right-wing world. Meckler was a founder of the Tea Party Patriots, one of the largest groups during the Tea Party mania; several members of his board were affiliated with conservative legal groups and think tanks that had devoted significant parts of their brainpower to testing the conservative limits of law. It's a mystery who has given them their massive, multimillion-dollar budget, but they certainly have friends in high places. I flipped to the last page, where I saw that dozens of the most powerful conservatives in the country had signed on in approval: Ben Shapiro. Greg Abbott. Marco Rubio. Sean Hannity. Sarah Palin. Ron DeSantis.

"This is genius," I texted Dan back, unnerved yet impressed by their audacity.

When I asked another researcher in eastern Washington State if he'd heard about the Convention, he immediately sent me everything he had. They were, apparently, recruiting teenagers to run mock simulations in a multiday seminar called the Patriots Academy. "If you're between the ages of 16–25 or know someone who is, this is for you!" the email read, with key selling points bolded. "Not only will you **participate in the nation's most realistic mock legislative session** (actual legislators train with them!) and **network with conservative movers and shakers,** your week will include speakers such as Rick Green, Nathan Macias, and more! Your tuition includes your lodging, meals, training, materials, and more." The Patriot Academy was holding mock legislative sessions in state capitols all over the country: Colorado, Arizona, Florida, Delaware, Idaho, Indiana, Texas. And I knew *exactly* the type of young person the Patriot Academy wanted to capture and mold: an ambitious recent college grad, immediately sent to work for a state representative somewhere, with the knowledge of how to work the legislative system in advance—navigating the system of writing bills and pushing it through a markup committee, learning the soft skills of negotiating with elected officials—with a ticking time bomb in their heads.

The Convention already has a detailed plan for the future, should they get the convention they desire. In fact, they've practiced it already. In November 2016, gathered symbolically in Colonial Williamsburg, the Convention ran a convention simulation with delegates from all fifty states, and successfully passed several amendments in the span of three days: abolishing the Sixteenth Amendment entirely (no more income taxes), reverting the Commerce Clause to its original meaning (no more federal enforcement of the Civil Rights Act), and allowing states, voting on a three-fifths majority, to reject federal laws altogether (no more Occupational Safety and Health Administration, Obamacare, Food and Drug Administration, and, basically, anything that Congress has ever passed).

I'd read an op-ed arguing for the revocation of birthright citizenship a few days earlier, published by my college professors in the *Claremont Review of Books.* The possibility that my beloved professors didn't think *I* deserved citizenship, or willingly supported people who thought the same, made me nauseous. As I flipped through the Convention's brochures, a thought then crossed my mind: could the Convention of States, if successful, rewrite the Citizenship Clause and prevent immigrants' children born in the US from automatically becoming Americans? It was one of those moments that sent my mind spiraling, again, into a million different branches of causality. Could they repeal the Nineteenth Amendment, which granted women the right to vote? Could they rewrite the Fifteenth Amendment, revoking Black suffrage? Could they spontaneously decide to abolish the Electoral College altogether, restructure the three branches of government, and install someone as president-for-life? The possibilities, says Meckler, are endless. "So long as a proposed amendment relates to limiting the power of the federal government," he wrote in one brochure, "the Convention of States itself would determine which ideas deserve serious consideration, and it will take a majority of votes from the states to formally propose any amendments."

Currently, nineteen state legislatures have already called for a convention. Later that night, as I stared at the ceiling in my hotel room, I realized: they only need fifteen more.

———

When I spoke to David Jolly, a former Florida Republican congressman who'd served with DeSantis, he noted that the CoS was one of those groups that you just had to work with, if you were a Republican. "I had advisors in my Senate race against DeSantis actually suggest that that would be the ultimate signal to conservatives," he told me. "It is this entire war on the federal government idea, wrapped in Constitutional speak and federalism."

Everyone kept telling me the conventional knowledge that DeSantis—Yale, Harvard Law, the US Navy, etc.—was a man who could speak MAGA and connect with the Trumpian base, while also having the discipline and temperament to act wisely and sagely and bring the

Republican Party back to normalcy. It was said that on his very first day in office, he sat down with a copy of Florida's laws and constitution and read through the entire thing. He leveraged every lever of power to punish corporations that stood in his way, stripping Disney World's tax-exempt status after they opposed a bill preventing teachers from introducing topics on same-sex marriage into elementary school curricula. And there was one key differentiator between him and Trump: he never tweeted, never spiraled in public, never even whispered a word against Trump, leaving the job of engaging with MAGA internet to an aide named Christina Pushaw. Of course, he coasted to reelection off the strength of how he'd handled the pandemic, maintaining a state of societal normalcy while the rest of the world melted down. Millions of people emigrated from blue states to the Free Republic of Florida, as my sources jokingly called it.

But the moment he returned to office, DeSantis went wild. He successfully bullied the College Board into changing its AP African American history curriculum to eliminate units about queer theory and intersectionality, deriding them as "woke." He went out of his way to seize an *entire state college*—the New College of Florida, in Sarasota—with the explicit goal of turning it into the next Hillsdale College, a midwestern school that has yielded a slew of Straussian academics and was closely affiliated with the Claremont Institute. He even appointed Christopher Rufo, a senior fellow at the Claremont Institute, to be on its board. "Unfortunately, like so many colleges and universities in America, this institution has been completely captured by a political ideology that puts trendy, truth-relative concepts above learning," DeSantis's office said in a statement announcing the change.

What would happen if this brilliant man got his hands on the US Constitution?

Now, as I write this book in the first half of 2023, I'm watching the next generation of MAGA unfold, creating their own parallel right-wing activist infrastructure to the nice(ish) libertarian one I'd grown up in. I spent the first week of the year following the inner workings of a new MAGA-aligned lobbying group, the Conservative Partnership Institute, as they backed the MAGA insurgency that held Kevin McCarthy's House speakership hostage in exchange for a set of hazy promises—never written down—about cutting spending on the Ukraine War, bringing the budget back down to 2020 levels, and, if they could, de-wokeifying the government. Like their fellow activist alumni, this group of new legislators had dedicated weeks to studying arcane congressional legislative procedure, allowing them to wrestle more and more power out of McCarthy's hands. I watched America First policy be codified and slipped into bills, and new MAGA interest groups formed under the radar. The new president of the famed Heritage Foundation, Kevin Roberts, swung the movement far away from the staid constitutionalism of Mike Pence into the hinterlands of nationalist-conservatism and America First politics. And I watched DeSantis, gingerly stepping into the presidential race, build a litany of anti-woke talking points against Disney, Target, and the holiday Juneteenth—and marveled as even *that* fell flat against the juggernaut of Trump in the primaries. (How did he end up in such a slump?!)

But nothing has ever pinged off my radar more than the Convention of States Project, which has several other projects going on outside of training young legislators.

For citizens who couldn't attend these mock sessions—or were simply interested in other ways to support the cause—the Patriot

Academy, a nonprofit run off donations, had extracurricular courses. There was Constitutional Leadership, the classes training young leaders to interpret the Constitution. There was the "Biblical Citizenship" multiweek seminar, available both in person and online, that provided coursework for churches interested in teaching Christian nationalist teachings: "You and your church can be the catalyst for restoring Biblical values in your neighborhood, State, and Nation." There was an option for the time-pressed sovereign citizen: the Constitution Coach course, a video series that one could literally host at home, Tupperware party–style: "As a Coach, literally all you have to do is get people into a room and press 'play'! The videos do all the teaching for you. You are free to learn along with the rest of the class!"

And then there was "Constitutional Defense."

A five-day course at the Patriot Academy Campus in Fredericksburg, Texas, Constitutional Defense was also run by Rick Green and taught enrollees a "unique blend of Firearms Defense combined with Constitutional education so that you get both the physical and intellectual training." Tuition was one hundred dollars for five days—heavily subsidized by donations through a 501(c)3 nonprofit—and teachers who wanted to bring Constitutional Defense to their hometowns could attend for free.

"We guarantee that you will be amazed at how much you will learn about the Constitution and liberty, while also improving your defensive handgun skills more than you can imagine," the site promised. "Even if you know nothing about the Constitution and you have no experience with a handgun, your Constitutional knowledge and your passion for American Exceptionalism, as well as your handgun skills, marksmanship and safety awareness will all dramatically improve."

That night, on that balcony under the moon by the beach, as the insider turned to talk to the bartender, the pinball machine of my mind shot off again.

I pictured myself on the road again, thinking about driving through the windswept Texas Hill Country, standing at a range next to the determined patriots learning valuable self-defense skills. I thought about the number of these programs multiplying across the country over months, years even; I thought about Ron DeSantis, Ben Shapiro, Mike Huckabee, Sean Hannity, dozens of other prominent Republicans endorsing these programs, as their comfortable oblivious billionaire patrons looked the other way, and what would happen if Trump ever caught wind of them. I thought about my path, the adorably naïve academic libertarian programs I'd enrolled in as a child, safe on the campus of an all-women's college in 2009, and how it could have possibly ended up at a gun range, forty miles outside of Austin, with the goal of rewriting the Constitution closer at hand.

I opened my eyes, finding myself back at the beach, looking at the vast, black ocean spread in front of me, wondering how long it would be until the storm rolled in again.

This, I realized later, was the first time I did *not* know what would happen next.

EPILOGUE:
TUCKER AND ME

The Heritage Foundation's Leadership Summit
Gaylord National Resort & Convention Center, Maryland
April 21, 2023

I yawned in the middle of the giant glass atrium, right outside the ballroom where CPAC was usually held,[1] drained after watching four Heritage Foundation–moderated panels about wokeism. Unlike Turning Point's youthful explosiveness, or CPAC's MAGA marketing convention atmosphere, Heritage's annual Leadership Summit was a gathering of the country's most established (and inevitably older) conservative activists, having serious fireside chats and conversations. I'd watched Ron DeSantis, on the cusp of running for president, sit for a fireside chat with the new Heritage president Kevin Roberts; a member of the Taliban Nineteen, a derisive nickname for the GOP congressmen who had held up Kevin McCarthy's speakership,[2] talked about how he was bringing Washington's horse-trading politics to heel. During the Q&A, an old man in the audience had wrested control of the microphone to ramble about 9/11 conspiracy theories before Mol-

221

lie Hemingway, now moderating a panel, asked him to politely calm down. The daytime programming was over, but I had one more decision: Did I want to see Tucker Carlson give a speech that night at the Heritage black-tie gala?

I hadn't known that he would be speaking until I saw the program, as well as a giant table with a TUCKER banner, staffed by some twenty-something-year-olds selling copies of his latest book. And I was surprised that he'd even set foot in Washington at *all:* he had notoriously fled DC in the summer of 2020, and now split his time between his summer house in Maine and his winter house in Florida, vowing never to live in an urban area again. He'd even convinced Fox News to build him a permanent studio in both locations. On the one hand, it would be fascinating to see him in person—we had not met up since 2016, shortly before he became a Fox prime-time host. On the other hand, the remarks were about five hours from now, and as a credentialed member of the press, I would only be allowed in the ballroom for thirty minutes *just* to watch his remarks, before being politely escorted out. The likelihood of saying hi to Tucker was slim. My apartment was forty-five minutes away by car. And this weekend was my *birthday*.

Crabbiness won out, as well as the need for a nap. *Screw it, I'm going home*, I thought, walking past several equally tired conference attendees wolfing down sandwiches and sushi, unaware that this was the weekend Tucker and Fox News would go into free fall.

No one knew whether he'd said something at the Heritage dinner that set off the Murdoch family. No one knew if it was part of Fox's settlement with Dominion Voting Systems—days before, a judge had awarded Dominion $787.5 million in damages over Fox's claims that the company had rigged the 2020 election. The HBO show *Succession* was on everyone's minds—journalists were obsessed with the show, which focused on an emotionally stunted billionaire family that owned a right-wing cable news network, and the final season was currently airing—and no one knew if there had been some sort of secret boardroom coup like the show would have depicted. All they knew was that on Monday morning, without warning, Tucker Carlson had been axed, and I found out via a *New York Times* push alert in the parking lot of my allergy doctor, the same time that everybody else did.

"BRO," I texted him. "WHAT."

He didn't respond.

———

In the past two years, Tucker's transformation into a hypernationalist, right-wing demagogue had made no sense to the bubble of journalists, media executives, lawyers, policy officials, and comms directors who had at one point seen Tucker as One Of Them. They'd breathed a sigh of relief when they saw him get a prime-time show at Fox News, thinking he'd bring a touch of class and sanity to the network of Bill O'Reilly and Sean Hannity, and held a glimmer of hope when it was revealed he'd convinced Trump to take COVID more seriously. But then, at some point in the summer of 2020, he sold his house in Northwest DC and left the Coastal Elites for good. And in my mind, the move to the deepest parts of MAGA Country was the key to his success: he now hosted the most popular primetime show in the country, averaging 3.2 million viewers a night in 2022, and had done so by leaning into the kind of stuff that I'd read on white nationalist forums and heard from the people in his new neighborhoods. And my friends, family, and everyone I knew who existed outside of the media *loved* him.

I was less on the Tucker Love/Hate Spectrum than I was fascinated with his metamorphosis. The last time I'd seen Tucker in person was over lunch in a quiet Italian trattoria on the Upper East Side in 2016, right after I joined *Vanity Fair* and before Trump was elected. The last time I'd seen Tucker live was in July 2022, when he Zoomed into a virtual panel with a journalist named Ben Smith[3] and took him to the wood chipper over accusations that he was a white nationalist. (To be fair to Tucker, unless the interviewee has a swastika tattoo, "Are you a white nationalist" is a stupidly broad question that few would ever openly answer in the affirmative.) And I wondered what it was like to be king of the MAGA world: he had the number one show on cable news.

One would *think* that he'd spend his time in pricey urban real estate near a major media center and five steak houses, like his Fox News rivals and predecessors did. But no, he told me on the phone, he would *never* live in a city, much less Washington or New York, again. "It's been a really bad several years, I would say, for the country, but my personal happiness has gone up just because I'm not around that stuff and I don't want to be around it ever again," he told me, the *fasten seat belt* alarm dinging in the background as he began his drive to work.

As we caught up over the phone, I noted there was a lot that was similar to the Tucker I'd met eleven years ago, such as his ability to nurse a grudge for years and craft a withering description of said grudgee: Ben "Reptile" Smith, Arianna "Narcissistic Rich Lady" Huffington, Bill "Never a Genius" Kristol, and at least three other people and publications we'd touched on during our conversation. I could tell what had made him an effective pundit to his viewers: the fact that he knew the media elite so well, *too* well, and could describe their foibles in the way that only a magazine writer with an acid pen could. (In the days of print magazines, the withering bon mot was the coin of the realm.)

I was curious about how he, a journalist from the print era, who'd flirted with digital, and now lived on cable, viewed the modern flow of information. After all, he'd been the one who suggested that the right needed their own version of the *New York Times*, back in 2005. Had the right met that challenge and followed the trajectory of what he hoped?

He paused briefly to greet a neighbor in his tiny town. "I don't know how interested in conservative journalism I am anymore, but not very," he went on. "What I'm interested in is freethinking open-minded journalism. And, to me, it's just super simple." What he hated: sites like the Daily Beast, where Andrew Kirell, my old Mediaite colleague and fellow escapee from libertarian journalism hell, was now an editor. "If the State Department says, 'Well, Assad has used chemical weapons against his own people,' I think a journalist would say, 'Okay, that sounds bad. Show me the evidence that proves that he did that.' The Daily Beast, rather than sort of running that story down, will find like the three people—in that specific case, one person, *me*—who questioned the story and asked for real evidence, and then denounce that person for being skeptical of whatever the official story is." What he liked: "Anyone who doesn't do that." That seemed broad, so I prodded. "I definitely don't think it's a matter of Republican versus Democrat or left versus right," he insisted.

"Or, like, conservative media versus MSM?"

"No! I don't *care* about that! I read The Grayzone every day. Do you know what that is?"

"No." I truly didn't.

"It's like some forbidden hard-left website run by Max Blumenthal and his wife or his partner, who are just absolutely wonderful people. And they have a different foreign policy perspective."[4]

Either Tucker had evolved to a new level of information diet, or this was the way that everyone outside the *New York Times*'s readership consumed the news, and I was panting in the distance, trying to catch up. *And I thought* I *was good at this.* "Wait, so what other sites are you reading besides that? Like what's in your daily information diet?"

"I do most of my reading, honestly, based on texts that I get. I do most of my communicating by text and I don't email."

I let him spin through another rant about Arianna Huffington ("Totally deep into frivolous bullshit . . . No one wants to hear your boring self-care lectures anymore"), the sanctification of Ukrainian president Volodymyr Zelensky and the perception that Tucker himself was pro-Putin ("No one asked any questions. *Zelensky was George Washington. If you don't agree, you're for Putin. Putin is evil*"), his wealthy liberal neighbors in DC hanging Black Lives Matter signs in their windows ("It was only about 'I'm a good person,' it was almost like going to SoulCycle for them"). But underneath his barbs and quips and grudges was a palpable, roiling anger against the former colleagues who'd made up his industry, their brains rotted by the incentive structure of the iPhone and the internet, and who'd turned him off the *New York Times* altogether and toward The Grayzone. "All the little feature pieces, all the soft feature pieces, are about the same class of people," he seethed. "This tiny class of people—and they're tiny; globally, it's like a hundredth of a percent [who] are affluent, well-educated, urban dwellers with Twitter accounts in American cities. That's just a sliver of world population. And yet, almost all media caters to them. And even if I didn't hate them—comma, *which I do*, comma—I would still find it totally disproportionate. I really would. I really, really would. Because it is."

So what's a white nationalist to you? I asked later.

"I literally have no fucking idea," he said, the exasperation clear in his voice. "No one's ever explained it to me. I assume, because it's nationalism—I mean, the word *nationalism* suggests a country—it's people who want an all-white country and they just want to expel everyone who's not white from the country? . . . I have kind of like very old-fashioned liberal views on race, like Dr. Seuss views—'we're all the same underneath our skin and all that,' which is actually my real view, which I've explained about a thousand times in public."

Granted, Tucker was a grown man who had curated his world so severely that he'd excised the mainstream media out of his daily life out of sheer spite. But I'd read a poll earlier that week from Gallup[5] with alarming statistics: only 16 percent of Americans trusted print media. Only 11 percent trusted television news. Ben Smith, big in the media but largely inconsequential to the rest of America, had a vision of a white nationalist in his head that Tucker barely recognized, and my understanding of the Proud Boys' rather violent, pro-white nationalist manifesto elicited a *whoosh* and a shrug from Tucker. ("I'm against picking fights, for sure. But I'm strongly for the Western civilization . . . But I think it's, you know, I'm a product of Western civilization. And I think I have the right to want to continue it. . . . [I]f you said to a Nigerian, you know, how far would you go to protect African civilization, he'd be like, what wouldn't you do?") It slowly dawned on me: Tucker, now a consumer of news instead of a creator, was the rule rather than the exception, knowing exactly what it was that the rest of his audience believed and reinforcing it rather than deigning to lecture that they were wrong. And that's why he was so popular.

"I think it's fair—again, as a fifty-three-year-old—to make my own judgments about everything," he said around the end of our conversation, as he was getting ready to tape his show. "I don't have to accept them uncritically from some low-IQ Cornell graduate from the *New York Times*. I can decide for myself, but I was not allowed to do that.

Like, why is it so hard to just get, like, a full list of QAnon pronounce-ments online? Why doesn't that appear on my Google search? Do you think that's weird? Is that information too dangerous for me? Or what? I can't be trusted with it?"

What. The thing I'd spent nearly half a year obsessing over, the thing he'd firmly thought was ridiculous and overblown—Tucker had never *read* it? "My algorithm definitely gives me everything Q," I said, baffled.

"Do you know a place? I just wanted to read it," he said. "I wanted to read what all these mystical predictions were. And I could never figure out how to [read] it. So I think at least on my Google machine, when I went in there, the first thirty responses were people hyperven-tilating over QAnon. But I just wanted to know what QAnon said, and I couldn't get to that . . . I mean, I read the Unabomber manifesto."

"Oh boy. Well, I could send you them," I said.

"I would love that. I've literally never read them in my life. And I don't know anyone who has, that's the other thing."

There was the distinct possibility that Tucker was lying to me. Last year, he'd done an interview with a right-wing podcaster named Dave Rubin, where Tucker admitted freely that he was not above lying if he was in trouble: "I mean, I lie if I'm really cornered or something," he admitted. "I lie. I really try not to. I try never to lie on TV. I just don't—I don't like lying. I certainly do it, you know, out of weakness or whatever." But there was also the possibility that he was not. When we hung up—after a surreal five minutes where I explained everything I knew about QAnon to the most influential person on television at the time, summarizing it as "an even worse version of *Bowling Alone*"—I opened my web browser and went to my preferred search engine, DuckDuckGo, and searched for "QAnon posts." The top search result was an Archive.org PDF of every single post that Q had ever written. I quickly sent it to Tucker. This had taken thirty seconds.

Our algorithms were now, indeed, vastly different.

————————

I had so many questions after I'd learned Tucker had been fired. Why would Fox throw out their biggest star at the height of his popularity and ratings, when he had the biggest audience in cable news, period? Were they aware that they risked losing a giant segment of their viewers, who'd watched the network for Tucker alone and were hypersensitive about cancel culture, especially if it was a decision made by New York City–based elites? Over the next few days of reporting, I still didn't get a good answer, either from the people in Tucker's orbit, who had their own theories, or from the people familiar with Fox's decision, whose answers seemed thin and inconsistent.

One explanation, reported by the *New York Times*, was that Fox leadership had read the texts that Dominion Voting Systems had subpoenaed from Tucker, and were horrified to see a text where he voiced his conflicted feelings about seeing an antifa protester get beaten up by three Trump supporters: "It's not how white men fight." It seemed rich, coming from Fox News, that they would let Tucker delve into the Great Replacement[6] theory on air over four hundred times, yet have a meltdown at this one text. *Vanity Fair*'s Gabriel Sherman, an old colleague of mine from the Hive and an author who'd written the definitive book about the network's founding, had reported several notably different theories floating around Fox's leadership: one claimed that Rupert Murdoch, the ninety-two-year-old owner of the parent company News Corp, had recently broken off his engagement to his would-be fifth wife, Ann Lesley Smith, after she had declared Tucker a "messenger from God." The firing, this theory went, was driven by jealousy: Rupert had purportedly watched Smith fawn over Tucker during a dinner that March, at once point asking them all to fall into prayer. A further theory claimed that when he watched Tucker's speech at the Heritage dinner, Murdoch was immediately reminded of Smith's messianic obsession with Tucker, and was "freak[ed]" out by the "spiritual talk," as one source told Sherman. I was initially dubious: Murdoch had run *Fox freaking News* for decades as a mouthpiece for conservatism, which required a high tolerance for even the wackiest segments of American Christianity.

But as I went through Tucker's speech again, I could see a situation where *someone* in Fox's leadership could have panicked over the speech: a Christianity-laced sermon implying that the forces of the left were spiritually evil, accelerating the destabilization and possible end of Western civilization itself. Loving Jesus was one thing; calling liberal politicians evildoers and ungodlike was one thing. Invoking theology to wage a holy war on the foundations of government was not.

When people, or crowds of people, or the largest crowd of people at all, which is the federal government, the largest human organization in human history decide that the goal is to destroy things, destruction for its own sake, "Hey, let's tear it down," what you're watching is not a political movement. It's evil.

So, if you want to assess, and I'll put it in non . . . And I'll stop with this. I'll put it in nonpolitical or rather nonspecific theological terms, and just say, if you want to know what's evil and what's good, what are the characteristics of those?

And by the way, I think the Athenians would've agreed with this. This is not necessarily just a Christian notion, this is kind of a, I would say, widely agreed-upon understanding of good and evil. What are its products? What do these two conditions produce?

Well, I mean, good is characterized by order, calmness, tranquility, peace, whatever you want to call it, lack of conflict, cleanliness. Cleanliness is next to godliness. It's true. It is.

And evil is characterized by their opposites. Violence, hate, disorder, division, disorganization, and filth. So, if you are all in on the things that produce the latter basket of outcomes, what you're really advocating for is evil. That's just true. I'm not calling for religious war. Far from it. I'm merely calling for an acknowledgment of what we're watching, which is not one . . .

And I'm certainly not backing the Republican Party. I mean, ugh. I'm not making a partisan point at all. I'm just noting what's superobvious. Those of us who were in our mid-fifties are caught in the past in the way that we think about this. One side's like, "No, no, I've got this idea, and we've got this idea, and let's have a debate about our ideas."

They don't want a debate. Those ideas won't produce outcomes that any rational person would want under any circumstances. Those are manifestations of some larger force acting upon us. It's just so obvious. It's completely obvious.

I hadn't heard that sort of talk in my work since November 2021, when I was in rural Washington with Joshua Feuerstein and he'd spoken about Jezebel and Ahab in the White House. (*Was Tucker secretly a member of the Patriot Church?* I wondered, half-seriously.) I also hadn't known Tucker to discuss the Athenians before; it sounded too much like a Claremont-influenced West Coast Straussian writing in American Greatness, a news site that Peter Thiel had backed as a high-minded alternative to the *National Review.* And though he would never praise

Hitler publicly or gin up derogatory names for minorities, Tucker was shrewder than my first mentor, John Elliott: he had, after all, been delivering in front of the conservative movement's moneymakers and super-activists (and a few dozen mainstream journalists).

Then I heard even *new* talk, the kind that I could report on for Puck: the possibility that Tucker was about to move to Twitter, flouting the porous boundaries of his noncompete, and become a right-wing *content creator.*

Chalk it up to my childhood as an internet baby, reading fanfiction and trolling on message boards, or my extremely early adoption of Twitter. But my best reporting was now about the online right-wing creator economy, which had birthed a universe of commentators who once had to slavishly ingratiate themselves with Fox News in order to gain prominence. Back in 2018, I spoke to an up-and-coming company called the Daily Wire, whose main talent, Ben Shapiro, was not just one of the top podcasters in the country, but was also a product of the conservative activist pipeline. His path was unusual at the time—conservatives were supposed to go into politics, and breaking into showbiz was impossible—but with the rise of the internet (and his connections to a right-wing activist web that included Andrew Breitbart, the David Horowitz Freedom Center, and right-wing billionaire Ferris Wilkes) he and his business partner realized an opportunity for an alternative distribution model for their right-wing beliefs. All the alternative media that's challenging the mainstream narrative—*The Joe Rogan Experience,* Elon Musk's ownership of Twitter, even Donald Trump launching his Twitter competitor Truth Social—can trace their inspiration straight to that moment. And the Wire itself had launched the careers of several young internet personalities: Michael Knowles, whom I'd once described as a "dapper, lib-triggering troll"; and Matt

Walsh, whose documentary *What Is a Woman?* was now single-handedly fueling the panic against transgender individuals nationwide. It had also become the permanent home of Candace Owens, a political commentator who seemed hellbent on outdoing her competitors, and who uniquely infuriated the left because she was Black. But they had never reached the prominence or reach of Fox News' hosts, much less Tucker's audience of three million a night, and Tucker announcing that he was launching a free online show—on Twitter, no less, a program even *more* buggy than Peter Thiel's free-speech YouTube competitor Rumble.

Days after Tucker was fired, he published an enigmatic video on Twitter, seemingly taped on an old iPhone while bunkered in his home studio in Maine, alluding to his cancellation (cancel-culture style) by Fox News—an organization, he implied, now allied with the powerful elites of both the Republican and Democrat parties. "Both political parties and their donors have reached consensus on what benefits them and they actively collude to shut down any conversation about it," he said, staring down his nose into the lens. "Suddenly the United States looks very much like a one-party state. That's a depressing realization, but it's not permanent . . . Where can you still find Americans saying true things? There aren't many places left, but there are some."

I had been taping a podcast and once I was done, I immediately ran off the street into a local coffee shop with my laptop, sending messages to sources and scouring Twitter for clues, my keyboard loudly clacking to the annoyance of the other patrons. And in the back of my mind, as I tapped away like a woman possessed, was an odd sense of irony mixed with wonder mixed with bafflement. All of my universes had started to concentrate down into one man—the man I used to dream of being, the man who had held grudges so deep that his hatred of a mutual associate of ours (from his childhood!) was the first thing he'd ever said to me. Yet our paths had diverged so wildly, looping past each other and into our opposing worlds. He was now the right-wing internet creator, brash and bold and twisting the world by the sheer force of his personality. I was now the magazine writer, observing the world in the background. I had gotten my childhood wish.

And yet nothing had changed. No matter how far I'd run from the movement, it had chased close behind me, ravenous to consume society. It was my entire world, once again—and now it was everyone else's world too.

I closed my eyes, took a deep breath, knocked back the rest of my coffee, and continued to type.

ACKNOWLEDGMENTS

I think it's safe to say that 99.999% of writers would never dream of writing a memoir in their early thirties: it seems arrogant for one to even *think* that they've had enough of an interesting life at that age to warrant a book, and public introspection at that age is, well, scary, which is why I have *so* many people to thank for helping me pull *The MAGA Diaries* out of my stubborn brain. Firstly: Jon Kelly, for sitting me down one day after Trump was elected and telling me that I should write a memoir about my time in the right. Aimee Bell at Gallery Books, who asked me one day in the *Vanity Fair* bathroom whether I had any pitches, and who immediately put me in touch with a literary agent at CAA when I described the memoir to her. And Mollie Glick, the aforementioned agent, who gave me a crucial piece of advice and always remained in my corner: *wait until you feel ready to write this book.* (It took two years and an attempted insurrection to get to that point.)

But I have to give the most credit to Julia Cheiffetz, Nick Ciani, and the Atria team at Simon & Schuster, who issued the most daunting challenge of all: telling my story and explaining MAGAworld to the widest possible readership—a lot of this culture only makes sense if you know it personally—in a way that was still true to myself. The best editors, I've been told, are also pretty good therapists, and Julia was key to helping me explain my story—even to myself. I can't imagine having done this without her support, guidance, and pushback against my desire to hide my truest self under a rock. I hope I haven't given you a heart attack.

There's also an army of people who supported me along the way: my colleagues and editors at *Vanity Fair, Politico,* and Puck, especially David Friend, John Homans, and Benjamin Landy, who never signed up to manage my chaotic life when we met eight years ago, but has been exceedingly patient and graceful along the way. I also must thank every other journalist and writer who's backed me up over the past two years, especially: the amazing fact-checking duo Emilio Leanza and Alice Herman, David and Danielle Frum, Claire Landsbaum, Kevin Nguyen, Elise Taylor, Adam Ciralsky, Mac William Bishop, Wesley Lowery, Kurt Bardella, and John Davis. A special shout-out to my beloved Puckettes Julia Ioffe, Tara Palmeri, and Teddy Schleifer—yes, Teddy is a Puckette—and Jonathan Karp at Simon & Schuster.

To my friends, who've been uncommonly understanding every time I've disappeared over the past two years, and watered my plants whenever I left town, thank you from the bottom of my heart and I promise that we'll spend quality time with each other. To my darling sisters, for believing in the purpose of this book and berating me over FaceTime whenever I lost faith in myself.

And to every one of my sources I've ever worked with, and everyone I've ever interviewed: thank you for guiding me through the world of the American right over the past eight years, and for trusting that I'll always try to capture it as accurately as I can. And now that you know my secret backstory, please keep talking to me after this.

NOTES

CHAPTER 1: THE YOUNG CLAREMONSTER

1. Derbyshire, a writer at *National Review* who drew criticism for his thoughts about "ethnic balancing" and women's emancipation, was fired from *National Review* in 2012 for suggesting in an article for Taki's Magazine that white and Asian parents warn their children about "ferociously hostile" Black people for their own safety. He now writes for VDARE, a notoriously white supremacist online publication.

2. It is much worse these days.

CHAPTER 2: PRESERVING THE IDEALS OF THE AMERICAN FOUNDING

1. Founded in 1969, the center was financed by Henry Salvatori, an oil industrialist who had sold his company in 1960 to devote more time to fund conservative activist causes. He was one of the first investors in *National Review*, the magazine founded by conservative luminary William F. Buckley in the 1950s, as well as one of the earliest supporters of Ronald Reagan. He also endowed the Henry Salvatori Professorship in Law and Community Service at Chapman University's law school,

which is currently occupied by John Eastman, the legal scholar who attempted to convince Vice President Mike Pence to overturn the results of the 2020 presidential election.

2. Strauss's philosophical works focused on the conflict between "Athens and Jerusalem," a metaphor for two diametrically opposed schools of Western political philosophy. Athens represented the "ancients"—Socrates, Aristotle, and so forth—who believed that justice was granted from an inherent set of "natural rights," a moral code determined by reason and enforced within the polity by mutual agreement. Jerusalem represented Christian philosophers—St. Augustine, St. Thomas Aquinas, etc.—who believed in "natural law," the concept that justice was dictated by an all-knowing yet inscrutable God and that government should reflect His word, but that it was also something that could be understood by humans through the lens of reason and natural rights. (This is an extremely truncated summary of the Athens-versus-Jerusalem debate and I apologize to the Straussians for condensing it.)

3. In the most simplistic terms, Straussianism, the philosophy of the German political philosopher Leo Strauss (1899–1973), is sort of an intense mind-reading exercise applied to the work of Western philosophers. Separated from the context of historicism—the values system of a modern scholar, tinging their interpretations of the text with their own moral relativism and philosophical views—how did the author see themselves and their world, and what was that author's particular purpose in writing their texts? (For a *very* simplistic and glib example, things like, say, applying Jungian psychoanalysis as to whether being the third son of an attorney shaped Machiavelli was not the Straussian way. Machiavelli, they would point out, would not have cared about such things, for Machiavelli would not have known such agonies existed.)

4. Without going too deep into the reasons for the schism, the West Coast Straussians, led by Leo Strauss's most gifted disciple Harry Jaffa, decamped to Claremont and established their own school of thought based on applying the Straussian method to the study and defense of the principles of the Founding Fathers, fighting against the moral relativism and nihilism of philosophers from Machiavelli to Friedrich Nietzsche. In their interpretation, the Founders were on par with

the ancients, and tried to preserve the Western philosophical ideal. Straussianism, in this case, was convenient in helping them claim that their interpretation of the Founders' writings reflected the true intent, which ironically makes it malleable to wayward political headwinds. (In 2008, for instance, Straussianism was associated with the nefarious, empire-building ways of the Bush-era neoconservatives; in 2009, it backed the limited government of the Tea Party. Later—in a bizarre twist of fate involving an anonymously published 2016 essay called "The Flight 93 Election," which called for the purging of multiculturalism in America—Straussianism became the realm of Trumpists.)

5. The National Journalism Center at the Young America's Foundation, the organization founded by William F. Buckley, has produced figures like Ann Coulter and Greg Gutfeld. It has also produced Malcolm Gladwell and Terry Moran, making it the least ideologically driven journalism program out there.

6. Charles and David Koch, the owners of the multibillion-dollar oil conglomerate Koch Industries and two of the richest people in the world, were the most powerful forces in the Republican Party at the time, founding and funding a series of nonprofits that focused on training and networking young libertarian and right-wing politicos—the Koch Network, funded largely by the Koch Foundation. But it wasn't surprising that I had no idea who the men were back then, because no one outside of their tiny circle of Republican confidants did. As Jane Mayer reported in her book *Dark Money: The Hidden History of the Billionaires Behind the Rise of the Radical Right*, members of the Koch network were, at the time, so paranoid about their activities being known that they operated in complete secrecy, even going so far as to operate white-noise machines during donor and activist events to prevent people from listening in.

CHAPTER 3: RIGHT-WING SUMMER CAMP

1. In 2023 numbers: $565.61 a week, with a $494.91 travel stipend. I lived pretty well that summer.

2. PJ Media, one of the OG right-wing blog networks and commentary sites, was founded in 2005 by two citizen journalists who'd forced the

famed anchor Dan Rather to resign from CBS after debunking his report claiming that George W. Bush had received preferential treatment to avoid fighting in the Vietnam War. In fact, the site got its name from a derisive comment a CBS executive made about their attempts to fact-check Rather: "You couldn't have a starker contrast between the multiple layers of checks and balances at *60 Minutes* and a guy sitting in his living room in his pajamas." (Incidentally, one of the founders and Rathergate debunkers is named Charles F. Johnson, a fact that irks both him and Chuck Johnson to no end.)

3. This is the real description of the essay prompt: a $10,000 prize for any college student who could "forecast a bachelor's degree holder's annual income in 2014, 2019, 2024 and 2034 after factoring in the cost of current government programs, including TARP and TALF, and stimulus packages."

4. Edmund Burke (1729–1797) is widely considered to be the philosophical father of modern conservatism in the West. The pillars of American conservatism, specifically, can be traced back to his 1790 book *Reflections on the Revolution in France*, wherein he argued that the extreme nature of overthrowing a government and upending a ruling structure (such as the aristocracy) as a means to obtain abstract natural rights (such as liberty, equality, and so forth) was a recipe for societal disaster. While he advocated for rulers to build in mechanisms to *slowly* change their mechanisms if the populace demanded (amendments and elections, for instance), Burke still argued in favor of upholding centuries of tradition—even if it seemed irrational—as a means to keep the societal fabric together: "When ancient opinions and rules of life are taken away, the loss cannot possibly be estimated. From that moment we have no compass to govern us; nor can we know distinctly to what port we steer." In the twentieth century, this criticism was eventually invoked by American conservatives as a rebuke to Bolshevism and Communism, and in the twenty-first century, you can see echoes of Burke's critiques in modern-day opposition to movements like Black Lives Matter, concepts like "diversity, equity, and inclusion" initiatives, and policies like affirmative action.

5. Adam Smith (1723–1790) is the great-granddaddy of capitalism and modern economics. He's largely known for his work *The Wealth of*

Nations, which recast wealth and trade as a sign of a nation's strength: prosperity, he argued, was not a reflection of a nation's divine right, but rather a reflection of their politics, technology, industry, and social order. His earlier work, *The Theory of Moral Sentiments* (the book I received), argued that humans were motivated by the immediate needs of "rational self-interest"—surviving without tearing each other to bits, regardless of everyone's access to personal resources—to properly divide their society's resources and wealth. You might be familiar with his phrase "the invisible hand" to describe his ideal distribution of wealth; consequently, you might understand why he was quite a favorite of free-market Reagan conservatives and Tea Party Libertarians.

6. Mollie Hemingway would eventually become the editor in chief of the Federalist, a prominent conservative online magazine, as well as a Fox News commentator.

7. Possibly the oldest youth talent incubator in the conservative movement, the Leadership Institute was founded in 1977 by Morton Blackwell with the explicit goal of identifying, training, and cultivating right-wing talent in the politics, policy, law, and media, paying close attention to cultivating college students. Some of their most prominent alumni include Senator Mitch McConnell, Mike Pence, and James O'Keefe. According to them, as of 2021, the Leadership Institute has trained over 230,788 activists.

8. The Collegiate Network is a project of the Intercollegiate Studies Institute, a nonprofit dedicated to spreading conservative ideas on college campuses by helping right-wing students print pamphlets, attend seminars, and bring speakers to their school. The Collegiate Network, specifically, funds and publishes roughly dozens of college publications across the country, including the *Dartmouth Review*, where Laura Ingraham and Dinesh D'Souza got their start, and the *Stanford Review*, where Peter Thiel got his. They also offer paid internships in journalism.

9. Yes, the one that also owns Fox News.

10. If there's any powerful right-wing group you'd recognize immediately, it's likely to be this one. The Heritage Foundation was arguably the intellectual engine behind Ronald Reagan's presidency and is by far the most powerful think tank in Republican politics these days, setting the policy agenda for the GOP *writ large* for decades. It also had one of the best-paid

college internship programs in Washington, with subsidized housing, free seminars, networking events, and speaker series with conservative professionals. In recent years, it's made a very conscientious effort to pivot toward MAGA populism, which is an entire drama in and of itself.

11. A giant chunk of the reason Americans for Tax Reform had such a chokehold on the GOP around this time was Norquist, who began his career in activism as a Leadership Institute–backed college student, coming up with the Taxpayer Protection Pledge—some variation of "I will oppose and vote against any and all efforts to increase taxes"—and convincing Republican lawmakers to sign it upon being sworn into office. It is very, very easy to use that pledge against someone.

12. The Susan B. Anthony List was founded in 1993, in direct response to the success of EMILY's List, an influential progressive group that worked to support and elect pro-abortion candidates, primarily women, to public office. In response, the SBA List, named after the prominent nineteenth-century suffragette, deliberately sought out anti-abortion candidates to support their runs for office, particularly women such as Sarah Palin.

13. Yes, it's *another* free-market libertarian policy think tank funded by the Koch Foundation and is *also* based out of George Mason University, to the tune of roughly $29 million per year. And to prove how attractive the idea of parody music videos were in the Republican Party around this time, imagine this: in 2010, the Mercatus Center published a YouTube video featuring a rap battle between free-market economist F. A. Hayek and the neoliberal John Maynard Keynes.

CHAPTER 4: THE DAILY CALLER

1. Reason.TV is affiliated with the libertarian magazine *Reason*, which has been published since 1986 and might be one of the few right-wing magazines with pure intent.

2. Swartz was one of the founders of the Open Access movement, which argued that the public had a right to read scientific research and called for academic publications to take down paywalls. At the time, he had been charged with several federal counts of fraud, facing up to $1 million in fines and thirty-five years in prison, for breaking into an MIT server and using his guest account to download several hundred articles from

JSTOR, an academic paper repository. Though he had an account with JSTOR as a Harvard research fellow, his intent was to distribute the works freely online. Swartz later died by suicide in 2013 after rejecting a plea bargain from the government; both the government and Swartz's lawyers have differing accounts as to why he was compelled.

3. The wife of Supreme Court justice Clarence Thomas, Ginni is known as a prominent conservative activist in her own right, and is controversially known for her work on the *Citizens United* decision, which removed caps on unlimited corporate spending in politics. She also was involved in several attempts to stop the 2020 presidential election from being certified for Joe Biden, and in a call to White House chief of staff Mark Meadows, Thomas referred to a QAnon conspiracy theory as the root cause.

CHAPTER 5: EXILE IN FRUMLAND

1. Most of Accuracy in Media's earliest activity involved its founder, Reed Irvine, writing crank letters to newspapers claiming bias. Over time, however, he learned how to infiltrate these groups to gather and publicize examples of their inherent bias: buying stock so he could sit in on shareholder meetings, and running pressure campaigns against television networks by writing to their advertisers. He died before the advent of social media, but AIM was evolving with the times, and Accuracy in Academia was as well.

2. I had been reminded frequently at the Career Center that one should have excellent, probing questions at the ready for the end of an interview when they would inevitably ask: *Do you have any questions for us?* In my interview with the Huffington Post, I immediately forgot all of my questions and instead asked whether it was true that they had a nap room. Do not do this.

3. Established in the late 1940s by a Milwaukee auto tycoon, the little-known Bradley Foundation is one of the biggest right-wing networks in the country, with an estimated $850 million endowment. At the time, they were pouring their money into more anodyne conservative issues such as school choice, health care, and teachers unions. By 2021, they would be known for funding at least eleven groups who have promoted conspiracies about election fraud.

4. The political advocacy arm of the Koch brothers' libertarian influence machine, and arguably its biggest: in 2010, AFP played a crucial role in elevating the Tea Party and swinging the House back to the control of the Republican Party, spending $40 million in the endeavor to do so. Not the Koch Foundation.

5. Two years later, a report from the Center for Public Integrity would reveal that in 2011, 95 percent of the Franklin Center's funding came from a right-wing dark money group called Donors Trust. It was the kind of group that was built specifically so no one knew, exactly, who had poured money into it, and it could keep those donors secret by running issues-based campaign ads. And in the span between my interview and that report, the Wisconsin Reporter had published stories fighting against Scott Walker's recall with a fury of misreported news, and separately alleged that several right-wing Republican groups in Wisconsin—the Club for Growth, Americans for Prosperity, and others—were under a government investigation. This was all while failing to mention that the Franklin Center's director of special projects was *also* in charge of those groups. The group is now called the Franklin News Foundation.

CHAPTER 6: ESCAPE FROM THE CONSERVATIVE GHETTO

1. Probably the most libertarian publication in the top-ranked conservative publications—and the least beholden to reinforcing the GOP party line, because libertarians have no gods—*Reason*, founded in 1968, is more along the lines of pot-legalizing, free-market-loving, anti-statist "everyone leave us alone" ethos than the Reaganite *National Review* or the neocon *Weekly Standard* or the anti-woke *Federalist*.

2. Kat Timpf climbed her way up the ranks at Fox News as a commentator and is now the cohost of *Gutfeld!*, Fox's late-night comedy talk show. It has been the most-watched late-night talk show in the country for nearly two years straight.

3. Yes, the one who became Donald Trump's campaign manager and political adviser.

4. Please watch the first forty-five seconds of the 1968 musical *Oliver!* for a faithful recreation of working at a 2014-era content factory.

CHAPTER 7: THE NEW LEADERS COUNCIL

1. If you've ever seen two separate bills on the same topic pop up in two separate states at the same time, chances are good that it came from this group. Founded by some of the same people who created the Heritage Foundation, the American Legislative Exchange Council (ALEC) is, essentially, a hub for right-wing state lawmakers to collaborate, draft, and pass conservative legislation in their home states Around this time in 2015, ALEC was under fire for writing bills that appeared too lenient toward their corporate donors; these days, they would like to rewrite the Constitution under an Article V convention to build a "conservative nation." More on that later.

2. If you've heard of the *Vanity Fair* Oscar Party, the private celebrity shindig after the Academy Awards, that was a Graydon Carter invention.

3. A college libertarian organization, similar to the Leadership Institute, except for people who love Ron Paul.

CHAPTER 8: THE LOWEST CLASS

1. Founded in 1988 as a reactionary think tank against Islamic jihadism, and blowing up online through sites like Jihad Watch and FrontPage Magazine, the David Horowitz Freedom Center, based in Southern California, is known these days as a far-right institution that combats the influence of "the political left" in culture, policy, and international relations. Miller had met Horowitz as a high schooler in Santa Monica, and in turn Horowitz, who recognized his talent as a rising nationalist firebrand, became his mentor, introducing him to top conservatives and cultivating his career. Miller eventually would go on to work for Trump at the White House, where he was known as the administration's most intense anti-immigration hard-liner. Among other things, he is responsible for the policy of separating migrant children from their parents at the southern border.

2. Before he became the podcasting megastar he is today, Ben Shapiro was the editor at large at Breitbart, working closely with Andrew before his death, and had done a stint at a site called TruthRevolt, a prototype

version of the podcast network the Daily Wire. Truth Revolt, incidentally, was funded by the David Horowitz Freedom Center.

3. Gateway Pundit was founded in 2004 as a fairly typical right-wing news blog. By 2016, they had a full staff and became a go-to read for Trump voters, primarily for their negative coverage (and conspiracy-mongering) of Hillary Clinton voters. When the Trump administration came into power, they took care to extend a White House press credential to Gateway Pundit—a move that horrified the press corps.

4. In 2016, Seth Rich, a twenty-seven-year-old employee of the Democratic National Committee, was shot and killed near his house in Washington, DC. Though police were never able to find the killers, right-wing influencers and personalities immediately began theorizing that Rich had been responsible for leaking a tranche of embarrassing emails to the public, and had been murdered by the Clintons in response. The conspiracy theory was repeated on Fox News for weeks by Sean Hannity and *Fox & Friends*, leading Rich's family to successfully sue the network for emotional distress in 2018. The claims have never been proven.

5. The *Claremont Review of Books*, long considered an arbiter of Smart Conservatism, shocked the right in 2016 when it published the infamous "The Flight 93 Election," an anonymous essay that gave the first intellectual argument for Donald Trump's presidency. The basic gist: this was *the* last election where the American people could save themselves from the perils of Democrat socialism, multiculturalism, and the influence of nonwhite minorities flooding over the borders, the current GOP establishment was inadequate in doing so, and the outsider neophyte Trump was the only person who could stop the decline of the Republic. Rush Limbaugh was so delighted that this populist message was printed in the *Review* that he spent an entire episode of his radio show reading the essay out loud.

CHAPTER 9: THE PROGRESSIVE SNOWFLAKE POWER HOUR

1. In 2011, Solyndra, a solar panel company that had received $535 million in stimulus money, went bankrupt, and its headquarters were soon raided by the FBI. House Republicans alleged that the White House had not done its due diligence on Solyndra, claiming they had actually

approved the loan in order to promote green energy spending, and spent years investigating the company. It was, indeed, a quaint throwback compared to the overwhelming investigation into Hillary Clinton's handling of the Benghazi attacks.

2. If you need Vietnamese-speaking Buddhist nuns who can conduct a Zen funeral service in the greater Boston area with five days' notice, I've got you covered.

3. Modern-day MAGA nationalists will get extremely offended if you call them "Nazis," because *technically* speaking they're right: while the Nazi Party of the 1930s promoted antisemitism, racial hierarchy, social Darwinism, authoritarian government, and so forth, as well as the social demotion and expulsion of all undesirables, it *also* called for *lebensraum*: the invasion of surrounding countries in order to unite the Germanic peoples into one nation and thus ensure the race's survival. While they've argued that anyone who entered the country after the 1962 Immigration Act is more likely to be less than sufficiently American, the MAGA movement, so far, has not called for America to invade other countries. (The social undesirables part is tbd.)

4. The Charlemagne Institute, devoted to defending and advancing "Western Civilization," is the result of a merger between two preexisting conservative groups: *Intellectual Takeout*, a conservative news blog launched in 2009, and the Rockford Institute, a group founded in 1976 that was affiliated with numerous famous white nationalists. In its heyday in the 1990s, the Rockford Institute literally had a program called the John Randolph Club, named after a nineteenth-century Virginia congressman who simultaneously disliked slavery yet fought to uphold the institution. "I am an aristocrat," he once declared. "I love liberty. I hate equality." Randolph is widely considered to be one of the conservative movement's forebears.

5. The fuller paragraph from the Alcuin Internship web page: "Today, those who control the levers of power in American culture have largely rejected our Judeo-Christian heritage. In education, media, business, and government, we are witnessing the vast promotion of postmodernism, globalism, and cultural Marxism. As a consequence, many Americans—especially our youth—are lost, lonely, and adrift. In response to this cultural crisis, Charlemagne Institute created the Alcuin

Internship to raise up the next generation of young Americans who will join us on our own long march to reclaim those institutions and our Republic."

6. In a response to Splinter, Elliott said, with phrases emphasized in bold font: "Some of the remarks were intended as jokes. But I realize that they are offensive and wrong. These emails were written during a period of time when I was underemployed and in a difficult space. I had networking meetings during this time with many people, including some of whom were on the 'Alt-Right.' To the extent I flirted with their ideology, I have since come to see it as wrong. I am sorry that I made any remarks that expressed support for it. Since coming to The Charlemagne Institute, I have embraced its view that Western Civilization is all-inclusive. I reject the concept of 'white nationalism' totally."

7. In a response to Buzzfeed News, Elliott denied that he'd played a role in McHugh's radicalization, even though he did invite her to dinners with British Holocaust denier David Irving. "I chose Katie to mentor as a libertarian, not as a member of the 'alt-right,' " he wrote to Gray. "The 'alt-right' didn't exist in 2011, and I've had no connection with the 'alt-right' since it was invented. I tried to be a mentor and a friend to Katie for a decade, even as she went down some of the dark paths of those fringe groups. But her decision to go down those paths had nothing to do with me. I truly feel bad for her."

CHAPTER 10: THE YEAR OF THE STORM

1. https://www.mediamatters.org/donald-trump/here-are-extremist-figures -going-white-house-social-media-summit

2. Apart from Portland, due to a geographical quirk that allows them easy access to that hipster city, it's rare for militias to make their way into a major metropolitan area. Despite their dramatic emergence in the media during summer of 2020, militia activities are largely limited to smaller cities—think Portland, Oregon, and smaller—as well as their sprawling suburbs and exurbs. It was partially geographical—trying to move a convoy into New York City is nearly impossible—but it was also a place where the message resonated the strongest: a suburb is the terrifying place to be without the police.

3. Yes, the mania over hydroxychloroquine *was* a random internet comment gone wild. I'd traced the trend back from Trump, through a Tucker Carlson segment, through a fake doctor, to a single Twitter conversation in late February 2020 between three people, wherein a "philosopher" mentioned that chloroquine could *possibly* be a prophylaxis.

4. Militia philosophy can best be reflected in the theory behind the American Redoubt movement, the antigovernment philosophy put forth on a blog run by James Wesley Rawles in 2011. He proposed that Christian conservatives migrate to the Pacific Northwest—remote, lacking natural hazards, and so sparsely populated—should the government declare martial law for any number of reasons. The government's response to the pandemic struck every single nerve that a militia member could possibly have—business restrictions, mask mandates, the fear of forced vaccinations, the involvement of Bill Gates—making the Redoubt suddenly more appealing. (When I was in Spokane, I ran into several real estate agents who were oriented toward Redoubters looking for prepper-worthy plots of land.)

5. Whereas groups like the Proud Boys and the Oath Keepers can point to their diverse memberships and claim they're trying to protect "Western civilization," the Groypers are explicitly white nationalists who want to protect "white America" and hate the mainstream Republican movement—even, say, a Jared Kushner figure—for being too tolerant of women and the LGBT community.

6. Media Matters, a liberal watchdog group, published a longer list of invitees: "Conservative radio host Bill Mitchell, a right-wing meme maker known online as Carpe Donktum, Turning Point USA founder Charlie Kirk, right-wing propaganda YouTube channel Prager University, pro-Trump cartoonist Ben Garrison (whose invitation has since been rescinded), Human Events publisher Will Chamberlain, Media Research Center founder Brent Bozell, conservative think tank the Heritage Foundation, Students for Trump cofounder Ryan Fournier, right-wing personality Ali Akbar (also known as Ali Alexander), discredited 'citizen journalist' James O'Keefe, Rep. Matt Gaetz (R-FL), Senator Marsha Blackburn (R-TN), right-wing commentator Tim Pool, Turning Point USA Chief Creative Officer Benny Johnson, far-right blog The Gateway

Pundit founder Jim Hoft, fringe social media platform Minds.com, conservative singer Joy Villa, anti-abortion activist Lila Rose, and YouTube conspiracy theorist Mark Dice." (Amazingly, this list is incomplete.)

7. I didn't know this at the time, but behind the scenes, Eastman had been asked by the Trump administration to turn these Twitter theories into a legal memo. Trump and Eastman then tried to use this memo to convince Pence to swing the count in his favor.

8. The self-cleansing cycle is a fixture of movement conservatism, dating from the early days of its founding. The John Birch Society, a once-powerful faction of the right that was just as conspiratorial as QAnon, got aggressively pushed out of Official Conservatism by the mid-1970s, defenestrated by Reaganites, led by William F. Buckley, who wanted to make the movement look more respectable.

9. After a multiyear investigation, four senior members of the Proud Boys, including leader Enrique Tarrio, were convicted in 2023 of seditious conspiracy in relation to January 6th. While it was made clear during the trial that the Proud Boys had participated heavily in storming the Capitol, and that Tarrio himself had encouraged a "spectacle" at the event, prosecutors were unable to prove that there had been deliberate coordination between the Proud Boys and other groups present at the Capitol, such as the Oath Keepers, or political figures like Donald Trump.

CHAPTER 11: THE ROAD TRIP

1. A nearby man helpfully explained to me that she was likely from a denomination that viewed the protester as someone *representing* Jesus, and she might have interpreted Zach's question as him asking whether the protester was actually the Son of God. After an hourlong conversation about St. Augustine's *Confessions*, during which I learned he was Catholic and had a son who was a priest, he wished me well on my travels and hoped that one day, I might accept Jesus. "There's a spiritual darkness descending upon this country," he added.

2. Newsom survived the recall attempt by a whopping 23 points.

3. A MAGA free speech social network, a progenitor to Truth Social.

4. As far as I can recall, he's correct.

CHAPTER 13: THE PATRIOT ACADEMY

1. I know we've discussed a great many right-wing groups in these notes by now—though I assume that the proliferation of these groups *is* the point—but the Federalist Society is one of the big ones. Established by a group of Harvard and Yale legal scholars in 1982, the Federalist Society is a well-funded, deeply influential network of right-wing legal theorists, lawyers, and academics who recruit young students in top law schools, train them in the profession of being a conservative legal activist, network them into prominent jobs, and send them into the world to influence American law and jurisprudence. The Federalist Society reached the height of its power during the Trump administration, when they vetted every one of his nominees to the Supreme Court, and as a result, five justices—Brett Kavanaugh, Amy Coney Barrett, Clarence Thomas, Samuel Alito, and Neil Gorsuch—are decades-long Federalist Society members.

EPILOGUE: TUCKER AND ME

1. Although CPAC had been held in Orlando, Florida, during the pandemic, the group had returned to Maryland in 2023, and for some reason my application that year had been denied. Not that I'd missed out on much, anyway: though no official attendance numbers had been released, attendees noted that giant barriers had been erected throughout the venue, making the vast rooms appear smaller (and therefore less sparse), the activist training sessions had been eliminated altogether, and the after-party scene had never been so barren. On the plus side, the main hall filled up for Donald Trump's speech, as usual, which one in the conservative movement would consider a win.

2. This nickname was bestowed on the twenty GOP congressmen who'd held up Kevin McCarthy's speakership, coined by disgruntled moderate Don Bacon. Their fans call them the "Mighty 20" and I do not believe they appreciate my nickname for them.

3. At the time of this interview, Smith was the founder of a news site called Semafor, but Smith had done the rounds throughout the mainstream media at this point: he'd been a reporter at *Politico*, media

252   NOTES

reporter for the *New York Times*, and, infamously, the BuzzFeed editor who published the dossier alleging that the Russians had a blackmail tape involving Trump, Russian hookers, and copious amount of urine.

4. Max Blumenthal had briefly been a journalist, writing for outlets like Media Matters and the Daily Beast, before launching the Grayzone, a site criticized for promoting authoritarian regimes. He frequently appears on Russian state-owned outlets RT and Sputnik Radio, has taken an anti-Ukraine stance in his reporting on the 2022 Russian-Ukraine war, and pushed back against the reporting on Syrian president Bashar al-Assad's chemical warfare campaigns. In a twist of irony, his father, Sidney Blumenthal, was a former ally of the Clinton family and worked for the Clinton Global Initiative.

5. https://news.gallup.com/poll/394817/media-confidence-ratings-record -lows.aspx.

6. Adapted from a similar French theory and primarily used by white nationalists and white supremacists, the "Great Replacement theory" posits that American political elites are attempting to use immigration laws and multiculturalism to increase the number of racial minorities in the country, thereby turning whites into a minority group themselves and dilute their power and standing. According to the *New York Times*, Carlson had mentioned the theory over four hundred times on his Fox show.

INDEX

Kelly, Jon, 124–26, 127, 131–32, 148, 149, 152, 164, 185, 210
Kesler, Charles, 40, 41, 52
Kirell, Andrew, 105–7, 110, 155–56, 157, 225
Kirk, Charlie, 4, 7, 139, 164, 249n6
Kleeb, Jane, 154–55
Klein, Ezra, 123
Kline, Mal, 94
Knowles, Michael, 232–33
Koch brothers (Charles and David), 53, 159, 239n6, 244n4
Koch Foundation, 46, 55, 96, 239n6, 242n13, 244n4
Koch Industries, 239n6
Koch Network, 99, 239n6
Kravis, Henry, 124
Kristol, William, 38, 224
Kushner, Jared, 131, 141, 206, 249n5

L

Labash, Matt, 71, 75
Lahmeyer, Jackson, 190
Lamont, Ned, 118
Landry, Jeff, 8
Lankford, James, 190
LaRouche, Lyndon, 178
Lazard Frères, 149
Leadership Institute, 58, 59, 119, 120, 124, 135, 241n7
lebensraum, 247n3
Levin, Brian, 175
Levinson, Alexis, 75
Lewandowski, Corey, 127
Lewis, Matt, 75, 80, 107
Lewis, Michael, 149, 150
libertarianism, 44, 55, 67–68, 80, 105, 106, 244n1
Lieberman, Joe, 118
Limbaugh, Rush, 213, 246n5
Lincoln Project, 3
Lindell, Mike, 174, 185–89, 196
LinkedIn, 153
Lippman, Daniel, 163, 178, 180–81, 182, 183
Louisiana State University (LSU), 7, 8

M

Macias, Nathan, 213–14
Madison, James, 49
Manning, Chelsea, 136–37
Mansfield, Harvey, 38
Markay, Lachlan, 56, 135
Martosko, David, 75, 79, 83, 87
Mason, George, 211
Maxwell (author's libertarian friend), 54, 55, 60–61, 62, 63, 93, 132

Mayer, Jane, 239n6
McArdle, Megan, 56
McCarthy, Kevin, 217, 221, 251n2
McConnell, Mitch, 120, 121, 213, 241n7
McElwee, Sean, 152
McHugh, Katie, 157, 159–60, 248n7
McInnes, Gavin, 135, 168
Mckesson, DeRay, 122
Meadows, Mark, 243n3
Meckler, Mark, 211, 212–13, 215
Mediaite, 77, 104, 105–6, 109–11, 113, 116, 155, 225
Media Matters, 249n6, 252n4
Melber, Ari, 141
Mercatus Center, 64
militias, 168–69, 176–77, 178, 248n2, 249n4
Milk N Cooks, 135
Miller, Stephen, 132, 245n1
Milton Academy, 23–24, 26, 27–30, 31, 46, 68
Minds.com, 249n6
Miranda, Matti, 115
Mitchell, Bill, 164, 249n6
Moen, Bill, 123
Molyneux, Stefan, 135
Moore, Amanda, 191–92, 194
Moran, Terry, 239n5
Morgenson, Gretchen, 56
Morning Hate, 156–60
MSNBC, 69, 104
Mueller investigation, 141
Munro, Neil, 74–75, 94, 108
Murdoch, Rupert, 229–30
Musk, Elon, 153, 167, 232
MyPillow, 174, 186

N

National Journal, 74
National Journalism Center at the Young America's Foundation, 46, 239n5
National Review, 31, 34, 40, 41, 45, 50, 56, 59, 138, 231, 237n1, 244n1
National Rifle Association, 61
natural law, 37, 238n2
natural rights, 238n2
Nazis, 1–4, 247n3
Netroots Nation, 118
New College of Florida, 216
New Democrats, 118
New Leaders Council, 116–24
New Orleans *Times-Picayune*, 50, 52
New Republic, 69
News Corp, 58, 229
Newsmax, 136, 174, 177
Newsom, Gavin, 189, 190, 250n2
New York, 141
New Yorker, 61, 69, 112

ABOUT THE AUTHOR

TINA NGUYEN is a national correspondent and founding partner for Puck, covering the world of Donald Trump and the American right. Previously, Nguyen was a White House reporter for *Politico*, a staff reporter for Vanity Fair Hive, and an editor at Mediaite. Nguyen graduated from Claremont McKenna College and lives in Washington, DC.